International Relations Theory

Written for advanced undergraduate and graduate students, this is the first textbook on international relations theory to take a specifically game-theoretic approach to the subject, and provide the material needed for students to understand the subject thoroughly, from its basic foundations to more complex models. International relations theory is presented and analysed using simple games, which allow students to grasp the concepts and mechanisms involved with the rationalist approach without the distraction of complicated mathematics. Chapter exercises reinforce key concepts and guide students to extend the models discussed. Drawing examples from international security, international political economy, and environmental negotiations, this introductory textbook examines a broad array of topics in international relations courses, including state preferences, normal form games, bargaining, uncertainty and communication, multilateral cooperation, and the impact of domestic politics.

Andrew H. Kydd is Professor in the Department of Political Science at the University of Wisconsin where he teaches courses on international relations theory, game theory and international relations, nuclear weapons and world politics, terrorism and conflict resolution. He has published articles in the *American Political Science Review, International Organization, World Politics,* and *International Security,* and his first book, *Trust and Mistrust in International Relations,* won the 2006 Conflict Processes Best Book Award.

International Relations Theory

The Game-Theoretic Approach

Andrew H. Kydd

CAMBRIDGE
UNIVERSITY PRESS

University Printing House, Cambridge CB2 8BS, United Kingdom

One Liberty Plaza, 20th Floor, New York, NY 10006, USA

477 Williamstown Road, Port Melbourne, VIC 3207, Australia

314-321, 3rd Floor, Plot 3, Splendor Forum, Jasola District Centre, New Delhi-110025, India

79 Anson Road, #06-04/06, Singapore 079906

Cambridge University Press is part of the University of Cambridge.

It furthers the University's mission by disseminating knowledge in the pursuit of education, learning and research at the highest international levels of excellence.

www.cambridge.org
Information on this title: www.cambridge.org/kydd

© Andrew H. Kydd 2015

This publication is in copyright. Subject to statutory exception and to the provisions of relevant collective licensing agreements, no reproduction of any part may take place without the written permission of Cambridge University Press.

First published 2015

A catalogue record for this publication is available from the British Library

Library of Congress Cataloging in Publication data
Kydd, Andrew H., 1963–
International relations theory : the game theoretic approach / Andrew H. Kydd.
   pages cm
ISBN 978-1-107-02735-0 (Hardback) – ISBN 978-1-107-69423-1 (Paperback)
1. International relations.   2. Game theory.   I. Title.
JZ1305.K92 2014
327.101´5193–dc23   2014031785

ISBN 978-1-107-02735-0 Hardback
ISBN 978-1-107-69423-1 Paperback

Additional resources for this publication at www.cambridge.org/kydd

Cambridge University Press has no responsibility for the persistence or accuracy of URLs for external or third-party internet websites referred to in this publication, and does not guarantee that any content on such websites is, or will remain, accurate or appropriate.

To Yoi, Amelia, and Tommy

Contents

List of figures page x
List of tables xii
Acknowledgements xiv

1 Introduction 1
   1.1 International relations theory 1
   1.2 Game theory and international relations theory 6
   1.3 Paradigm wars and problem oriented research 7
   1.4 The utility of a partial view 10
   1.5 Conclusion 10

2 What states want 11
   2.1 Utility theory 12
   2.2 Issue spaces 17
   2.3 The shape of utility functions 21
   2.4 The state as unitary actor 28
   2.5 The national interest 30
   2.6 Conclusion 34
   Exercises 34

3 Varieties of strategic settings 36
   3.1 Normal form games and Nash equilibria 37
   3.2 The Prisoner's Dilemma 39
   3.3 The Assurance game 44
   3.4 Coordination 46
   3.5 Chicken 47
   3.6 Matching Pennies 49
   3.7 Conclusion 53
   Exercises 53

4 Bargaining 55
- 4.1 Extensive form games 56
- 4.2 A Bargaining game 59
- 4.3 Adding a status quo 61
- 4.4 Bargaining and conflict 63
- 4.5 War as a binary lottery 66
- 4.6 War and intermediate outcomes 69
- 4.7 Conclusion 73
- Exercises 73

5 Power change and war 75
- 5.1 The problem of preventive war 77
- 5.2 Power change with bargaining in the future 81
- 5.3 Power change with bargaining in the present and future 85
- 5.4 Bargaining over power 89
- 5.5 Conclusion 90
- Exercises 90

6 Private information and war 92
- 6.1 Modeling uncertainty 93
- 6.2 Bargaining with uncertainty over the cost of conflict 94
- 6.3 Game forms and game free results 100
- 6.4 The problem of mistrust 101
- 6.5 Uncertainty over the balance of power 104
- 6.6 Conclusion 110
- Exercises 111

7 Arms competition and war 112
- 7.1 Costly deterrence 114
- 7.2 The risk–return tradeoff and deterrence 120
- 7.3 Conclusion 125
- Exercises 126

8 Cooperation theory 127
- 8.1 The problem of cooperation 129
- 8.2 Discounting future payoffs 130
- 8.3 Finitely repeated games 132
- 8.4 Indefinitely repeated games 134
- 8.5 Tit for Tat and Contrite Tit for Tat 136

8.6 Monitoring   141
8.7 A Tariff Barrier game   143
8.8 The folk theorem and multiple equilibria   145
8.9 Empirical investigations   146
8.10 Conclusion   147
Exercises   147

9 Diplomacy and signaling   149
9.1 Communication in international relations   149
9.2 Updating beliefs and Bayes' Rule   151
9.3 Cheap talk and diplomacy   154
9.4 Costly signals and crisis bargaining   164
9.5 Conclusion   175
Exercises   176

10 Multilateral cooperation   177
10.1 Public goods   178
10.2 The Tipping game   187
10.3 Conclusion   192
Exercises   192

11 Domestic politics and international relations   194
11.1 The impact of domestic politics   194
11.2 Domestic constraints in bargaining   197
11.3 Two-sided constraints   202
11.4 Cheap talk and negotiation with domestic constraints   206
11.5 Conclusion   210
Exercises   210

References   211
Index   227

Figures

2.1	Utility functions	*page* 20
2.2	The Edgeworth Box	21
2.3	Risk attitudes	23
2.4	Prospect theory utility function	25
2.5	Status quo and greedy states	26
2.6	Two status quo states	27
2.7	A case of ethnic conflict	28
3.1	Equilibria in the Competition for Power with Costs game	43
4.1	The Deterrence game	57
4.2	The issue space	60
4.3	The Bargaining game	60
4.4	Bargaining with a status quo	62
4.5	Bargaining with a status quo and conflict option	63
4.6	The bargaining range	64
4.7	The bargaining outcome	66
4.8	The bargaining range with war as a lottery	67
4.9	Utility functions that devalue intermediate outcomes	70
4.10	War with an indivisible good	71
5.1	The Power Change game without bargaining	77
5.2	Power change equilibria without bargaining	79
5.3	The Power Change game with bargaining in the future	82
5.4	Power change equilibria with future bargaining	84
5.5	Power change equilibria with present and future bargaining	88
6.1	Bargaining with private information over costs	95
6.2	The bargaining range with incomplete information	95
6.3	Equilibria in the Bargaining game with incomplete information	99
7.1	Arms race equilibria: complete information	119
7.2	Arms–War game with uncertainty: risk–return equilibrium	125
8.1	The Tariff game issue space	144
9.1	Bayes' Rule with continuous probability	152

9.2	Types in the Treaty game	156
9.3	Cost cutoff points with scientific uncertainty	160
9.4	The Costly Signaling game	165
9.5	Costly Signaling game: complete information equilibria	167
9.6	Costly Signaling game: strategies for each state/type	168
9.7	Bluffing equilibrium in the Costly Signaling game	172
9.8	Comparative statics in the bluffing equilibrium	173
10.1	The N person Prisoner's Dilemma	182
10.2	Military spending among allies	186
10.3	The Tipping game	188
10.4	Landmines Convention game	190
10.5	Multilateral arms control with interior equilibria	191
11.1	A two-dimensional bargaining space of tariff levels	198
11.2	Bargaining with ratification	199
11.3	Equilibrium in the Two-Level Bargaining game	201
11.4	Bargaining with two-sided ratification	203
11.5	Equilibrium with two-sided constraints	204
11.6	Issue space with uncertainty about state 2's legislature	206
11.7	Communication and bargaining with domestic constraints	208

Tables

2.1 Different state utility functions *page* 16
3.1 The Prisoner's Dilemma 39
3.2 The Prisoner's Dilemma: general notation 40
3.3 The exchange game 40
3.4 The Assurance game 45
3.5 The Pre-emptive War game 46
3.6 The Coordination game 47
3.7 The Standard Setting game 47
3.8 Chicken 48
3.9 The Nuclear Crisis game 48
3.10 Matching Pennies 50
3.11 The D-Day game 51
3.12 The Pre-emptive War game 53
3.13 A Nuclear Crisis game 54
4.1 SPNE in the Bargaining game 61
4.2 SPNE in the Bargaining game with a status quo 62
4.3 SPNE in the Bargaining game with conflict 65
5.1 Equilibria in the Power Change game without bargaining 78
5.2 Equilibria in the Power Change game with bargaining in the future 83
5.3 Power Change game with present and future bargaining: no revision equilibrium 85
5.4 Power Change game with present and future bargaining: revision in the future equilibrium 86
5.5 Power Change game with bargaining in the present and future: double revision equilibrium 87
5.6 Power Change game with bargaining in the present and future: preventive war equilibrium 88
6.1 No war, no revision equilibrium 96
6.2 Equilibria when both types have a credible threat to fight 97
6.3 Equilibria when only low cost type has credible threat to fight 98

6.4	The Preventive War game with mistrust	102
6.5	Four types of state	104
6.6	The Mutual Optimism game, version 1	105
6.7	The Mutual Optimism game, version 2	108
6.8	The Trust game	111
7.1	Payoffs in the Arms–War game	115
7.2	The Arms–War game: no build equilibrium 1	116
7.3	The Arms–War game: no build equilibrium 2	117
7.4	The Arms–War game: deterrence equilibrium	118
7.5	The Arms–War game: war equilibrium	118
7.6	The Arms–War game with uncertainty: risk–return equilibrium	122
8.1	The Prisoner's Dilemma	129
8.2	A Coordination game	132
8.3	A Modified Prisoner's Dilemma	133
8.4	A one-round deviation from Tit for Tat	137
8.5	A one-round deviation from Contrite Tit for Tat	139
8.6	The Prisoner's Dilemma	147
9.1	The Treaty game	155
9.2	The truthful communication equilibrium with scientific certainty	157
9.3	The truthful communication equilibrium with scientific uncertainty	161
9.4	The truthful communication equilibrium with uncertainty over sender's motivations	163
10.1	Different types of goods	179
11.1	Equilibria in the Bargaining game with domestic constraints	200
11.2	Equilibria in the Bargaining game with two-sided constraints	203
11.3	Equilibria in the Constrained Bargaining game with uncertainty	208

Acknowledgements

Authors of textbooks owe their greatest debts to their teachers and their students. I had my first brush with international relations theory in Kenneth Oye's Introduction to World Politics class at Princeton in the mid 1980s. The class was held in the biggest classroom on campus and there were over 400 students. His lectures were so good we applauded after every one, not just the one at the end of the semester. After a few years I went to the University of Chicago where I learned international relations theory and game theory from James Fearon, Charles Glaser, Charles Lipson, John Mearsheimer, Duncan Snidal, Daniel Verdier, Stephen Walt, and In-Koo Cho. Retracing my steps, I presented the first three chapters at the PIPES workshop at the University of Chicago in May 2012. I thank the participants there for their many helpful comments. It is always a treat to come home.

I first started teaching a course such as the one this book is based on at the University of California at Riverside. However, I only started working on the textbook a few years ago at the University of Wisconsin. I would especially like to thank the graduate students in my classes who read draft chapters in the early stages. In the first year they were: Roseanne McManus, Mark Toukan, Steven Wilson, Mason DeLang, Jason Ardanowsky, and Mert Kartal. The second generation were: Budak Bugrahan, Patrick Kearney, Richard Loeza, Susanne Mueller, Ryan Powers, and Anna Weisfeiler. The next year I taught it through the iTV consortium to students at Ohio State and Illinois; the roster was Caitlin Clary, Gina Martinez, William Massengill, William McCracken, Yoshiki Nakajima, Marzia Oceno, Jason Duu Renn, Ashlea Rundlett, Daniel Silverman, Daniel Wollrich, Joshua Wu, Iku Yoshimoto, and Nikolaj Zemesarajs. The last year's cohort was Anne Anderson, Sarah Bouchat, Clarence Moore, and Nathaniel Olin.

I would also like to thank a number of anonymous referees at Cambridge for their comments on the proposal and early drafts of some chapters, and John Haslam for taking a flier on the project.

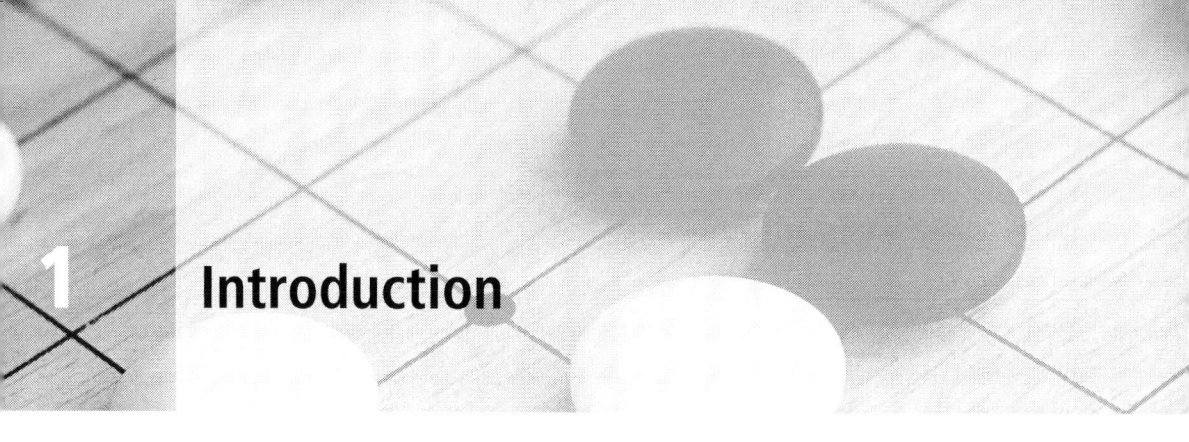

1 Introduction

> The ideas of economists and political philosophers, both when they are right and when they are wrong, are more powerful than is commonly understood. Indeed the world is ruled by little else. Practical men, who believe themselves to be quite exempt from any intellectual influence, are usually the slaves of some defunct economist.
>
> John M. Keynes (1936)

WHAT causes war? Why do states sometimes trade freely and other times protect their domestic industries? Why are some environmental treaties successful and others fail? Wars, international trade, and environmental treaties shape the lives of people around the world. Whether people live or die, are prosperous or poor, have a clean environment or a polluted one, all are affected by international relations. Mistaken beliefs about how the world works can lead to flawed policies, which can cause unnecessary harm to millions.

This book presents an approach to international relations that yields at least some tentative answers to questions such as these. The approach analyzes international relations through the lens of game theory, the mathematical study of strategic interaction. In this introduction, I discuss international relations theory, why game theory is useful for studying it, how the approach fits into the overall international relations theory landscape, and why an acquaintance with the approach may be of use even to those who do not pursue it in depth.

1.1 International relations theory

Why would we want a theoretical approach to international relations when an empirical one would seem more practical and useful? Theory helps guide our thoughts when we approach the world for empirical answers. If our theoretical ideas are confused or inconsistent, we are unlikely to find solid answers to questions we might pose about world events (Mearsheimer and Walt 2013). Theory helps us formulate models or mechanisms of international processes that we can then compare with reality to see if they seem to capture what is going on. For this reason, theory has been important to all scientific disciplines, from physics to economics, as well as in international relations. As Keynes famously argued, even those who consider themselves immune to abstract speculation are usually guided by unconsciously held theoretical perspectives, which appear to them merely as principles, or rules of thumb. We might as well get these perspectives as clear and coherent as possible.

Theories are deductive logical frameworks that imply potential laws, or more modestly, hypotheses, about how the world works (Waltz 1979, 5–7). As such, they must start with a set of core assumptions, or postulates. What counts as a core assumption and what as an auxiliary (or even unstated) assumption is somewhat arbitrary, but there is a fair amount of convergence in the rationalist international relations theory world about what the central ideas are.[1] I focus on three in particular.

1. *States* are the most important actors. State actions determine war and peace, and set the conditions under which economic activity takes place. Other actors are clearly important, but in the models of this book they will matter through their influence on state preferences or behavior. This makes the theory "state centric," which has obvious limitations (Ashley 1984, 238–242). Some rationalist scholars interpret the actors in the models as state leaders rather than states per se, and hence adhere to an individualist ontology (Bueno de Mesquita *et al.* 2003). States are still primary, however, because the individuals that matter are the ones who occupy important decision-making roles in the state.

2. States interact in a context of *anarchy*. This implies that states may fight each other if they wish, but it also means that they cannot make *commitments* that they do not wish to keep in the future. In well-ordered states, the legal system enables private agents to make contracts that bind them to behave in certain ways, even when they would prefer not to. Between states, there is no such option – states will only agree to things that they want to do anyway, or can enforce upon each other through threatened punishments.

3. States are *rational*. What this means exactly will be spelled out in Chapter 2. For now, let it be understood as an assumption that states make decisions based on their evaluations of the consequences of their actions, rather than via an evaluation of the appropriateness of the behavior (March and Olsen 1998).

While the first two assumptions are fairly accurate, in my view, the third one is clearly false, as a descriptive matter. However, it may be close enough for certain contexts, and

---

[1] For the realists, see Waltz (1979, Chapter 5), Mearsheimer (2001, 30), and Glaser (2010, 28); for neo-liberal institutionalism, see Keohane (1984); and for the constructivist approach, Wendt (1999, 1).

is useful to produce coherent theories. The status of the assumption is open to debate, in the social sciences in general as well as in international relations in particular, and the conditions under which it is more or less accurate are subject to investigation (Kahler 1998, MacDonald 2003, Camerer and Fehr 2006). I omit from the above list the common realist assumption that states are *unitary* actors. It will hold for the majority of the book, but will be relaxed in Chapter 11, where I examine the influence of domestic actors. I also omit from the above a specific assumption about the content of state preferences, or what it is that they seek to maximize. I will discuss this issue in the next chapter; the models in the book will accommodate multiple interpretations on this point.

Theories exist to explain some things, the dependent variables, with reference to other things, the independent variables. What does the theory of this book try to explain, and with reference to what? At the broadest level, game theory attempts to explain *strategic choice*, or *behavior*, with reference to *preferences* and *constraints*. This behavior could be the initiation of wars, setting tariff levels, forming alliances, joining multilateral treaties, accepting offers of compensation, etc. The rationality assumption implies that states are choosing the best option available to them, from a set of possible options, or strategies. Rational choice theorists are, therefore, interested in *optimization* or the mathematical problem of selecting the value of a variable (the strategy choice) that maximizes the value of a function (the actor's *utility* or happiness). All the actors in the models considered below will be attempting to maximize their utility, or make themselves as well off as they can, given the constraints posed by the structure of the game and the actions of the other players.

As a result of this commitment to the idea that individuals are maximizing their utility, rational choice theorists are especially puzzled by – and interested in explaining – *inefficiency* or outcomes that leave both sides worse off than they could have been. Inefficiency is viewed as unambiguously bad because at an inefficient outcome, everyone could be made better off, so no one would be harmed by a change. In international relations theory, this concern for efficiency often leads to a focus on *conflict* and *cooperation*. Conflict is assumed to be inefficient in comparison with cooperation, that is, more costly for both sides than alternative outcomes that are at least in theory available to the players in a strategic situation. Conflict, be it war, the interruption of trading relations, or economic sanctions, is assumed to impose costs on both sides. If the same outcome could be achieved without conflict, and so without the costs of conflict, both sides would seem to be better off. Note, this assumes that decision makers do not enjoy war or conflict for its own save, which is probably true for most leaders in the current era, but it is clearly not always true. Cooperation is assumed to be efficient, in that it avoids the costs of conflict.

There are two principal contexts in international relations in which cooperation and conflict arise: *bargaining* and *implementation* or *enforcement* (Fearon 1998a). In bargaining, conflict can take the form of prolonged bargaining, rather than quick agreement, and negotiations that fail to reach an agreement at all. Negotiations that fail can impose costs to all, associated with the foregone economic benefits of cooperation. In the international security context, failed negotiations can even lead to war. In the implementation of an agreement, conflict can arise when one side fails to fulfill its obligations, leading the other side to reciprocate. If there are short-term incentives to exploit the other side, it may be hard to sustain cooperative behavior over time that honors an agreement. For instance, a national leader may be tempted to impose non-tariff barriers on foreign goods in violation of a trade treaty in order to please a domestic constituency, knowing that this will harm another state and possibly cause it to retaliate.

There are five main explanations of inefficiency in international relations. The first three derive from the bargaining theory of conflict as articulated by Fearon (1995), while the last two are associated with the literature on enforcement, usually known as cooperation theory (Oye 1986).

1. *Undervalued or non-feasible intermediate outcomes* means that if states simply do not value intermediate or compromise solutions very highly, or such solutions are not feasible or absent altogether, then they may fail to cooperate because each side prefers to take a chance on getting all or nothing, rather than settling for compromise. This is sometimes known as the "indivisible goods" issue, although the problem is more general, as we will see in the next chapter.
2. *Private information* means people operate with different beliefs, which may prevent them from coming to agreement in bargaining situations. If one state underestimates another's resolve to prevail over a certain issue, it may be too intransigent in the bargaining process, which may then break down in conflict. Mistrust can also prevent cooperation in implementation settings if each side thinks the other side is motivated to exploit them rather than reciprocate the cooperation. If private information is combined with incentives to misrepresent knowledge, as it often is in bargaining and in the mistrust context, the parties will have difficulty overcoming their uncertainty and may fail to cooperate.[2]
3. *Changing power* can also cause bargaining to fail if a state fears it will lose power in the future and wishes to attack while it is strong rather than allow itself to decline and then have to make concessions from a position of weakness. This is the logic of preventive war. Changing power is often referred to as "the commitment problem"

---

[2] This corresponds to the problems of uncertainty over preferences and the state of the world, as discussed in Koremenos *et al.* (2001).

following Fearon (1995) and Powell (2006). I prefer to think of the inability to commit as a general implication of anarchy that underlies all the models considered in various ways.

4. *Monitoring problems* can also cause inefficiency if states cannot immediately detect efforts to exploit them and so fail to cooperate because it makes them vulnerable to exploitation. This is particularly problematic in implementation and enforcement questions and is what makes cooperation risky in the Prisoner's Dilemma game, analyzed in Chapters 3 and 8. If states were able to perfectly monitor each other's behavior, there would be no such thing as surprise, and in particular no surprise attacks or surprise defections. States would, therefore, be able to mirror each other's actions as closely as they like, and thereby eliminate the fear of being suddenly exploited. This problem is especially salient in the fields of peacekeeping and arms control verification (Bailey 1995, Lindley 2007, Fortna 2008, Debs and Monteiro 2014).[3]

5. *Impatience* can also cause inefficiency in the enforcement context. When there are short-term temptations to exploit the other side, states can still cooperate if they value future payoffs sufficiently and fear that exploiting the other side will lead to mutual defection in the future. This "shadow of the future" can keep states cooperating, but only if they care about the future (Oye 1986). If they are too focused on the short term, because of personal or institutional characteristics, they may not care about future punishment and seize the short-term gains from exploiting the other side.

These explanations of inefficiency may seem rather incomplete at present, but they will be developed at much greater length in the succeeding chapters, in a variety of settings, and will hopefully become clear.

A special form of conflict is *war*. Empirical scholars define war as sustained combat involving at least 1,000 fatalities (Sarkees 2000). I assume that war, like conflict more generally, is inefficient because it imposes costs on both players, so that both participants could be made better off by something other than fighting (Fearon 1995). War can be divided into two types, *non-decisive* and *potentially decisive*. Non-decisive wars are competitions in the infliction and absorption of costs, and the key feature is that no side can lose except by voluntarily making concessions or giving up the object in contention. A state can always keep fighting if it wants to. Such wars are sometimes called wars of attrition, because they involve the competitive destruction of value.[4] The same kind of analysis that applies to such wars can be applied to non-lethal contests of will,

---

[3] This assumes that states cannot change their policies discontinuously and instantaneously. This problem is called uncertainty over behavior in Koremenos *et al.* (2001).
[4] Real wars of attrition can be potentially decisive; however, if each side has a stock of resources to fight with, once exhausted this leaves them incapable of further fighting.

such as trade wars or lengthy bargaining more generally. A key question, however, is why states in a bargaining session would choose to impose on each other the radically greater costs involved in a real war rather than continue to bargain.

Potentially decisive wars embody a mechanism that may eliminate one side from the game by disarming it. In a potentially decisive war, a state can lose even if it wishes to keep fighting, and its preferences will no longer matter because it loses the ability to affect the other side. As we will see in more detail in Chapter 4, the simplest model of a potentially decisive war is a costly lottery between victory and defeat. The costs reflect the losses involved in fighting, and the lottery reflects the fact that if a state's troops are victorious, the enemy can no longer offer resistance. Potentially decisive wars are even more puzzling events because not only do they greatly increase the costs of bargaining, they dramatically increase the variance, since they introduce the possibility of total loss and total victory, which is absent in non-decisive wars where states must lose voluntarily. Why states would choose a high cost, high variance method of resolving their disputes is a deep puzzle, since we usually assume that states dislike both cost and risk.[5]

1.2 Game theory and international relations theory

The particular theoretical approach of this book is based on formal, rational choice theory, in particular, game theory.[6] Formal theory just means theory that is expressed in mathematical terms. The advantages of doing so are the increased logical rigor that results from harnessing the power of mathematical language. Mathematicians have established many helpful tools that can be applied to thinking about processes of all kinds, including international relations. Rational choice theory is based on a particular conception of the processes being modeled. The premise is that social processes such as international relations can be best thought of in terms of the choices made by actors that have goals and are trying to achieve them rationally. Game theory is the subset of rational choice theory that deals with strategic interaction, that is, situations in which what each player wants to do depends in part on what it thinks others will do.[7]

The assumptions of game theory line up particularly well with the assumptions of international relations theory. As a branch of rational choice theory, game theory

---

[5] Non-decisive wars may become potentially decisive if the combatants escalate and start fighting potentially decisive battles. Most low intensity warfare is non-decisive.

[6] The founding book is Von Neumann and Morgenstern (1944). A good text that could be read with this book is Osborne (2004). Gill (2006) and Moore and Siegel (2013) provide overviews of mathematics in political science.

[7] For the debate over the merits of rational choice in security studies, see Brown *et al.* (2000b). For a survey of early game theoretic applications to international relations, see O'Neill (1994).

assumes that actors are rational and choose the strategy that will make them best off in terms of the consequences of their behavior. Game theory also assumes no special abilities to make commitments between the actors, and so is appropriate for studying anarchical contexts.[8] Also, there are relatively few important actors in many international interactions. Many international events are bilateral, and the two national leaders are the most important decision makers. Models with two or three actors are much more tractable than models with more players, although large numbers of players can be studied in simplified settings where the strategies available are not too complex, as in the models of Chapter 10.

Game theory alone, pursued in the abstract, can only provide limited insights into any specific empirical domain such as international relations. The complexity of the world ensures that there is enormous variation in strategic contexts across different disciplines, such as economics, sociology, and political science, and within political science between domestic and international politics, and within international relations. To really generate useful ideas or testable hypotheses, we must build models with these specific contexts in mind. Models highlight mechanisms that are thought to be important in producing the results that we observe.

Models are usually more complicated than the games pure game theorists study, but of course are radically simpler than reality. The additional complexity, motivated by substantive knowledge of a particular domain, makes the model useful for generating insights for that domain, and possibly even testable hypotheses. The simplification is equally necessary, in order to abstract away from complications and study problems in their simplest form, before building up more complex models to deal with the possibly confounding details.

Formal models are mathematical, and we often need to solve equations or prove propositions to draw out the implications of a model. However, the key to insight in modeling is choosing what the structure of the model will be, which determines what equations are set up in the first place. What is the underlying structure in a given situation, what is going on? For this reason, this book develops international relations theory together with the formal models. The game theoretic tools provide a language for thinking clearly about international relations and developing a rich, complex theoretical framework for understanding.

1.3 Paradigm wars and problem oriented research

Theory has traditionally been conceived of in international relations in terms of "paradigms," or schools of thought. E. H. Carr drew a distinction between realism

---

[8] Technically, this is true of *non-cooperative* game theory. The alternative, *cooperative* game theory, does allow for commitments.

and idealism (Carr 1946), where realism was held to constitute a tradition of thought stretching back to Thucydides (1954), and including luminaries such as Machiavelli (2003) and Hobbes (1968 (1651)). Hans Morgenthau's *Politics among Nations* expounded the realist view at length in the early Cold War period (Morgenthau 1948). The most prominent late Cold War exponent was generally acknowledged to be Kenneth Waltz who was said to have turned realism into a proper social scientific theory (Waltz 1954, 1979). Waltz's theory was based on the assumptions that the world was anarchic and states wished to survive, and led to the conclusion that cooperation, except against common enemies, was rare, war frequent, and that states formed recurrent balances of power. After the Cold War, fissures developed within realism leading to a schism. Offensive realists, most prominently John Mearsheimer (2001), were most loyal to Waltz's assumptions and conclusions and they attempted to fill in the logic. Defensive realists, such as Charles Glaser (2010) and Stephen Van Evera (1999), held to the assumptions, but abandoned the conclusions when it became apparent that security seeking under anarchy did not necessarily lead to war, or even conflict. A third school dubbed neo-classical realism attempted to return to the roots of realism by admitting the importance of domestic politics and the variety of human motivations (Rose 1998).

Meanwhile, idealism as realism's foil was replaced first by neo-liberal institutionalism (Keohane 1984) and then by liberalism tout court (Moravcsik 1997). The former allied itself with the emerging literature on the repeated Prisoner's Dilemma game (Axelrod 1984), and argued that institutions provided information that could ameliorate the negative effects of anarchy. The latter argued that preferences and domestic politics are more important than international interaction. The more radical paradigmatic alternative was once Marxism, but, since the end of the Cold War, constructivism has largely supplanted it (Wendt 1999, Hopf 2013). Constructivism focuses on state identities and argues that anarchy can be ameliorated and eventually transcended though transformations in state identity.

By the turn of the millennium, if not before, it had become apparent to many scholars that paradigmatic warfare had run its course as a mode of research. Realism and liberalism no longer seemed to have distinct identities worthy of paradigmatic status, and had been reduced to strands of rational choice analysis applied in different contexts, e.g. political economy vs. security, that emphasized different variables, domestic politics vs. international factors. Rationalism vs. constructivism emerged as the new grand debate,[9] but skepticism almost immediately emerged from two leaders of the respective camps (Fearon and Wendt 2002). References to the paradigms gradually dropped out of articles, and eventually even from introductions and abstracts.

---

[9] See the 50th anniversary issue of *International Organization* Volume 52, No. 4.

A survey of academics revealed that the discipline was still perceived to be dominated by paradigms, but this was increasingly not the case in the actual journal articles being published (Maliniak et al. 2011). Gradutate students were taught to scorn paradigmatic thought where they had once been encouraged to choose sides. In a recent expression of this train of thought, David Lake characterized paradigmatic debate as "evil" and a hindrance to progress (Lake 2011).

The modern alternative to paradigmatic warfare is "problem oriented research." The eager graduate student now is supposed to pick a problem of interest and importance and consider what the best approach would be to tackle it. Theories are brought in eclectically as needed (Sil and Katzenstein 2010) and empirical methods, likewise, determined by the problem at hand. The goal is to explain the phenomenon rather than to validate a particular theory, in crude statistical terms to maximize the R^2 rather than the t statistic of your favorite variable.

The game theoretic approach stands athwart this trend, not exactly shouting stop, but certainly not offering any encouragement. The rational choice approach to politics is subject to many of the same critiques levied by the critics of paradigmatic debate (Green and Shapiro 1994, Brown et al. 2000b). It is theory driven. It seeks to expand and develop a particular perspective rather than understand a particular problem. Its practitioners do not wonder what would be the best way to tackle a new research question, they wonder what would be the best way to model it within the traditional framework. The boundaries of the approach are flexible, and can be expanded to include phenomena such as bounded rationality, other regarding preferences, and a concern for fairness. However, the bulk of applied work is in the traditional mode, focusing on national actors with self-regarding preferences.

One aspect of the modeling enterprise sets it apart from its predecessor paradigms, namely the rigor that goes along with mathematical formulation. This rigor allows it to progress and cumulate in a way that was difficult to discern, although not entirely absent, in the verbal theoretical debate. For example, when prominent rational choice scholars published an article in a leading journal of political science and a graduate student found a mathematical error that vitiated their results, their response was to acknowledge the error – an exchange that would be unthinkable in verbal paradigmatic debate (Bueno de Mesquita et al. 1997, Molinari 2000).[10] This ability of the theory to correct itself also enables it to cumulate. Once a model is well formulated and solved correctly, it is done, and there is no need to wonder what it really means or write an exegesis of it. It can be built upon and extended by future scholars in a way that more closely resembles a body of work rather than an endless debate.

---

[10] The fact that the correction itself contained an error either strengthens or undermines the point, depending on one's perspective.

1.4 The utility of a partial view

This book is necessarily only a partial view of international relations and the theory thereof. It would be difficult to write a truly synoptic theory of international relations at present, given the diversity of approaches and the relatively fluid state of the field.[11] The usefulness of such an introduction will be most apparent for those already committed to, or at least interested in, the rationalist approach to international relations: liberals, realists, political economists, and the like.

I would argue that it may still have utility for those indifferent to or even hostile to the rationalist view. Problem oriented scholars, with no commitment to any particular theoretical perspective, nonetheless benefit from the availability of coherent theories and associated empirical hypotheses for testing. Game theoretic models often reveal strategic interdependencies or selection issues that are not apparent at first blush, and require careful consideration of the threats to inference (Signorino 1999). Scholars working in the psychological approach benefit from the identification, at least at the theoretical level, of a "rationalist baseline" for behavior. That is, when we know what behavior can be rationalized under certain conditions, we can begin to assess more carefully the role of psychological biases in cognition and decision making. Even constructivists, who might seem to have the least to gain from a rationalist textbook, may benefit by having a clear and coherent exposition of the position they find themselves in opposition to. The interchange between Wendt and Fearon on the rationalist–constructivist debate illustrates how greater communication between the two camps can dispel mistaken conceptions of what divides them (Fearon and Wendt, 2002).

This book should be read alongside other approaches, both theoretical and empirical. If it can contribute to strengthening the understanding of the game theoretic approach, both by adherents and opponents, it will have achieved an important aim.

1.5 Conclusion

The goal of this book is to provide a clear, structured understanding of rational choice theory as it is currently applied to international relations. The approach will be to develop families of models on the main topics that have been investigated with game theory in as systematic and understandable a way as possible. It cannot hope to be comprehensive – there will be many deserving models and whole topics that are not covered or even cited here, but I hope it will serve as a useful doorway into the field.

---

[11] See Carlsnaes *et al.* (2002), Reuss-Smit and Snidal (2008), and Dunne *et al.* (2013) for some broad surveys.

2 What states want

INTERNATIONAL relations is primarily concerned with the actions of states, understood as organizations that exercise a near monopoly of large-scale force within certain territories. Other actors are also important, such as individuals, interest groups, firms, and international organizations. Domestic political actors such as lobbying groups can affect foreign policy by advocating for protectionism, and international actors such as the International Atomic Energy Agency (IAEA) can affect international events by providing information on states's nuclear programs. However, most of these actors affect international relations indirectly by influencing the behavior of states, so state behavior remains of paramount importance.

States are so important because their behavior affects us all. When a state attacks another state, thousands or even millions may die. When states lower their trade barriers, import competing firms go out of business and workers at those firms lose their jobs, while consumers are able to purchase a broader variety of imported products at a lower cost. The field of international relations is, therefore, mainly interested in explaining state behavior.

How do we explain state behavior? The approach I will take to this question is to assume that states have certain goals or preferences, and seek to attain them through their actions. That is, states act instrumentally to achieve certain ends. While this approach is not the only one, it has proven to be a very fruitful way of looking at the subject. It situates international relations within the broader rational choice paradigm shared with economics and political science.

This chapter will, therefore, focus on the fundamentals of the rationalist approach as it applies to international relations, the actors, and their preferences. I will define what it means for a state to be rational, and consider what the logic of consequences implies for state choice. I will discuss the theory of preferences, expected utility theory, how states can be differentiated in various ways by their preferences, how states can be thought of as unitary actors, and what states have preferences over, or what they want.

2.1 Utility theory

The basic postulate of utility theory is that people, and by extension states, have preferences over how the world should be, and act to satisfy those preferences as best they can. The theory can be divided into two branches: choice under certainty or over known outcomes, and choice under uncertainty or expected utility theory.

2.1.1 Utility theory under certainty

The actors in international relations are assumed to have preferences over the possible outcomes of their interactions, which in turn determine their behavior.[1] For instance, we can posit three possible outcomes of war: victory, stalemate, and defeat. The set of outcomes can be denoted X, and if we write V for victory, S for stalemate, and D for defeat, we can define the set of outcomes as $X = \{V, S, D\}$. Outcomes are also sometimes called "states of the world."

Typically, we think states prefer victory to stalemate to defeat. One way of representing such preferences is with the relation denoted $\succeq$, where $V \succeq S$ is defined as "V is at least as good as S." This may seem a rather feeble way of expressing how most states feel about the comparison between victory and its alternatives, and to reflect this we denote $\succ$, so that $V \succ S$ is read as "V is preferred to S" and is defined as $V \succ S \Leftrightarrow (V \succeq S \text{ and not } S \succeq V)$.[2]

The key properties that preferences must have to be characterized as rational are *completeness* and *transitivity*. Completeness just means that every element in X can be ordered via the relation $\succeq$, so that no possible outcomes are simply incomparable. Transitivity means that if, say, victory is as good as stalemate, $V \succeq S$, and stalemate is as good as defeat, $S \succeq D$, then victory is also as good as defeat, $V \succeq D$. Preference orderings with these properties satisfy our ordinary understanding of what it means to be rational; someone who preferred victory to stalemate, stalemate to defeat, and defeat to victory would be unable to make a reasonable choice of what to pursue.

Definition 2.1 *A state has rational preferences, $\succeq$, over the outcomes in set X if they are:*

- *complete, that is, for all $x_i, x_j \in X$, we have either $x_i \succeq x_j$, or $x_j \succeq x_i$, or both:*
- *transitive, that is, for all x_i, x_j, and $x_k \in X$, if $x_i \succeq x_j$ and $x_j \succeq x_k$, then $x_i \succeq x_k$.*

---

[1] For an introduction to preference theory, see Mas-Colell *et al.* (1995, Chapter 1), or McCarty and Meirowitz (2006, Chapter 2).
[2] For $\Leftrightarrow$, read "if and only if." It might seem more straightforward to start with $\succ$ but starting with $\succeq$ has become customary because it makes various proofs in preference theory simpler, so is retained here for consistency with the field.

An implication of rational preferences is that strict preferences are also transitive, that is, if the preferences $\succeq$ are rational, then $\succ$ is also transitive, so that if $V \succ S$ and $S \succ D$, then $V \succ D$.

The big payoff for having rational preferences over a set of outcomes is that there will exist at least one outcome that is at least as good as all the others, and outcomes like that would be chosen by a rational state if it were simply a matter of choice. Sometimes these elements or outcomes are called maximal, or more simply best outcomes. In contrast, there is no reason to choose an outcome that is not as good as another one in the outcome set.

Theorem 2.1 *If state has rational preferences $\succeq$ over a finite outcome set X, then there exists at least one outcome that is as good as all the others.*

Proof Proceed by induction. If the set X only has one member, x_1, then we know from completeness that $x_1 \succeq x_1$, so trivially we have an element that is as good as all the others. Now assume that X has n elements and that there is at least one element as good as any of the others, call it x_m. We know that $x_m \succeq x_i$ for all $x_i \in X$. Now consider the set $X' = X \cup y$. By completeness, either $x_m \succeq y$, or $y \succeq x_m$ or both. If $x_m \succeq y$, then x_m is at least as good as anything in the new set X'. If $y \succeq x_m$, then by transitivity, since y is as good as x_m and x_m is as good as anything in X, y is as good as anything in X'. Therefore, by induction, for any finite set there exists an element that is as good as any other. □

With somewhat more complicated math, this result can be extended to continuous outcome spaces.

Thus, rational preferences that are complete and transitive enable us to speak of a best outcome for a player, or at least a set of best outcomes, which they should rationally choose. Completeness and transitivity may seem easily violated in practice. Some options may be so unfamiliar or uncertain in their implications that it is hard to order them. However, this can be modeled by explicitly bringing uncertainty into the picture, assuming that the fundamental objects or outcomes can be ranked. Transitivity may also appear to be violated, especially by collectivities and over time, but again this can be explicitly modeled using multiple player games. Heroic or not, these assumptions underlie most of rational choice theory in economics and political science.

Preference orderings are the foundation of utility theory, and there are interesting issues that can be addressed by considering them directly. However, real numbers are easier to deal with than more general orderings, so in applied settings it is customary to use utility functions to represent preference orderings.

An actor's *utility function* assigns numbers to outcomes that represent how much a state likes or dislikes that outcome. It is a function, $u(x)$, from the set of possible outcomes, X, to the set of real numbers, $\mathbb{R}$, denoted $u : X \to \mathbb{R}$. Higher numbers correspond to higher utility or happiness, so an outcome that gives a utility of 5 is preferred to one that gives a utility of 2.

Definition 2.2 *A function $u : X \to \mathbb{R}$ is a utility function representing the preferences $\succeq$ if, for all $x_i, x_j \in X$, $u(x_i) \geq u(x_j) \Leftrightarrow x_i \succeq x_j$.*

If an actor has a preference ordering $\succeq$ defined over X, it is very easy to construct a utility function that represents it. Each outcome x is given a utility number $u(x)$, where outcomes that are strictly preferred to another get a higher number and those that are tied get the same number. Such a utility function is sometimes called "ordinal" because it reflects the order of the outcomes in a preference relation.

2.1.2 Expected utility theory

Ordinal utility functions can actually get us quite far in studying strategic interaction, and the games of Chapter 3 are often analyzed in terms of ordinal utility. However, states with identical preference orderings might still behave differently. This is because ordinal preferences give no information about how much states want certain things, and this can be vital. For instance, a state that prefers victory to stalemate but only by a little bit should not exert itself to break out of the stalemate, while another state that found the stalemate intolerable might be motivated to escalate the war in pursuit of victory. The theory of expected utility enables us to think about how much actors prefer various outcomes.[3]

The building block of the theory is the "lottery," which is a probability density over the space of outcomes, X. An example of a lottery is a war in which there is a 10% chance of defeat, a 70% chance of stalemate, and a 20% chance of winning. A different lottery would attach different probabilities to the possible outcomes, such as 40% chance of defeat, 10% chance of stalemate and a 50% chance of victory. There are as many different lotteries as there are different probabilities that can be assigned to the outcomes. The sum of the probabilities of all the potential outcomes must equal 1.

Definition 2.3 *A lottery associated with a finite set of outcomes, X, with number of elements equal to $|X| = n$ is a vector $L = (p_1, \ldots, p_n)$, where $p_i \in [0, 1]$ is interpreted as the probability that outcome i occurs, so that $\sum_i p_i = 1$.*

---

[3] See Mas-Colell et al. (1995, Chapter 6), and McCarty and Meirowitz (2006, Chapter 3) for introductions to expected utility theory.

2.1 UTILITY THEORY

The fundamental assumption underlying expected utility theory is that actors have preferences defined over the space of lotteries over outcomes, denoted $\mathscr{L}$, just as they do over the outcomes themselves. That is, if you ask a state whether it would prefer a lottery with a 10% chance of victory and a 90% chance of defeat or a 20% chance of victory and an 80% chance of defeat, it would be able to provide you with an answer (presumably the second lottery beats the first).

Let us then define a preference operator, $\succeq$, over the space of lotteries $\mathscr{L}$ defined on X and think about how to represent it with a utility function. What should such a function look like? It would have to produce a real number utility value for the lottery that would be a function of the probabilities and utilities for the pure outcomes, p_i and $u(x_i)$. An extremely convenient function that does this is the expected utility function. An expected utility function assigns every lottery a utility equal to the expected value of the utilities of the components of the lottery.

Definition 2.4 *The expected utility of a lottery L based on a finite outcome set X is defined as the expected value of the utilities of the outcomes*

$$EU(L) \equiv \sum_{i=1}^{n} p_i u(x_i)$$

Let's say we have an actor willing to answer a lot of questions about their preferences over lotteries, so we know $\succeq$. The question then becomes: Can this preference relation be represented by the expected utility function? And since the lotteries are defined by the probabilities, this in turn leads to the question: Can we pick a utility function over outcomes, $u(x)$, that enables the expected utility function to faithfully represent the preference relation $\succeq$? The answers were provided by Von Neumann and Morgenstern (1944) in their foundational work on game theory, and are given in the following theorem:

Theorem 2.2 *Given a preference ordering $\succeq$ over the set of lotteries $\mathscr{L}$ defined on an outcome space X, a utility function over the outcomes $u(x)$ exists such that the expected utility of any lottery, $EU(L)$, reflects the preference ordering, that is, $L_1 \succeq L_2 \Leftrightarrow EU(L_1) \geq EU(L_2)$ if the following conditions hold:*

1. *The preference ordering $\succeq$ is complete and transitive.*
2. *Different lotteries that assign the same value to the outcomes are equivalent.*
3. *If $L_1 \succ L_2$, then all lotteries sufficiently close to L_1 are also preferred to L_2.*
4. *If $L_1 \succ L_2$, then adding an equal chance of obtaining L_3 to both sides does not alter the preference.*

Table 2.1 Different state utility functions

	Value for		
	Victory	Stalemate	Defeat
State 1	1	0.9	0
State 2	1	0.5	0
State 3	1	0.1	0

The conditions are somewhat technical, and I refer the reader to longer discussions of expected utility theory for more formal statements and proofs. The key point to take away is that under seemingly reasonable conditions, any actor that can rank lotteries over outcomes can be treated as if they are maximizing the expected utility of those outcomes.

An example of how to derive such utility functions is illustrated in Table 2.1. Say we have three states, all considering the three outcomes we have been considering, V, S, and D. All three states have the same preference ordering, $V \succ S \succ D$. Let us, therefore, assign the best and worst outcome payoffs of 1 and 0 respectively, $u_i(V) = 1$ and $u_i(D) = 0$. Then we simply ask our states: What lottery over the best and worst outcomes would they find equivalent in preference to S for sure? State 1 responds that a 90% chance of victory and 10% chance of defeat would be equivalent to stalemate for sure, so we assign a utility for stalemate of $u_1(S) = 0.9$. This state thinks the stalemate is quite good, and could hardly be improved on even by victory. Defeat, on the other hand, is disastrous. Such a state will be reluctant to invest much in victory. State 2 answers that a 50–50 lottery between victory and defeat would be about the same as a stalemate, so we assign $u_2(S) = 0.5$. This state thinks the stalemate is right in the middle between victory and defeat. State 3 answers that even a 10% chance of victory and a 90% chance of defeat would be as good as a stalemate, so $u_3(S) = 0.1$. State 3 thinks the stalemate is pretty bad, only slightly better than defeat and much worse than winning a war. Such a state would be highly motivated to pursue the war.

This type of utility function is called "cardinal," and it produces information about the strength or intensity of preferences. In the previous example, player 3 cares much more about breaking out of a stalemate than player 1 does, even though both prefer victory to stalemate.

2.1.3 Efficiency

With utility functions defined over outcome spaces, we can define clearly what it means for an outcome to be *efficient*.

Definition 2.5 *Given a set of actors with utility functions u_i defined over an outcome space X, an outcome $x' \in X$ is* efficient *if for any other outcome $x'' \in X$ that makes some player i better off, $u_i(x'') > u_i(x')$, there must be some other actor j that is worse off, $u_j(x') > u_j(x'')$.*

If an outcome is efficient, therefore, joint gains are not possible by moving to another outcome. If one player is made better off by switching to some other outcome, this will come at the expense of at least one other actor. By contrast, for every inefficient outcome there is at least one efficient outcome in which at least one actor is made better off and no one is harmed. Inefficiency, therefore, seems unambiguously bad, and to be avoided if possible. As discussed in the previous chapter, conflict is often believed to be inefficient because of the costs involved, whereas cooperation is thought to be efficient. Inefficient outcomes, therefore, seem especially problematic from the rationalist point of view, and deserving of explanation. Efficiency is sometimes called Pareto efficiency after the Italian economist Vilfredo Pareto. Associated terms include: Pareto optimal, meaning an efficient outcome; Pareto inferior, meaning not efficient; Pareto improvement, meaning moving from one outcome to another where at least one actor gains and no one loses; and Pareto frontier, meaning the set of Pareto optimal points in certain contexts.

A related concept is *zero sum*.

Definition 2.6 *A set of outcomes X and utility functions u_i defined over it is* zero sum *if every $x \in X$ is efficient*

A zero sum situation is one in which mutual gains are not possible. Hence, bargaining in zero sum situations involves clear conflicts of interest, rather than a search for mutual benefits. A *positive sum* situation is one that is not zero sum, that is, in which mutual gains are possible.

2.2 Issue spaces

The different possible states of the world over which preferences are defined can be either finite or infinite, I discuss each in turn.

2.2.1 Indivisible goods and finite issue spaces

So far, we have been assuming that the set of possible outcomes, X, is finite. The simplest case would be an "indivisible good," which both sides want but only one side can have. Finite issue spaces are worth considering for three reasons. First, as Fearon (1995) pointed out, bargaining may be more likely to fail with indivisible goods, because their indivisibility makes compromise solutions impossible and it may be that neither side will be content with not having the good if they think they have a chance of winning it through war. Therefore, bargaining over indivisible goods may differ from bargaining over divisible ones.

Following on from this insight, some scholars have argued that many international issues are not easily divisible, or are at least socially constructed to not be divisible (Hassner 2003, Toft 2005, Goddard 2006). Perhaps the most frequently discussed current example is the status of Jerusalem, particularly the Temple Mount/Haram al Sharif, in negotiations between Israel and the Palestinian Authority. A religious site may be viewed as indivisible by those bargaining over it, since sharing it with those of another faith destroys its value. Relatedly, there may be structural reasons why some goods are hard to divide. It may be hard to draw boundaries in regions of flat terrain because such boundaries are easily challenged. Hence, states may end up locating boundaries on rivers or mountain ranges (Schelling, 1960). Language patterns and other national identity markers make some territorial units difficult to divide, particularly in the modern era. For France to annex German-speaking provinces in some territorial bargain with Germany would be extremely difficult. In the modern era, pre-existing administrative boundaries have had enormous influence on subsequent boundaries when they are changed (Beissinger 2002, Carter and Goemans 2011).

Finally, finite issue spaces may simply be a convenient and acceptable simplification of a more continuous reality. In many models of international deterrence, the good being implicitly bargained over is assumed to be indivisible (Bueno de Mesquita and Lalman 1992, Zagare and Kilgour 2000). For instance, nuclear deterrence models study the process of deterring an adversary from attacking, either a state itself or some other international interest. The defender is assumed to possess some good that the challenger wants, but no intermediate divisions of the good are on the table. Rather, the defender either keeps the good or gives it up to the challenger as a whole. This way of modeling is more from convenience rather than any philosophical commitment to the idea that the objects of international negotiation are really indivisible.

For these reasons, it is worthwhile considering how to model indivisible goods and finite issue spaces. One way is to conceive of a set of goods, G, each element of which may be owned by each of the actors. In the simplest case, the set G has one element, call it A, so there are only two states of the world. Player 1 has the good and player 2 does not, and vice versa, denoted A_1 and A_2 where the subscripts indicate which actor has the good. If the good is positively valued, it will be easy to rank for the two players – each player will prefer to have the good. However, there will not be any intermediate possibilities, which may make bargaining hard.

However, there may be more than one good at stake in a given context. Consider a world with two goods, $G = \{A, B\}$, and two actors, player 1 and player 2. There are then four possible states of the world: player 1 has both, A_1B_1; player 1 has A but not B, A_1B_2; player 1 has B but not A, A_2B_1; and player 2 has both, A_2B_2. Already, this fills in the interval between the extremes, now there are two intermediate states of the world, A_1B_2 and A_2B_1. If the players value the goods equally, both of the intermediate outcomes will be valued the same. However, if one good is more valuable than the other, then there are two distinctly valued intermediate outcomes.

With three goods, $G = \{A, B, C\}$, and two actors, there are eight possible states of the world, $A_1B_1C_1, A_1B_1C_2, A_1B_2C_1, A_1B_2C_2, A_2B_1C_1, A_2B_1C_2, A_2B_2C_1$, and $A_2B_2C_2$. More generally, with a set G of goods, the number of goods is $|G|$ and with two actors the number of possible states of the world is $|X| = 2^{|G|}$. With three actors, the number is $3^{|G|}$, and with n actors, $n^{|G|}$. Thus, the number of possible states of the world increases exponentially with the number of underlying goods to be distributed.

An important special case is where all the goods have the same value. For instance, let's say two actors are bargaining over a stack of dollar bills. One dollar bill has the same value as any other, so what matters is not which dollar bills one gets but how many. In this case, if there are a set G of goods of equal value, the number of meaningfully distinguishable divisions is just $|G| + 1$. If there are 100 dollar bills, an actor can have none of them, all of them, or any number between 0 and 100. Note, if we assume that no dollar bills are left on the table, that is, each one ends up in someone's pocket, the resulting outcome space is zero sum. Since the players only care about how many bills they get, there are no Pareto improvements to be made over any outcome that fully distributes the cash.

It is easy to see that as the number of discrete goods increases, the resulting issue space begins to resemble a continuous issue space between the extremes of one side having all the goods and the other side having them all. Therefore, if we think that there are many goods to be bargained over, a continuous interval may be a reasonable approximation of the issue space for some purposes. However, for small numbers of indivisible goods, it may be worthwhile modeling the resulting discrete issue space explicitly.

2.2.2 Continuous issue spaces

Utility functions can also be defined over infinite and continuous sets. For instance, utility functions are often defined over the unit interval, the real numbers between 0 and 1, $X = [0, 1]$. This outcome space is used to represent the proportion of something in dispute that one actor gets as opposed to another. For instance, two states might have conflicting preferences over where to draw the border between them. We

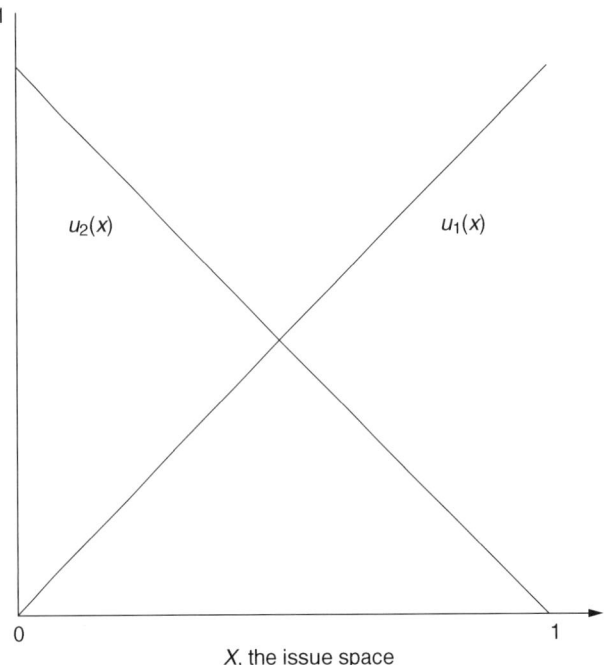

Figure 2.1 Utility functions

can let x represent the proportion that goes to player 1 and $1 - x$ be the proportion that goes to player 2. If both sides want more territory, then player 1's utility function, $u_1(x)$, will be increasing in x, while player 2's utility function, $u_2(x)$, will be decreasing. In the simplest case, illustrated in Figure 2.1, the functions could be linear, such that $u_1(x) = x$ and $u_2(x) = 1 - x$.

2.2.3 Multidimensional issue spaces

Of course, states often care about multiple issues in any international interaction. We can represent multiple issues easily in an issue space with the requisite number of dimensions. For instance, consider Figure 2.2, known as an "Edgeworth Box," after the nineteenth-century Irish economist, Francis Ysidro Edgeworth, who introduced it. Here the X axis represents one issue, say territory, and the Y axis represents another, say wealth. The axes measure how much of each good player 1 receives, with player 2 getting the remainder. So for any point in the box, (x, y), player 1 gets x and y and player 2 gets $1 - x$ and $1 - y$. Consequently, the upper right corner is the ideal point for player 1, because there it gets all of both goods, while the lower left corner is the best for player 2, because there player 2 gets all of both goods. Each player has utility functions over the points in the plane, $u_i(x, y)$, represented by the indifference curves illustrated. Player 1's utility increases as outcomes move north east, player 2's utility

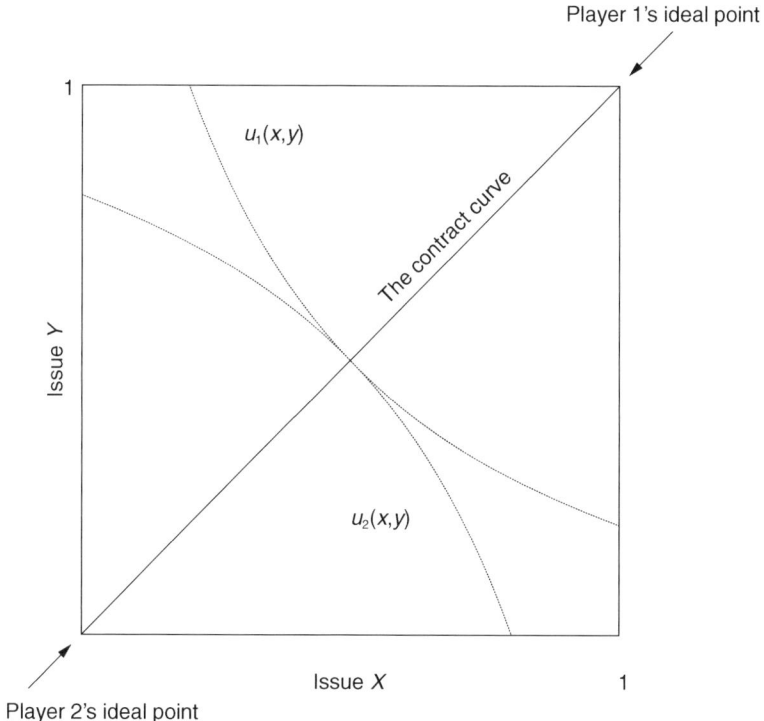

Figure 2.2 The Edgeworth Box

increases as the outcome shifts south west. Each player is willing to trade off one good for another, but would prefer to have more of both. The points where the indifference curves are tangent to each other is sometimes called the "contract curve," and it represents the points that are Pareto optimal, or efficient. Departing from the curve involves a loss in utility for both players.

An interesting feature of the contract curve is that it is unidimensional, and so if we assume that the two players would not consider outcomes that are Pareto inferior, which makes a certain degree of sense in a bargaining context, the contract curve reduces the two-dimensional problem to a one-dimensional problem. We can simply map the contract curve into the unit interval and return to the issue space illustrated in Figure 2.1. For instance, if the contract curve is the function $y(x)$, then the utility associated with outcome x is simply $u_i(x, y(x))$, and the parties can bargain over x with the appropriate value of y determined by the contract curve.

2.3 The shape of utility functions

The shape of a state's utility function will have enormous influence on the choices it makes. As a result, there are debates over what these utility functions ought to look like, and a variety of ideas on what types of utility function lead to what types of behavior.

2.3.1 Risk attitudes and intermediate outcomes

Scholars often explain state behavior with reference to attitudes towards risk. If a state leader initiates war, she is thought of as taking a risk and the inference is made that she is risk acceptant. A leader who pursues a cautious strategy is often described as risk averse. These terms need to be more precisely defined.

Consider two possible members of a set of outcomes $X = [0, 1]$: x' and x'' where $x' < x''$. Consider the lottery in which there is a p chance of getting x' and a $1 - p$ chance of getting x''. The expected utility of this lottery is $pu(x') + (1 - p)u(x'')$. The utility of the expected value of the lottery is $u(px' + (1 - p)x'')$.

Definition 2.7 *An actor is:*

- risk neutral *if* $pu(x') + (1 - p)u(x'') = u(px' + (1 - p)x'')$,
- risk averse *if* $pu(x') + (1 - p)u(x'') < u(px' + (1 - p)x'')$,
- risk acceptant *if* $pu(x') + (1 - p)u(x'') > u(px' + (1 - p)x'')$.

The three different risk attitudes are illustrated in Figure 2.3. An actor is risk neutral if the value of the lottery equals the utility of the expected value of the lottery, that is, when $pu(x') + (1 - p)u(x'') = u(px' + (1 - p)x'')$. The straight line utility function illustrates a risk-neutral actor. The utility function is $u(x) = x$. In this case, the expected value of the lottery is $pu(x') + (1 - p)u(x'') = px' + (1 - p)x''$, while the utility of the expected value is $u(px' + (1 - p)x'') = px' + (1 - p)x''$. They are, therefore, the same. Intuitively, the risk-neutral actor is indifferent between 50% of a good and a 50–50 lottery between all or nothing.

A risk-averse actor values the utility of the expected value more than the expected value of the utilities. That is, for the risk-averse actor, $pu(x') + (1 - p)u(x'') < u(px' + (1 - p)x'')$. A risk-averse utility function is illustrated above the risk-neutral one. Such utility functions are said to exhibit diminishing marginal returns, because the state is getting less and less additional utility from each additional unit of x. An implication of risk-averse preferences is that the actor likes compromise solutions in preference to risky gambles on all or nothing. A risk-averse actor prefers to get 50% for sure rather than take a 50–50 gamble on getting all or nothing.

A risk-acceptant actor values the utility of the expected value less than the expected value of the utilities. For the risk-acceptant actor, $pu(x') + (1 - p)u(x'') > u(px' + (1 - p)x'')$. A risk-acceptant utility function is illustrated below the risk-neutral one.

2.3 THE SHAPE OF UTILITY FUNCTIONS

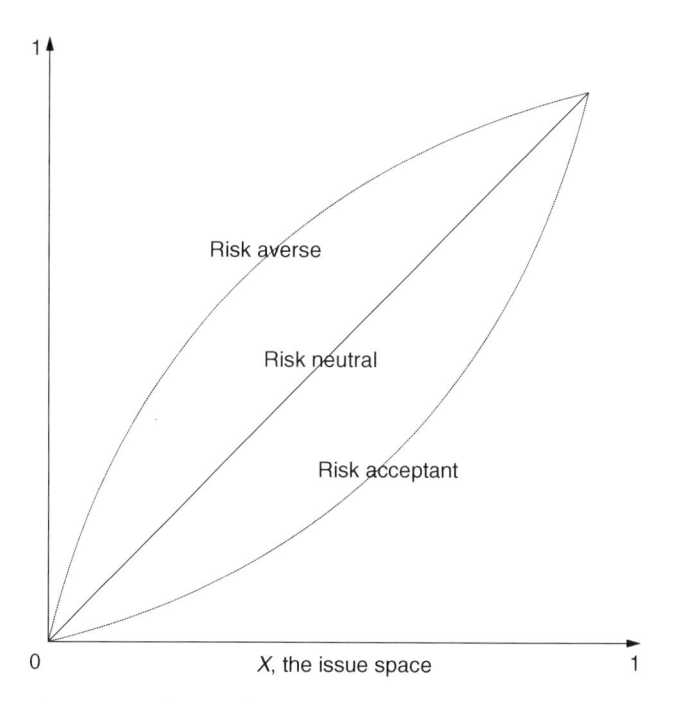

Figure 2.3 Risk attitudes

Such preferences have increasing marginal returns. A risk-acceptant actor prefers to take a 50–50 chance on all or nothing to getting 50% for sure.

This discussion has been predicated on the assumption that the underlying issue space, X, is some meaningful measure of something, usually money in the economic context. In the international security context, the usual illustrative referent is land. However, many things involved in international relations negotiations have no such interpretation, such as power, prestige, security, etc. O'Neill (2001) argues that the standard definition of risk attitudes makes no sense without such a measure, and hence is of limited value in international relations. He proposes alternative definitions that make more sense without an underlying metric. Another interesting debate on risk attitudes is whether risk aversion, at least as exhibited by real people, is consistent with expected utility maximization. Rabin and Thaler (2001) point out that experimental subjects display levels of risk aversion over small sums that would lead them to reject bets with minimal downsides and multibillion dollar upsides, which seems irrational, or at least not what people would do in practice. Because of its analytical simplicity, we will often make use of risk-neutral preferences, that is to say, linear preferences over the issue in dispute; however, we will also often consider alternatives.

A related concept that is well defined, even if the issue space is not a meaningful ratio measurement space, is the following. Posit two actors and an issue space $X = [0, 1]$. Define utility functions $u_i(x)$ such that $u_1(\cdot)$ is weakly increasing and continuous, while

$u_2(\cdot)$ is weakly decreasing and also continuous. Normalize the utility functions so that $\min(u_i(x)) = 0$, and $\max(u_i(x)) = 1$. We then make the following definition.

Definition 2.8 *The actors sufficiently value intermediate outcomes if* $\sum_i u_i(x) \geq 1$, $\forall x \in X$.

It is easy to show that a pair of actors who are either risk averse or risk neutral sufficiently value intermediate outcomes, while a pair of risk-acceptant actors do not. However, a risk-acceptant actor paired with a sufficiently risk-averse one could still sufficiently value intermediate outcomes. This means that the presence of a risk-acceptant actor need not cause conflict – if paired with a risk-averse actor; the two could conceivably bargain and reach an agreement. Note, it is impossible to say of one actor in isolation whether or not they sufficiently value intermediate outcomes. The property applies to pairs of actors. This idea will be developed further in Chapter 4.

2.3.2 Prospect theory

Extensive critiques of expected utility theory have been made in psychology. One of the most salient in international relations is prospect theory (Kahneman *et al.* 1982, Farnham 1995, Levy 1997, McDermott 1998). Prospect theory argues that risk attitudes differ depending on whether facing gains or losses. Prospect theorists argue that people are risk acceptant over losses and risk averse over gains, defined with reference to the status quo, S, as in the example illustrated in Figure 2.4. However, prospect theorists argue further that the location of the "status quo" is not objectively fixed by the current state of the world, but rather subjective and influenced by "framing." By posing dilemmas with different frames, establishing different reference points, people can be induced to make different decisions in the same objective circumstances.

An interesting phenomenon that can be observed in international relations is that the status quo may be easier to adjust upwards rather than downwards. A state that conquers a new province rapidly incorporates it into its status quo and would take great risks to retain it. A state that loses a province may not adjust so quickly, and may still see the status quo as where it was before the loss, and hence be willing to fight to get it back.

2.3.3 The status quo, satiated and greedy states

An important concept in many models of international relations is the status quo, or the way things are currently. Any game starts with an initial state of the world. States

2.3 THE SHAPE OF UTILITY FUNCTIONS

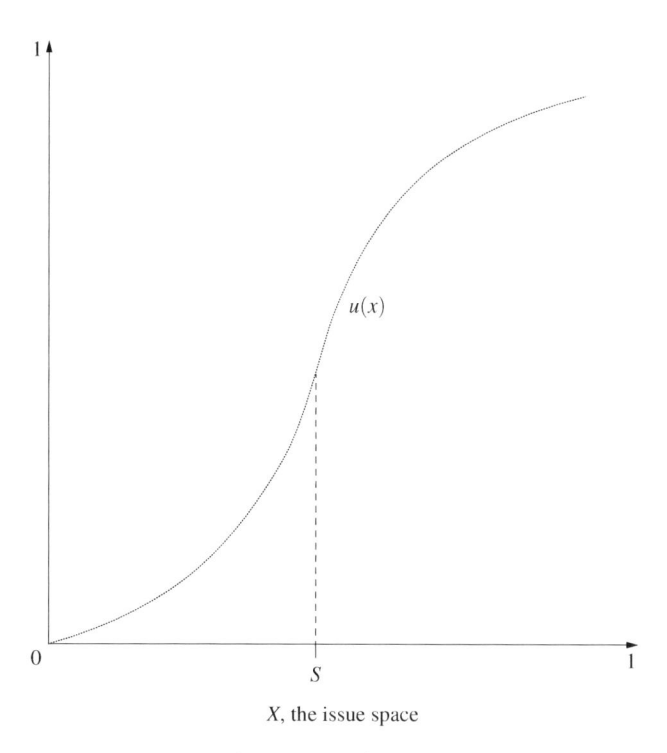

Figure 2.4 Prospect theory utility function

then may try to improve their situation, or simply defend what they have. States that are generally satisfied with the status quo, and do not greatly value gains in territory or power, are sometimes called status quo, or satiated states. States that are greatly dissatisfied with the status quo and want more territory or power are sometimes called expansionist, revisionist, or greedy (Wolfers 1962, Glaser 1995). Schweller combines this dimension with the relative power of the state to produce four types: wolves, who are strong revisionists; jackals, who are weak revisionists; lions, who are strong status quo states; and lambs, who are weak status quo states (Schweller 1996, 1998).

We illustrate these ideas in Figure 2.5 with the two different utility functions. The straight line utility function, $u(x) = x$, represents a state that gets a constant increase in utility with each additional amount of x it receives, from the first to the last. This could represent a "greedy" state in Glaser's terminology – it always wants more, no matter how much it has (Glaser 1995, 2010).

In contrast, the curved utility function indicates a state that cares differently about x depending on how much it already has. Before reaching the point s, it places great value on getting more. Then, after s, it gets disutility from additional increments. Such a state wants to have s, but doesn't care that much about getting more. If s represents the status quo, or how much the state already has, this state will be satisfied with the way things are and have no desire to get more. It will be very reluctant to give up what

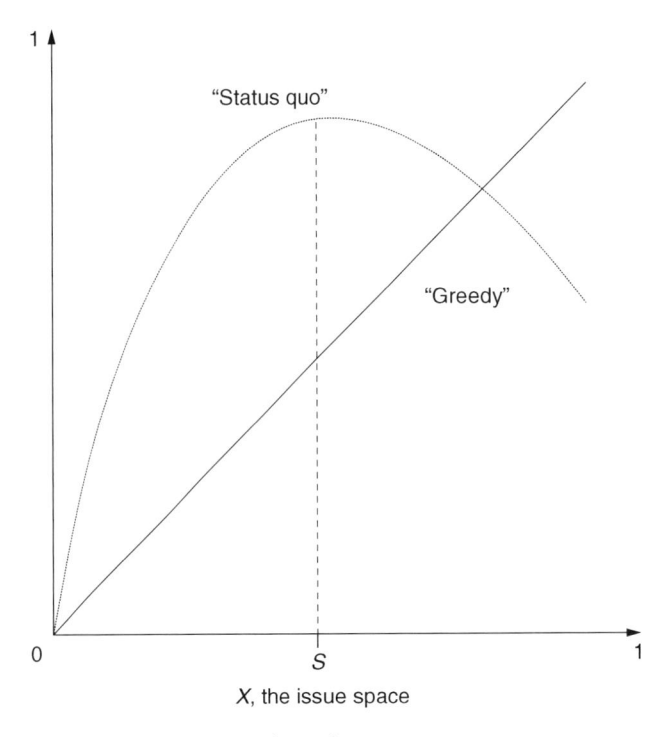

Figure 2.5 Status quo and greedy states

it has, however, so it will be difficult to force it down below s. We can argue that in the pre-nationalist era, states valued territory in more or less a linear fashion, more was better and there was nothing special about any particular border.[4] Since the onset of nationalism, they value territory more like the curved utility function, where achieving control of the homeland is strongly valued, and additional gains are unimportant or even harmful. More territory could be unwanted because the inhabitants are considered foreigners and the state does not wish to incorporate them (or commit genocide against them) (Schultz and Goemans 2014).

If we compare Figure 2.5 with Figures 2.3 and 2.4, we note several things. First, a risk-neutral state can be greedy, in the sense that it always wants more, without reference to the status quo. Second, a status quo state may exhibit both risk acceptance and risk aversion, as prospect theory suggests. A status quo state may be risk acceptant over outcomes below the status quo, and would prefer to gamble rather than make concessions. However, the same state could be risk averse over gains, and prefer sure limited

---

[4] Although the concept of the loss of strength gradient implies that even in the pre-national age there were diminishing returns from territorial expansion (Boulding 1962), in fact it might be possible to reconstruct something like an S shape if it is considered that it was important to reach a certain size, similar to the local competitors, in order to survive and beyond that a loss of strength gradient would kick in.

2.3 THE SHAPE OF UTILITY FUNCTIONS

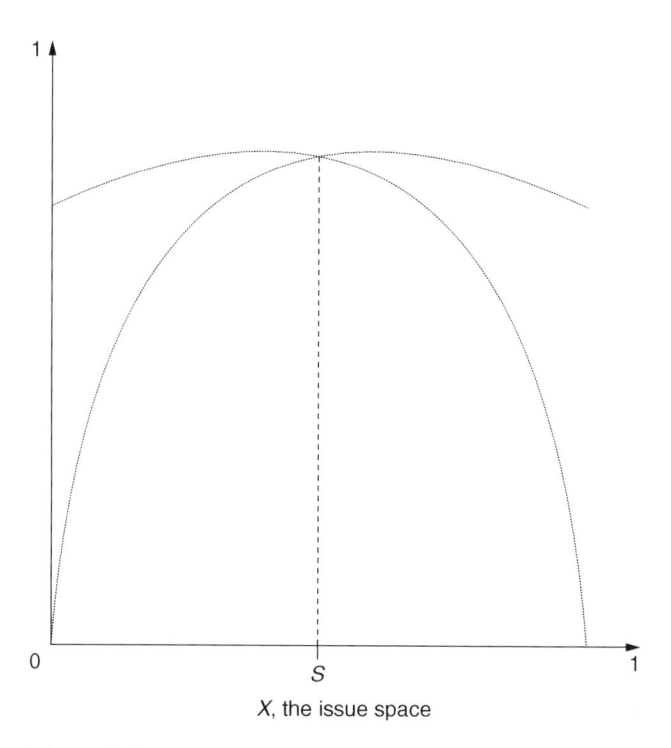

Figure 2.6 Two status quo states

gains rather than risky gambles on big gains. It may be advantageous in international bargaining contexts to be believed to have such a utility function, as it conveys only moderate desire for gain but great resolution to avoid losses. Finally, risk-acceptant states are quite greedy, they are hard to satisfy with compromise solutions and tend to want all or nothing gambles.

The utility functions of two status quo states are illustrated in Figure 2.6. Assuming that s marks the status quo, say the current territorial boundary, it is clear that in this case the two states are basically satisfied with the way things are. They may benefit from further expansion, but not that much, and they would actually suffer from taking over the entire issue space. Furthermore, each would suffer great losses in utility if the status quo were altered against them, so they are likely to resist encroachment. This represents two states in the age of nationalism in which their ethnic groups are well separated and the state boundaries correspond to ethnic boundaries, so the states have few conflicting claims to territory.[5]

In contrast, consider the states in Figure 2.7. Although these states could be satisfied short of obtaining the whole bargaining space, they are both deeply dissatisfied with

---

[5] One could make Figure 2.6 look more like (though not identical to) Figure 2.1 by rescaling it such that 0 is the maximum of player 2's utility function and 1 is the maximum of player 1's. With multiple types, we could pick 0 and 1 to represent the maxima for the most extreme types on each side, with more moderate types having interior maxima.

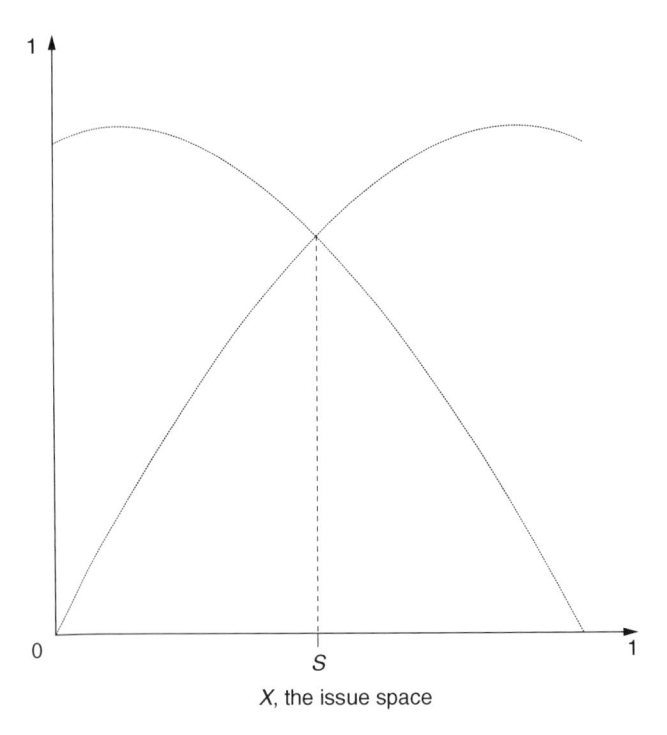

Figure 2.7 A case of ethnic conflict

the status quo. Each side would gain considerably by further expansion. This could represent a case of territorial conflict in which both states view the contested territory as part of their homeland, and hence are willing to expend great resources to acquire it. An example might be the long-running dispute between India and Pakistan over Kashmir.

2.4 The state as unitary actor

An obvious objection to talking of states as having preferences is that they are composed of many individuals. National governments often contain executive branches and legislatures, which both have a say in foreign policy making. Legislatures are composed of many members. The executive branch is an enormous bureaucracy. Treating the state as a unitary actor seems to violate methodological individualism, a fundamental premise of the rational choice approach (Kydd 2008). How can we justify treating states as unitary actors with transitive preferences? The problem was discovered in the eighteenth century by Condorcet: with three or more actors and three or more options, voting can produce cycles where $A \succ B \succ C \succ A$, and so forth, violating transitivity (McLean and Urken 1995). Black (1948) showed that cycles will be avoided if the options can be arrayed on a single dimension and the players have "single peaked preferences" that decline from an ideal point. In this case, the voter with the median ideal point will prevail. The median voter theorem is often invoked to justify modeling a legislature as a single decision maker, its median member. However, Arrow (1970) proved that with more than one dimension such cycles cannot be ruled out by any normatively desirable preference aggregation mechanism, such as majority rule (see Gaertner (2009) for an introduction to social choice theory). Thus, the problem of group preferences is real and profound.

There are three main responses to it. First, dictatorship trivially solves the problem by making one individual's preferences those of the state. This solution has the advantage of being realistic for some states, in that dictatorships exist, but it is not universal or normatively desirable. We would probably not want to covert democracies to dictatorships to solve the preference aggregation problem. A weaker version of this solution is to argue that national leaders, though constrained in various ways domestically, are relatively unconstrained internationally and so can act more or less like dictators within certain boundaries (Bueno de Mesquita 1981, 27).

A second approach is to argue that, while preference aggregation in the usual sense does not guarantee transitive preferences, certain structures of decision making can produce chief executives that act as if they maximize utility functions. Achen (1988) examined a model in which bureaucratic players pressurized the decision maker and showed that the result was a leader who acted in a unitary rational fashion (see also, Downs and Rocke 1990, 92–100). Subsequent models of trade protection developed along similar lines, with domestic interest groups offering a schedule of rewards to the leader for moving policy in the preferred direction (Grossman and Helpman 1994).[6]

The third approach is to explicitly model the domestic actors thought to influence international relations and the structures through which they exert their influence. This approach gained popularity after Putnam (1988) introduced the "two-level game" metaphor. It has also become popular in analyses of international crisis bargaining and decisions over war (Schultz 2001a, Bueno de Mesquita *et al.* 2003). Such models often feature leaders for whom a substantial motivation is to get reelected and so continue to enjoy the benefits of office holding. Of course, the domestic actors modeled are themselves composed of multiple actors, so this approach cannot claim complete fidelity to methodological individualism. However, the insights it generates are often worth the cost of the additional complexity.

For the purposes of developing a theory of international relations, analytical common sense mandates starting with simple cases and moving on to the more complex. This justifies focusing on states as unitary actors as a first cut, and adding detail about

---

[6] See Braumoeller (2012) for a non-rationalist version applied to great power politics. See also Hug (1999).

their internal structure as warranted subsequently. I will, therefore, focus primarily on models of unitary states, but will introduce domestic actors in Chapter 11.

2.5 The national interest

If states are to be thought of as unitary actors with preferences, what are these preferences? States are often thought to have a "national interest" but opinions diverge on what that comprises. Thucydides, and, following him, Hobbes, famously argued that men quarrel for three reasons: competition over scarce goods, fear for their safety or security, and love of glory or pre-eminence (Thucydides 1954, Hobbes 1968 (1651)). Other scholars have come up with other lists.[7] The four things perhaps most frequently mentioned are: territory, power, security, and wealth.

2.5.1 Territory

Territory is in some ways the fundamental goal for states, given that most states throughout history have been territorial entities, closely identified with control over a particular allotment of territory.[8] Territory is also limited in supply because with minor exceptions, such as Holland, they aren't making any more of it. Territory was often equated with power in the pre-industrial age, when wealth was regarded as fixed and came primarily from taxing geographically fixed assets, such as peasant labor. The relationship between territory and power is more variable today, but strategic territory can still convey power advantages, particularly if it is fortified or "consolidated" (Carter 2010).

In the literature on balance of power, states are often thought of as maximizing their share of the available territory (Wagner 1986, Niou et al. 1989, Acemoglu et al. 2008). The total territory is often denoted R and state i's share is denoted r_i. States then may attack or defend, devote resources against one adversary or another. These models are quite complicated, but one general result that tends to emerge is that if one state approaches having half the world's resources, the other states will ally against it, lest they be destroyed in the next round. In these models, territory is zero sum.

In the modern era of nationalism, states develop strong attachments to particular pieces of territory, their national homeland. This leads them to greatly value their homelands, and not value other territory as much, regardless of factors such as economic value or strategic location (Shelef 2014). In the many instances where these

---

[7] Wolfers (1962) has an interesting discussion of national goals, see Chapters 5 and 10.
[8] See Spruyt (1994) for an interesting analysis as to why this is the case.

attachments do not overlap, this facilitates peace by reducing the conflicts of interest states often engaged in over territory in the past, when territory was viewed more pragmatically for its economic value. However, these attachments may clash, which can lead to even greater problems. When two states develop national attachments to the same piece of territory, compromise may be difficult. Many wars continue to be fought over territory (Huth 1998). An interesting literature has emerged on the size of states. Alesina and Spolaore (2003) argue that states gain an efficiency boost from larger size, but that the increasing heterogeneity of the population over which they rule imposes costs, and the optimal size of the state is governed by these competing factors. Cederman (1997) takes a computational approach to a similar set of questions, asking what conditions foster the emergence or breakdown of states and balances of power.

Interestingly, territory is usually considered to be (at least) two dimensional, yet most models of bargaining and conflict have only one dimension, interpreted as the share of the territory each side has. Note, this cannot be finessed with the Edgeworth Box analysis presented above, since that was about adding two unidimensional goods, rather than a single two-dimensional one. In bargaining over territory, it is clear that some square kilometers are more valuable than others, and the valuation may differ across actors. This issue has not been adequately treated so far in international relations, though there is work on bargaining and dividing multidimensional goods from other perspectives (Brams and Taylor 1996).

As a result, although territory is sometimes thought to be a zero sum good, and even modeled as such, in reality it is not. States value some territories more than others, and, therefore, Pareto improvements are possible. If, contrary to fact, the US owned Normandy and France owned Florida, a trade would presumably make both states better off because France values Normandy more than Florida, and vice versa for the US. Even in the pre-national age when territory was less freighted with ideational baggage, territory closer to the national center was more valuable than territory farther away, because it was less costly to rule and more important for defense of the center.

2.5.2 Power

In the realist tradition, international anarchy is viewed as dangerous and power is the key to survival (Morgenthau 1948, Mearsheimer 2001). Power is viewed as inherently relative, for one state to gain more, another must lose (Waltz 1979, Grieco 1988). There are many different conceptions of power in international relations (Barnett and Duvall 2005). One interpretation of power in the military realm is to interpret it as a state's share of total military capabilities. For instance, consider two states in a world in which tanks are the decisive unit of military power. Each country's military power could be measured as its share of the total number of tanks. If state 1 has m_1 tanks and state 2 has m_2, then state 1's utility function would be $u_1(m_1, m_2) = \frac{m_1}{m_1+m_2}$ and state 2's would equal $u_2(m_1, m_2) = \frac{m_2}{m_1+m_2}$ (Powell, 1999a, 49).[9] In a world with $n > 2$ states, if we write the vector containing each state's absolute amount of military power $\mathbf{m} = (m_1, m_2, m_3, \ldots, m_n)$, then state i's utility will equal its share of the world total

$$u_i(\mathbf{m}) = \frac{m_i}{\sum_{j=1}^{n} m_j}$$

Power is relative, or zero sum. For one state's power to increase, other states' power must decrease. This makes cooperation impossible in two player games, but cooperation among coalitions is possible with more than two players (Snidal 1991a).

Some states may genuinely want power for its own sake. However, most if not all states temper their pursuit of power because they value the alternative uses of wealth that is spent on gaining power. That is, their utility functions include both wealth and power, so that money spent on power is felt as a cost. If this were not the case, states would devote their entire national income to military spending, which is rarely approached even in the midst of total war. If we assume that each unit of military power m_i costs γ_i, we can write an example of such a utility function as follows

$$u_i(\mathbf{m}, c_i) = \frac{m_i}{\sum_{j=1}^{n} m_j} - \gamma_i m_i$$

Note that with this utility function, power is no longer zero sum, since all states view military spending as a cost and can increase their welfare together by reducing military spending proportionally, so as to leave the power balance unchanged. This kind of utility function underlies many analyses of arms races.[10]

The tradeoff between wealth and power is also a theme of many analyses of the rise and fall of nations over time (Kennedy 1987). Kennedy depicts a cycle in which rising economic powers acquire greater territory, but this generates greater burdens of empire, which call for more military spending, which eventually outstrips the economic value of the territory gained, which leads to contraction or collapse.[11] This kind of tradeoff between power and wealth is modeled by Hirshleifer (1995). He lets states allocate their resources between predation, power directed outwards to steal the resources of others, and production, or investment in own production. Depending on the technology of war, either multiple states can form a steady state equilibrium or the system will collapse as one state consumes all the others.

---

[9] This is one specific version of a contest success function, generalizations of which have been extensively studied in economics, see Hirshleifer (1989).

[10] A somewhat unusual feature of this function is that zero spending on each side is the only Pareto optimal level of mutual spending (and that only if we define the function to be ≥ 1 at that point, which because of the 0 in the denominator is otherwise undefined), so there is no contract curve in this case.

[11] See also Gilpin (1981).

2.5.3 Security

Security is the goal often stressed by modern Realists, because the insecurity of the anarchic world would seem to make security of pre-eminent interest for states. (Waltz 1979, Mearsheimer 2001). Security is often equated with power, but it is in fact quite distinct. There are varying ways to formalize security, but one way is to think of it as the probability of continued survival. We can conceive of this as 1 minus the probability of being deprived of sovereignty through defeat in war (Kydd 1997b). If we let w stand for war, d stand for defeat, e stand for elimination, we can use conditional probability notation and write security s as

$$s = 1 - p(e|d)p(d|w)p(w)$$

A state is therefore secure to the extent that any of the three probabilities is low. If war is unlikely, then a state is secure even if it were likely to lose. If a state is unlikely to be defeated if a war occurs, it is still secure, even if war is likely. If it is unlikely to be eliminated even if it is defeated, it still has some security, for it can hope to retain its sovereignty after the war, as France did in 1944 and Iraq did in 1991, though they were defeated by their opponents. While producing some insights, this utility function is unusual in that it does not map from some set of goods or things of value to utility, but rather from a set of (subjective) probabilities to utility. Alternative understandings of security focus on safety from harm, human security as opposed to national security, and ontological as opposed to physical security (Paris 2001, Mitzen 2006, Kadercan 2013).

Power can increase security, by decreasing the likelihood of defeat in war. However, efforts by a state to increase its power by threatening other states may cause the other states to react in ways that make war more likely, decreasing state security in a process known as the security dilemma (Jervis 1978, Kydd 2005, Booth and Wheeler 2008). Security is positive sum, in that all states can be simultaneously made more secure. If no state ever attacks another, the probability of war is 0, $p(w) = 0$, for everyone, and all enjoy perfect security, $s = 1$. Nonetheless, conflict is possible over security if there is uncertainty about state motivations (Kydd 1997b).

2.5.4 Wealth

Wealth is the goal emphasized by the Liberal tradition, as well as much political economy (Moravcsik 1997). Wealth is easier to cooperate over, in the modern understanding, because it is positive sum, since cooperation can increase wealth for all players in the system. However, even with positive sum goods, competition can sometimes be fierce. Some argue that wealth, or "absolute gains," is primary to states' utility functions, and that power enters in only instrumentally as a means of protecting or acquiring wealth (Powell 1991).

2.6 Conclusion

The model of states as decision makers that try to advance their interests in the world is spare, but useful. The main task of this book will be to investigate how the strategic environment and the threats and opportunities that confront states lead to different kinds of behavior, and generate models that shed light on why states do what they do. In Chapter 11, I will relax the unitary state assumption to consider how domestic politics affects the picture.

EXERCISES

2.1 Consider the problem of utility over territory. Let's start simply with a one-dimensional representation. Consider two actors, 1 and 2, with utility functions defined over a single-dimensional issue space $X = [0, 1]$, but where the actors can own sections or "provinces" of the interval. The boundaries between sections are defined by a vector $B = (b_1, b_2, b_3, \ldots, b_n, 1)$. Thus, there are $n + 1$ provinces. Define a "size" vector containing the lengths of each province, $S = (b_1, b_2 - b_1, b_3 - b_2, \ldots, 1 - b_n)$. Define for each actor an "ownership" vector O_i with 1s in the place of the provinces that it owns and 0s elsewhere.

1. Assume that each actor's utility function is a simple sum of how much of the space they own so

$$u_i = \sum_{j=1}^{n+1} o_j s_j$$

   (a) Can the players both be made better off by exchanging existing provinces?
   (b) Can the players both be made better off by altering the boundaries of the existing provinces while preserving the ownership structure?
   (c) Can the players both be made better off by reducing the number of provinces – for instance, by consolidating contiguous provinces that are owned by the same actor?

2. Now assume that the utility function is a function of the sum of the squares of the provinces owned, indicating that there are increasing returns to the size of a province

$$u_1 = \sum_{j=1}^{n+1}(o_j s_j)^2$$

(a) Can the players both be made better off by exchanging existing provinces (without doing anything else)?
(b) Can the players both be made better off by reducing the number of provinces – for instance, by consolidating contiguous provinces that are owned by the same actor?
(c) If the actors are free to adjust both the number of provinces and the ownership structure, what set of boundaries is Pareto optimal with this utility function?

2.2 Consider two states, state 1 and state 2, which can unilaterally set their tariff rates on imported goods, $t_i \geq 0$. Each state has an ideal level for its own tariff, $t_i^i > 0$, and prefers that the other side's tariff be 0, $t_j^i = 0$. Assume that each side's utility declines with the distance between the tariff levels and their ideal point, as follows

$$u_i(t_1, t_2) = -\sqrt{(t_1 - t_1^i)^2 + (t_2 - t_2^i)^2}$$

1. Draw the t_1, t_2 quadrant and draw in the ideal points for each player.
2. Draw in sample indifference curves for the two states around their ideal points. What shape are they?
3. Draw in the contract curve between the two ideal points. What shape is it and why? What equation describes it?
4. The contract curve divides the t_1, t_2 quadrant into two regions. How do they differ in terms of how the players could realize joint gains in each region?

2.3 Consider the utility function $u(x) = x^\rho$, where $\rho > 0$ and $x \in [0, 1]$. Under what conditions would a player with such preferences be risk acceptant, risk neutral, and risk averse?

3 Varieties of strategic settings

WHEN states interact with each other in the international arena, they do so in a variety of strategic settings. In the context of an arms competition, states feel an imperative to keep up with their adversary, and surpass them, if possible. In international trade, states often have an incentive to protect domestic industries but a conflicting interest to widen markets for their exports. States attempting to coordinate on an international standard wish to harmonize their policies, but preferably on their own terms.

Each setting will present states with a different set of incentives and strategic opportunities. The primary question of interest in each case is how states will respond to these incentives and opportunities, or how they will behave. Some outcomes, called *equilibria*, will be stable or self reinforcing, in that if the players think they will occur, they have an incentive to fulfill that expectation and make them occur. Not all outcomes in a strategic setting have this property. Non-equilibrium outcomes are thought to be less likely to occur than equilibria, so by locating equilibria we can begin to make predictions about behavior.

More specifically, we can ask whether states will *cooperate*. Keohane (1984, 51) defined cooperation as a process by which policies that were not in harmony to start with are brought into conformity through a process of policy coordination. More formally, we can identify cooperation with the achievement of Pareto efficient outcomes by the players in a setting in which inefficient outcomes exist. That is, if a setting is positive sum, so that there is a possibility for joint gains, then it can serve as a model of a cooperation problem. If a Pareto optimal outcome is also an equilibrium, then cooperation is more likely in that setting than if the Pareto optimal outcomes are not equilibria.

These different strategic settings can be represented by simple two player, two strategy normal form games. The variety of preferences the actors may have over the four possible outcomes provides a wealth of different possibilities. Five of these normal form games have particular importance for international relations theory: the Prisoner's Dilemma, the Assurance game, the Coordination game, Chicken, and

Matching Pennies. There are many other possibilities (Rapoport and Guyer 1966, Kilgour and Fraser 1988, DeNardo 1995) but these five have been applied most widely.

The literature that has applied these simple games to the problem of international cooperation is large. Snyder and Diesing (1977) used these games to study crisis bargaining. Jervis (1978) used the Prisoner's Dilemma and Assurance game to study the security dilemma. Stein (1982a) introduced the distinction between Coordination and Collaboration games, which was further explored by Snidal (1985a).[1] Martin (1992) used Collaboration and Coordination games, along with the Assurance game and what she calls a "suasion" game[2], to study multilateral cooperation. The games of this chapter also figure in some popular accounts of the history of game theory and of one of its greatest contributors, John Nash (Poundstone 1992, Nasar 1998).

In this chapter, I first define the class of games under consideration and then discuss the *solution concepts* used to solve them, primarily the *Nash equilibrium*. Then I will discuss the five games and some simple applications to specific issues.

3.1 Normal form games and Nash equilibria

When players interact with each other, they have strategies available to them, or actions they can take. These actions, in combination with the actions of other states, lead to the outcomes of the game. The players have preferences over these outcomes, which will influence what actions they select. These are the elements of a normal form game. The simplest versions have two players with two strategies each, leading to four possible outcomes.

Definition 3.1 *A finite normal form game is a set of n actors, each with a finite set of strategies, S_i, and a utility function $u_i(\cdot)$ defined over the set of outcomes that results from the strategies selected by the players, $S_1 \times S_2 \times \cdots \times S_n$.*

What strategies should players choose in a normal form game? There are a variety of different solution concepts that have been suggested to help answer this question. Two have proven particularly useful, the concept of dominant strategies and the Nash equilibrium.

Some strategies may lead to a worse outcome for a player than an alternative strategy, no matter what the other players do. Such strategies are called *dominated* strategies, and it seems reasonable to suppose that no player would choose one. Let s denote a *strategy profile*, a vector with a strategy choice for each player. That is, s is an outcome in the

---

[1] See also Stein (1982b) and Wagner (1983).
[2] Similar to the deterrence game introduced in the next chapter.

game, $s \in S_1 \times S_2 \times \cdots \times S_n$. Let s_{-i} be a strategy profile for every other player in the game aside from player i. Write (s'_i, s_{-i}) for the strategy profile $(s_1, s_2, \ldots, s'_i, \ldots, s_n)$. We can then define a dominated strategy.

Definition 3.2 *A strategy s_i for player i is dominated by s'_i if $u_i(s_i, s_{-i}) < u_i(s'_i, s_{-i})$, for all s_{-i}.*

The most basic solution concept in game theory is that players should not choose dominated strategies. So one way to analyze a game is to go through eliminating dominated strategies one by one. Then the solution to the game is whatever is left, there could be several possibilities or there could be only one. In the Prisoner's Dilemma, we will see that we are lucky and can solve the game in this fashion. A related concept is the *dominant strategy*, which is a strategy that is best for an actor no matter what the other states do. A dominant strategy would seem particularly likely to be chosen since it does not depend on beliefs about what the other side will do.

While some games have dominated, or are even dominant strategies, many of the more interesting ones do not. The Nash equilibrium concept applies much more broadly, in fact it applies to all games.[3] A Nash equilibrium is a strategy profile such that no player has any incentive to switch their strategy if they expect the other players to play their respective strategies in the equilibrium.

Definition 3.3 *A Nash equilibrium is a strategy profile such that for all players, $u_i(s_i, s_{-i}) \geq u_i(s'_i, s_{-i})$, for all $s'_i \in S_i$.*

That is, in a Nash equilibrium, no player has an incentive to *deviate* to another strategy. Given what the other players are doing, each player is at least as well off with their strategy as with any other available to them. Another way of expressing this is that a Nash equilibrium consists of strategies that are *best responses* to each other, in that players cannot improve on their response to what the other players are doing. Nash equilibria seem to be stable because, once arrived at, there is no incentive to deviate. Thus, in situations where people are used to playing the game and have tended to implement the Nash equilibrium, there is little reason to suppose they would change their behavior.

With normal form games defined and solution concepts in hand, we can proceed to analyze the five two-by-two normal form games mentioned previously, the Prisoner's Dilemma, Assurance game, Coordination, Chicken, and Matching Pennies.

---

[3] See Kuhn (1997) for Nash's original contributions and other foundational papers in game theory.

Table 3.1 The Prisoner's Dilemma

		Player 2	
		Cooperate	Defect
Player 1	Cooperate	3, 3	1, 4
	Defect	4, 1	2, 2

3.2 The Prisoner's Dilemma

This game is is the most widely studied in game theory, and is the one game that non-specialists may have heard of. Common empirical applications include tariffs on imported goods and arms racing. It features a dominant strategy to not cooperate, which is a particularly compelling prediction of how the game should be played, although not an especially accurate one. The dominant strategies also constitute a Nash equilibrium.

The Prisoner's Dilemma is illustrated in Table 3.1.[4] Player 1 chooses the row and player 2 chooses the column. The numbers in the cells are utility values or payoffs for the actors, with player 1's payoff listed first and player 2's second. Higher numbers signify higher utility.

The Prisoner's Dilemma is a positive sum game. Specifically, mutual cooperation is better than mutual defection for both players. Both get their second best payoff, 3, rather than their next to worst payoff, 2. This means that cooperation is well defined in this context – both players would be better off if they both cooperated, rather than both defected.

Unfortunately, both players have a dominant strategy to defect. If the other side is expected to defect, cooperation gives a payoff of 1 and defection gives 2, so defection makes sense. If the other side is expected to cooperate, cooperation gives 3 but defection gives 4, so again defection is better. So no matter what the other side does, each side prefers to defect. Eliminating dominated strategies, therefore, leaves only mutual defection as the solution. Mutual defection is also the unique Nash equilibrium to the game. If the other side is expected to defect, defection is a best response.

While the numbers shown in Table 3.1 reflect the Prisoner's Dilemma preference ordering, they are specific and hence do not allow the preferences to be treated as variables. The Prisoner's Dilemma is often written more generally as shown in Table 3.2, where R stands for the reward of mutual cooperation, P is the punishment of mutual defection, T is the temptation to exploit the other side, and S is the sucker's payoff of being exploited. The payoff ordering $T > R > P > S$ defines the Prisoner's Dilemma.

---

[4] The story behind the name describes two prisoners being interrogated by a police officer and who are being offered incentives to testify against their counterpart.

Table 3.2 The Prisoner's Dilemma: general notation

		Player 2 Cooperate	Player 2 Defect
Player 1	Cooperate	R, R	S, T
	Defect	T, S	P, P

Table 3.3 The exchange game

		Player 2 No NTB	Player 2 NTB
Player 1	No NTB	$b-c, b-c$	$-c, b$
	NTB	$b, -c$	0, 0

3.2.1 The exchange problem

One example the Prisoner's Dilemma can be applied to is situations where the two players are arranging some exchange of concessions, where there are opportunities to cheat or not fulfill your side of the deal. For instance, in the trade context, the policy of interest might be tariff levels on the exports of the other country (Conybeare 1984). Both sides would be better off lowering their tariffs on each other's goods. However, each side would be even better off if the other side lowered its tariffs while it cheated and maintained a non-tariff barrier (NTB) to protect its import competing industries. We can model this by assuming that if one side lowered its tariffs, this would confer a benefit worth b to the other side, at a cost c to itself where we assume that the benefit is greater than the cost, $b > c > 0$. The game then looks as illustrated in Table 3.3. It is easy to see that the resulting preferences have a Prisoner's Dilemma ordering, since $b > b - c > 0 > -c$.

3.2.2 Competition for power

Weapons acquisition, or arms races, have been analyzed with game theory since the approach was invented. Let us consider one possible representation of this problem with two players who care about relative power. Let each player's absolute military power be denoted m_i and their utility function be the ratio of their military capabilities to the total

$$u_i(m_1, m_2) = \frac{m_i}{m_1 + m_2} \tag{3.1}$$

Let's assume that each side can vary their level of absolute military power between a minimum level, a_i, and a maximum level, b_i, so that $0 < a_i < b_i$, and $m_i \in [a_i, b_i]$.[5] What is the Nash equilibrium level of military power? If we take the derivative of player 1's utility with respect to its military power, we get the following[6]

$$\frac{du_1}{dm_1} = \frac{m_1 + m_2 - m_1}{(m_1 + m_2)^2}$$

$$= \frac{m_2}{(m_1 + m_2)^2} \quad (3.2)$$

This is positive, so player 1's utility increases the more power it has, no matter how much it starts with, and no matter how much power player 2 has. Therefore, the unique Nash equilibrium in the game is $m_1 = b_1$ and $m_2 = b_2$, and each side will maximize its level of power.

This is an example of a zero sum game. There is no room for cooperation, no outcome can simultaneously make both players better off than any other outcome. Therefore, this game is not a version of the Prisoner's Dilemma. The Prisoner's Dilemma is positive sum, because both sides are better off cooperating than defecting.

3.2.3 Competition for power with costs

The game just examined may seem odd in that the power that each side builds is not perceived to cost anything, so each side maximizes its power. Given that most countries spend less than 3% of their national income on the military, this would seem to be an unacceptably unrealistic assumption. Consider a modified arms competition where each side wants to be stronger but each unit of military power comes at a cost γ_i. The utility function now looks like this

$$u_i(m_1, m_2) = \frac{m_i}{m_1 + m_2} - \gamma_i m_i \quad (3.3)$$

The optimal level of military power for player 1 can be found by taking the derivative of its utility with respect to m_1 and setting it equal to 0.

$$\frac{m_2}{(m_1 + m_2)^2} - \gamma_1 = 0$$

$$\frac{m_2}{(m_1 + m_2)^2} = \gamma_1$$

$$(m_1 + m_2)^2 = \frac{m_2}{\gamma_1}$$

---

[5] These are continuous strategy spaces, but normal form games and Nash equilibria are still well defined. Having $a_i > 0$ prevents having to deal with the complication that the function is undefined where $m_1 = m_2 = 0$.

[6] From the quotient rule: $\frac{d\frac{u}{v}}{dx} = \frac{v\frac{du}{dx} - u\frac{dv}{dx}}{v^2}$.

$$m_1 = \sqrt{\frac{m_2}{\gamma_1}} - m_2 \tag{3.4}$$

A parallel function can be found for player 2

$$m_2 = \sqrt{\frac{m_1}{\gamma_2}} - m_1 \tag{3.5}$$

The Nash equilibrium to the game can be found by substituting one into the other and solving

$$m_1 = \sqrt{\frac{m_2}{\gamma_1}} - m_2$$

$$m_1 = \sqrt{\frac{\sqrt{\frac{m_1}{\gamma_2}} - m_1}{\gamma_1}} - \left(\sqrt{\frac{m_1}{\gamma_2}} - m_1\right)$$

$$\sqrt{\frac{m_1}{\gamma_2}} = \sqrt{\frac{\sqrt{\frac{m_1}{\gamma_2}} - m_1}{\gamma_1}}$$

$$\frac{m_1}{\gamma_2} = \frac{\sqrt{\frac{m_1}{\gamma_2}} - m_1}{\gamma_1}$$

$$\frac{\gamma_1}{\gamma_2} = \sqrt{\frac{1}{m_1 \gamma_2}} - 1$$

$$\left(\frac{\gamma_1}{\gamma_2} + 1\right)^2 = \frac{1}{m_1 \gamma_2}$$

$$m_1 = \frac{1}{\gamma_2 \left(\frac{\gamma_1}{\gamma_2} + 1\right)^2}$$

$$m_1^* = \frac{\gamma_2}{(\gamma_1 + \gamma_2)^2} \tag{3.6}$$

Symmetrically, we know that player 2's equilibrium level of spending will be

$$m_2^* = \frac{\gamma_1}{(\gamma_1 + \gamma_2)^2} \tag{3.7}$$

These levels of power represent the Nash equilibrium of the game. Neither side can improve its payoff by spending more or less on arms, given that the other side is spending its equilibrium amount. Thus, in this simple game, we can already show that states that care about power will not simply maximize their power simply because they live in an anarchic system in which others are also powerful. If power comes at a cost, there will be optimal interior levels of spending.

The analysis is illustrated in Figure 3.1. The axes are the player's level of power, m_1 on the horizontal axis and m_2 on the vertical. The curve labeled $m_1(m_2)$ is player 1's

3.2 THE PRISONER'S DILEMMA

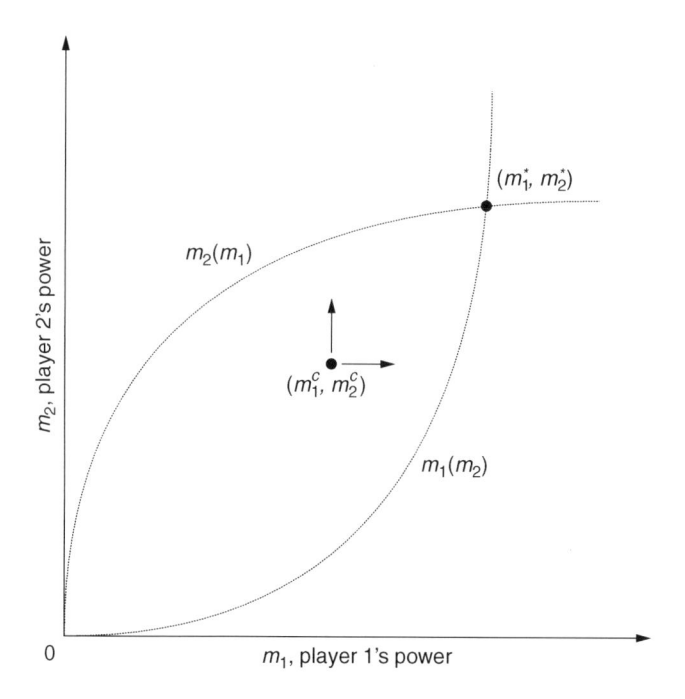

Figure 3.1 Equilibria in the Competition for Power with Costs game

optimal level of power as a function of how much power player 2 has, and $m_2(m_1)$ is the optimal level of power for player 2 as a function of how much player 1 has. These curves are sometimes called *reaction functions* as they indicate how each state will react to the other's choice. Where the reaction functions intersect is the equilibrium point, designated (m_1^*, m_2^*).

It is easy to see that the Nash equilibrium of the modified game is Pareto inefficient in that both sides could be made better off by reducing their spending. For instance, an arms control treaty that required the two sides to reduce their level of spending to a proportion $r \in (0, 1)$ of its former value. The resulting spending levels, denoted m_i^c for cooperation, are

$$m_i^c = rm_i^* \qquad (3.8)$$

and are illustrated by the point in the interior of the lens in Figure 3.1.

Substituting this level of spending into the utility function, we get

$$u_i(m_1^c, m_2^c) = \frac{m_i^c}{m_1^c + m_2^c} - \gamma_i m_i^c$$

$$u_i(m_1^c, m_2^c) = \frac{rm_i^*}{rm_1^* + rm_2^*} - \gamma_i rm_i^*$$

$$u_i(m_1^c, m_2^c) = \frac{m_i^*}{m_1^* + m_2^*} - \gamma_i rm_i^*$$

Note, the mutual reductions leave the balance of power unchanged, but reduce absolute military spending to a fraction r of its previous value. Therefore, the resulting level of power is Pareto superior to the Nash equilibrium. The problem is that it cannot be achieved, because at that level of power each side has an incentive to increase its spending, as indicated by the arrows in Figure 3.1. Player 1 wishes to increase m_1 to $m_1(m_2^c)$, and player 2 ants to increase m_2 to $m_2(m_1^c)$. Therefore, neither side has an incentive to abide by the treaty. The payoff structure, therefore, resembles the Prisoner's Dilemma, in that each side has an incentive to deviate from the cooperative treaty level to a higher level of power until the two sides return to the equilibrium level.[7]

3.3 The Assurance game

The Assurance game is illustrated in Table 3.4.[8] The strategies are conceptualized in the same way as for the Prisoner's Dilemma – one is cooperative and the other more competitive. Like the Prisoner's Dilemma, mutual cooperation is better for both players than mutual defection, so the game is not zero sum and cooperation is well defined.

However, the Assurance game differs from the Prisoner's Dilemma in having no dominant strategy and two Nash equilibria. If one side thinks the other will defect, the best response is to defect. Therefore, mutual defection is a Nash equilibrium in the Assurance game as it is in the Prisoner's Dilemma. However, if one side thinks the other will cooperate, it prefers to cooperate rather than defect in response. This means that mutual cooperation is also a Nash equilibrium. In the Assurance game, each side prefers to reciprocate the behavior of the other, returning defection for defection and cooperation for cooperation. Therefore, there are two Nash equilibria in the game – mutual defection and mutual cooperation. This raises the problem of equilibrium selection and poses a challenge to the predictive power of Nash equilibria. With more than one Nash equilibrium in a game, how can we predict what the players will do? The concept of Pareto optimality may help here. Since both players prefer the cooperative equilibrium to the non-cooperative one, we may suppose that at least with communication they may be able to attain the Pareto superior mutual cooperation equilibrium.

---

[7] Conversely, if the two states started out at higher levels of power than the equilibrium level, they would both be willing to engage in unilateral reductions until they reached the equilibrium from above.
[8] The Assurance game is sometimes also called the Stag Hunt, from a parable told by Rousseau about hunters cooperating to hunt a deer.

Table 3.4 The Assurance game

		Player 2	
		Cooperate	Defect
Player 1	Cooperate	4, 4	1, 3
	Defect	3, 1	2, 2

3.3.1 Pre-emptive war

The Assurance game is often applied to the security dilemma in international relations theory (Jervis 1978). Broadly speaking, if states want security, they can achieve it by leaving each other alone or by engaging in more competitive behavior. The more competitive equilibrium is worse for both sides, but the more cooperative equilibrium may be vulnerable if the two sides do not trust each other.

A specific instance of this kind of logic is the issue of pre-emptive war. Pre-emptive war is war motivated by the fear that the other side is about to attack, and the belief that there are advantages to striking first. These advantages include surprise, the ability to choose the opening scene of battle, and to seize the initiative. There are, of course, also disadvantages to striking first, including the fact that offensive operations typically require local force advantages and result in higher casualties, since defensive forces can take advantage of cover while offensive forces must expose themselves to enemy fire (Biddle 2006). There are also diplomatic drawbacks to attacking first, as it can seem aggressive and would be wrong in terms of international law. The belief that there are offensive advantages is often said to aggravate the security dilemma and is believed by some to have helped cause the First World War (Jervis 1978, Miller et al. 1991). Critics argue that there have been very few wars that can be plausibly interpreted as pre-emptive (Reiter 1995). The issue took on great salience in the nuclear era, because the short reaction times dictated by ICBM flight times seemed to leave no time for consideration and raised the chance that a false warning could lead to pre-emptive war (Schelling and Halperin 1961).

The pre-emptive war problem is illustrated in Table 3.5. If neither side attacks, peace results and the players receive their status quo payoffs, denoted s_i for player i. If both sides attack, war occurs and the payoffs are denoted w_i. If one side attacks and the other does not, the attacker achieves a first strike and the payoff increases to w_i^f while the side going second has a payoff equal to w_i^s. To reflect the first strike advantage, we assume that

$$w_i^f > w_i > w_i^s \tag{3.9}$$

If we assume that $w_i < s_i$, then both sides prefer the status quo to a war without first strike advantages, so, like the Prisoner's Dilemma and Assurance games,

Table 3.5 The Pre-emptive War game

		Player 2	
		Don't attack	Attack
Player 1	Don't attack	s_1, s_2	w_1^s, w_2^f
	Attack	w_1^f, w_2^s	w_1, w_2

a Pareto improvement over mutual attack is possible, and there is room for cooperation.

What are the equilibria in the game? We know that since $w_i > w_i^s$, if one side thinks the other is going to attack, it prefers to attack as well. Therefore, mutual attack is one equilibrium. If $w_i^f < s_i$, then the game has Assurance game payoffs, since both sides would also prefer not to attack if they thought the other side would refrain from attacking. If this condition is not true for a player, then it has Prisoner's Dilemma payoffs, and the only equilibrium in the game will be the mutual attack equilibrium.

3.4 Coordination

The Coordination game also features multiple equilibria but the players often disagree over which one is better. Coordination games are often used to study international standards where countries differ over which standard to adopt but all benefit by adopting some common standard (Stein 1982b, Snidal 1985a, Buthe and Mattli 2011).

Consider a simple version of the Coordination game, shown in Table 3.6. Here the strategies are not conceived of as cooperation or failing to cooperate, but as alternative ways to cooperate. Player 1 has a preference to coordinate on A, while player 2 has a preference to coordinate on B. However, both players prefer to coordinate their policies rather than fail to do so, so the game is positive sum and cooperation is possible. If they fail, however, player 1 would prefer to keep A and player 2 B. Thus, coordinating on A gives player 1 the highest payoff, while coordinating on B gives 2 the highest payoff. Each failing to coordinate on their preferred outcome is third best, while switching to the other side's preferred way and still failing to coordinate gives the worst payoff.

As in the Assurance game, there are two Nash equilibria in the Coordination game. Unlike in Assurance, however, both are Pareto superior to the non-equilibrium outcomes, and neither is Pareto superior to the other. Hence, unfortunately, Pareto optimality cannot tell us which seems more likely, or better in a general sense.

Table 3.6 The Coordination game

		Player 2 A	Player 2 B
Player 1	A	4, 3	2, 2
	B	1, 1	3, 4

Table 3.7 The Standard Setting game

		Player 2 A	Player 2 B
Player 1	A	$b_1 + r_1 + r_2, b_2 - c_2$	r_1, r_2
	B	$r_2 - c_1, r_1 - c_2$	$b_1 - c_1, b_2 + r_1 + r_2$

3.4.1 International standards

As an example of the Coordination game, consider two countries attempting to agree on an international standard for a communications technology. Each country has developed its own contending technology. Either one would make an acceptable international standard. Therefore, if the two sides agree to coordinate, they get a coordination benefit of b_i. In addition, each state will receive an additional revenue benefit, r_j, for each country that adopts its technology as a result of the sales that will accrue to its domestic companies that have pioneered the technology. Finally, each will pay a cost c_i if they are forced to transition to the other side's technology. This game is represented in Table 3.7.

We can see that both sides will be happy to avoid the worst non-coordinated outcome, where each side opts for the other's technology, since $r_j - c_i < b_i + r_i + r_j$. Both sides will further be willing to coordinate rather than stick to their own technology if $b_i - c_i > r_i$; the benefits of coordination minus the transition costs must outweigh the revenue that would accrue from sticking to one's own technology. If this is the case, then coordination is Pareto efficient, and there will be two equilibria in the game, both play A and both play B. However, the two equilibria cannot be ranked in terms of efficiency.

3.5 Chicken

The game of Chicken also features multiple equilibria that cannot be ranked by efficiency.[9] The matrix is shown in Table 3.8. This game is similar to the Coordination

---

[9] The name comes from teenage California dare rituals. Two drivers head towards each other and the first to swerve is a chicken.

Table 3.8 Chicken

		Player 2	
		Cooperate	Defect
Player 1	Cooperate	3, 3	2, 4
	Defect	4, 2	1, 1

Table 3.9 The Nuclear Crisis game

		Player 2	
		Back down	Hold firm
Player 1	Back down	s_1, s_2	0, 1
	Hold firm	pt1, 0	$-d_1, -d_2$

game in structure – if you rotate Chicken 90 degrees clockwise, the resemblance is clear. However, the strategies are typically conceived of as in Prisoner's Dilemma and Assurance, that is, each side cooperates or defects. Mutual cooperation is preferred to mutual defection, as in Prisoner's Dilemma and Assurance. However, neither mutual cooperation nor mutual defection is an equilibrium. Mutual cooperation is not an equilibrium because each side would prefer to exploit the cooperation of the other side by defecting. Mutual defection is not an equilibrium because it is so bad each side would rather cooperate and let the other side achieve the best outcome in the game rather than face mutual defection. Like coordination, the equilibrium outcomes are asymmetrical and, therefore, unranked by efficiency.

3.5.1 Chicken and Nuclear Crises

The chicken metaphor has long been used to analyze nuclear crises (Russell 1959, Kahn 1960, Rapoport and Chammah 1966). Consider the version shown in Table 3.9. Think of the two sides being involved in a dispute over an issue with three possible resolutions: victory for one side, victory for the other, and a continuation of the status quo. Each side gets a payoff of 1 if it wins, 0 if it loses, and $s_i \in (0, 1)$ for the status quo. If one side backs down while the other holds firm, the side holding firm wins. If both sides back down, then the status quo remains in place. If both sides hold firm, the result is a nuclear war with payoff $-d_i$ for each player, and we assume $d_i > 0$.

Since the disaster of nuclear war is worse than giving in, both sides will prefer to back down if the other side is expected to hold firm. If the other side is expected to back down, each side wants to hold firm, since $1 > s_i$. This gives the Chicken payoff ordering and the multiple equilibria associated with it. The secret to getting the equilibrium

3.6 Matching Pennies

In the Matching Pennies game, one side wants to avoid coordination with the other. This has been applied to situations of war and defense against terrorist attacks in which the defender wishes to match the attacker so as to block the attack, and the attacker wishes to avoid the defender so that the attack is successful.

Consider the game illustrated in Table 3.10.[10] If player 1 plays A, player 2 will wish to play B. If player 2 plays B, player 1 will wish to play B. If player 1 plays B, player 2 will wish to play A. And if player 2 plays A, player 1 will wish to play A, completing the cycle. Player 1 wants a match and player 2 wants a mismatch. The game is zero sum, there is no outcome that is a Pareto improvement on any other in the game. More problematic, this game has no Nash equilibrium in the sense we have so far been employing – no pair of strategies are best responses to each other. However, there is a clear incentive in this game to keep the other side guessing about what you will do. This implies that it might be a good idea to randomize over your strategies, or flip a coin about what to do. This is indeed the case, and the concept of mixed strategy has been developed for such situations.

A mixed strategy involves players randomizing over their set of strategies, now denoted *pure* strategies.

Definition 3.4 *A mixed strategy is a lottery over a player's set of strategies, $p_1, p_2, \ldots, p_n$, such that $p_i \in [0, 1]$, and $\sum_{i=1}^{n} p_i = 1$.*

Every normal form game has a Nash equilibrium, but some only have *mixed strategy equilibria*. In a mixed strategy Nash equilibrium, each player chooses a mixed strategy

---

[10] The story comes from a game in which each player has a penny, and they can show heads or tails. If the coins match, player 1 gets them; if the coins do not match, player 2 gets them.

Table 3.10 Matching Pennies

		Player 2 A	Player 2 B
Player 1	A	1, 0	0, 1
	B	0, 1	1, 0

and these strategies form best responses to each other. The fundamental feature of a mixed strategy equilibrium is that each side must be willing to randomize over its strategies so that each side must get equal utility from playing each of its strategies. Otherwise, if one strategy produced a higher utility than the others, the player would select it for sure and not be willing to play the other ones. In order for each player to be willing to randomize over their strategies, the other player's randomization must be calculated so as to make the first player indifferent among their strategies, and vice versa. That is, each player chooses a lottery over its strategies that makes the other side indifferent between its pure strategies, and hence willing to adopt a mixed strategy in turn.

The Matching Pennies game is easily solved in this manner: Let player 1 play A with probability p_1 and B with probability $1 - p_1$, while for player 2 the probabilities are q_1 and $1 - q_1$. To be willing to mix, or select a strategy at random, each player must be indifferent between playing its two strategies. The probabilities must, therefore, be calculated to make the other side indifferent between its options, and hence willing to randomize over them. For player 2, the calculation equates the payoff for playing A and B given that player 1 plays A with probability p_1

$$\text{Payoff for A} = \text{Payoff for B}$$
$$p_1(0) + (1 - p_1)1 = p_1(1) + (1 - p_1)(0)$$
$$1 - p_1 = p_1$$
$$p_1 = 0.5$$

Player 1, therefore, chooses A with a 50% chance and B also. Since the game is symmetrical, player 2 does so as well. The unique Nash equilibrium in the game is, therefore, for each side to play each strategy at random, 50% of the time.

3.6.1 The invasion of France, 1944

An example of Matching Pennies logic at work can be found in the realm of military strategy. It is June 1944, and the Allies are preparing an invasion of German-occupied France. There are three possible invasion sites: Calais, Normandy, and Brittany. Each

3.6 MATCHING PENNIES

Table 3.11 The D-Day game

		Player 2 (Germany)		
		Defend Calais	Defend Normandy	Defend Brittany
Player 1	Attack Calais	0, 1	1, 0	1, 0
(Allies)	Attack Normandy	$1 - c_n, 0$	$-c_n, 1$	$1 - c_n, 0$
	Attack Brittany	$1 - c_b, 0$	$1 - c_b, 0$	$-c_b, 1$

side must choose where to deploy the majority of its forces. If the Allies invade where the Germans are defending, they lose and Germany wins. If the Allies invade where the Germans are not expecting them, they win and Germany loses. While these are the dominant considerations, because Calais is closest to Britain, Normandy in the middle, and Brittany farthest away, there are additional costs c_n for invading Normandy and c_b for invading Brittany, above and beyond the cost of invading Calais where $c_n < c_b$. We assume the three targets are equally costly for the Germans to defend. We can draw up a game matrix for this situation, which is shown in Table 3.11.

Note that this game has a very similar flavor to Matching Pennies. Wherever Germany is thinking of defending, the Allies want to attack somewhere else. Wherever the Allies are thinking of attacking, that is just where the Germans want to defend. So the Allies want the pennies not to match, and the Germans want them to match.

To calculate the equilibrium, let $p_1(\cdot)$ be the probability player 1 attacks a given target and $p_2(\cdot)$ the probability that player 2 defends it. Player 1's probabilities are calculated to make player 2 indifferent between defending the three sites, so we have

Defend Calais Defend Normandy Defend Brittany
$$p_1(c)1 + p_1(n)(0) + p_1(b)(0) = p_1(c)(0) + p_1(n)1 + p_1(b)(0) = p_1(c)(0) + p_1(n)(0) + p_1(b)1$$

which implies that

$$p_1(c) = p_1(n) = p_1(b) = \frac{1}{3} \qquad (3.10)$$

so we know that player 1 must be equally likely to attack all three sites. As a result, it was vital to keep the Germans guessing even after the final decision was made to invade Normandy. Hence, the Allies launched a massive and successful intelligence campaign to confuse the Germans as to the location of the eventual assault (Brown, 1975). The operation was so successful that the Germans were convinced that the Normandy landings were a feint even after they took place, and retained forces at Calais to repel the eventual "main" invasion.

Player 2's defense probabilities must make player 1 indifferent between attacking the three sites

$$\text{Attack Calais} \qquad \text{Attack Normandy} \qquad \text{Attack Brittany}$$
$$p_2(c)(0) + p_2(n)1 + p_2(b)1 = p_2(c)1 + p_2(n)(0) + p_2(b)1 - c_n = p_2(c)1 + p_2(n)1 + p_2(b)(0) - c_b$$

or

$$p_2(n) + p_2(b) = p_2(c) + p_2(b) - c_n = p_2(c) + p_2(n) - c_b$$

Since we know the probabilities must sum to 1, let us substitute in $p_2(b) = 1 - p_2(c) - p_2(n)$, to get

$$p_2(n) + 1 - p_2(c) - p_2(n) = p_2(c) + 1 - p_2(c) - p_2(n) - c_n = p_2(c) + p_2(n) - c_b$$

which simplifies to

$$1 - p_2(c) = 1 - p_2(n) - c_n = p_2(c) + p_2(n) - c_b$$

From the first equation, we know that $p_2(n) = p_2(c) - c_n$. Substituting this into the relation between the first and third terms, we get $1 - p_2(c) = p_2(c) + p_2(c) - c_n - c_b$, which implies that

$$p_2(c) = \frac{1 + c_n + c_b}{3} \qquad (3.11)$$

Substituting this back in, we can see that

$$p_2(n) = \frac{1 + c_n + c_b}{3} - c_n \qquad (3.12)$$

and

$$p_2(b) = \frac{1 + c_n + c_b}{3} - c_b \qquad (3.13)$$

We see that these three sum to 1, as they should. In addition, from this we can easily see that $p_2(c) > p_2(n) > p_2(b)$. Therefore, to keep the Allies willing to attack all three sites, Germany must place more emphasis on defending Calais than on Normandy, and more emphasis on Normandy than on Brittany, which is indeed what they did (Zaloga 2007).

Closely related games, called "Colonel Blotto" games, have been widely applied to the analysis of allocating defensive resources against attacks, both in the general military context and in the field of counter-terrorism (Roberson 2006, Powell 2007a, 2007b, 2009, Kydd 2011). The defender's decision in many of these games is modeled as a problem of allocating defensive resources to the various targets, rather than choosing which one to defend and which to leave undefended. The problems are essentially identical, and the defense allocations end up tracking the mixed strategy probabilities of defense.

3.7 Conclusion

The five normal form games explored here may seem simple, even simplistic. They are at best metaphorical models of any real strategic interaction, particularly in complicated contexts like international relations. However, each one lays out an important strategic dynamic that is often recognizable in more realistic or complex settings. Recognizing a situation as like a Prisoner's Dilemma or like a Matching Pennies game will give immediate insight into how it can be fruitfully modeled, even if there are features of the situation that make a simple two-by-two normal form game inadequate. Elements of these games will be present in the more complicated models that follow.

EXERCISES

3.1 Consider the arms competition game with costs illustrated in Figure 3.1.

1. What happens if γ_2 increases? Which reaction function shifts, and in what direction? Draw the old and new reaction functions.
2. What happens to the equilibrium level of power for each side? Deduce this graphically.
3. Confirm your analysis by analyzing what happens to the equilibrium levels of power in Equations (3.6) and (3.7).

3.2 Consider the Pre-emptive War game illustrated in Table 3.12. Assume that for player 1, $s_1 > w_1^f > w_1 > w_1^s$ and for player 2, $w_2^f > s_2 > w_2 > w_2^s$.

1. Solve this game by the iterated elimination of dominated strategies.
2. Identify all Nash equilibria in the game.

3.3 Consider the Coordination game illustrated in Table 3.7. Assume that for player 1, $b_1 - c_1 > r_1$ and for player 2, $b_2 - c_2 < r_2$.

1. Solve this game by the iterated elimination of dominated strategies.
2. Identify all Nash equilibria in the game.

3.4 Consider the Nuclear Crisis game in Table 3.13. If both sides back down, the status quo remains in place with payoffs of $s_i \in (0, 1)$. If one side holds firm and the other backs down, the side that holds firm gets 1 and the side that backs down gets 0. If both sides hold firm, disaster happens, with payoffs of $-d_i$ where $d_i > 0$.

Table 3.12 The Pre-emptive War game

		Player 2 Don't attack	Player 2 Attack
Player 1	Don't attack	s_1, s_2	w_1^s, w_2^f
	Attack	w_1^f, w_2^s	w_1, w_2

Table 3.13 A Nuclear Crisis game

		Player 2	
		Back down	Hold firm
Player 1	Back down	s_1, s_2	0, 1
	Hold firm	1, 0	$-d_1, -d_2$

1. Find the mixed strategy equilibrium of the game. Let p_i be the probability that player i backs down. Solve for p_i.
2. How does p_i vary with the other side's level of satisfaction with the status quo, s_j? Convey the intuition for why this is the case.
3. How does p_i vary with payoff for disaster, d_j? Convey the intuition for why this is the case.

4 Bargaining

BARGAINING is ancient and pervasive in international relations. Thucydides describes several instances of international bargaining in the Peloponnesian War. In one of the most famous incidents described, the Athenians attempted to persuade the Melians to surrender their city and ally with Athens (Thucydides 1954, 400). The Athenians threatened that if the Melians did not accept their offer, they would attack. The Melians, hoping for aid from Sparta, refused, so the Athenians besieged the city and eventually prevailed at great cost to the inhabitants. The ancient Greek city states signed peace treaties, trade agreements, and alliances with each other, as did Rome, Carthage, and other important states of the ancient world. The first treatise on diplomacy in the modern period was entitled, "The Art of Negotiating with Sovereign Princes" (de Callières 1994). Today, states bargain over territory, trade barriers, arms control, pollution, and many other issues. This chapter will examine a simple extensive form model of bargaining and some of its implications for international relations.

There are two basic questions we can ask about bargaining. First, when does bargaining succeed and when does it fail? Bargaining that succeeds usually results in an agreement of some kind, sometimes a written treaty in the international context, but sometimes a more informal understanding. When bargaining fails to generate an agreement, the parties may simply continue with the status quo or they may engage in more active forms of conflict such as war, as the Athenians and Melians did. States are usually motivated to negotiate with each other because the status quo is unsatisfactory, at least to one side, or because they wish to avoid the costs of conflict. If there are joint gains to be had by reaching an agreement, it seems wasteful for bargaining to break down. More pointedly, it seems to require some explanation: why would states fail to come to an agreement that would make them both better off than the alternative, be it war or the status quo?

Second, if there is an agreement, what explains how well each side does in the bargaining? Negotiations can lead to a multitude of outcomes. How many missiles does each side get to keep? How much should each side reduce its tariffs? Should greenhouse gas treaties apply to developing states or not? The concept of bargaining power or leverage is often used to explain these distributional questions. States that are more powerful or have more leverage get a deal that more closely approximates their preferences, while weaker states with less leverage have to put up with a deal that offers less of what they want. But the nature of bargaining leverage, where it comes from, and how it is distributed will vary in different contexts. States that appear strong may actually lack leverage in a particular issue area because they are not able to bring their overall strength to bear on their negotiating partners. Conversely, states that are weak overall may have surprising leverage in a certain context (Kivimaki 1993). For instance, a weak regime facing a civil war and negotiating with a great power patron for assistance may have leverage precisely because it is weak and the great power cannot afford to see it fail. We will begin to address questions like these in this chapter, but we will also raise new questions that require additional tools for answers.

Powell (2002) and Reiter (2003) provide useful surveys of the formal bargaining approach to conflict in international relations. The most extensive development of the approach is Powell's analysis of bargaining in the shadow of war (Powell 1999a).[1] Because of its practical importance and coverage by programs in international law, there are many textbook and case study treatments of bargaining and negotiation (Cooper *et al.* 2013, Watkins and Rosegrant 2001, Sebenius 1984).

In this chapter, I first define extensive form games and their main solution concepts, the subgame perfect Nash equilibrium. Then I discuss a simple Bargaining game known as the ultimatum game. I then consider how adding a status quo and a possibility for inefficient conflict alters the equilibria in the game. I conclude by discussing how insufficiently valued or unavailable intermediate outcomes can lead to inefficient war, the first explanation of inefficient outcomes noted in Chapter 1.

4.1 Extensive form games

While the normal form games of the previous chapter are very useful representations of many strategic situations, an alternative representation of strategic interaction, *extensive form games*, is often preferred especially for dynamic games, or games that take place over time. An example is illustrated in Figure 4.1. In the Deterrence game, player 1 moves first, either challenging or not. If player 1 challenges, player 2 gets a move, either fighting back or not. Similar games have been used to represent Cold War crises between the superpowers. Challenging could be interpreted as doing something that undermines the other side's interests, like supporting rebels against a client regime or even starting a limited war, such as the Korean War. Fighting back is responding with force to such a challenge, risking the possibility of war. If player 1 decides not to

---

[1] See Muthoo (1999) for a general textbook on bargaining theory.

4.1 EXTENSIVE FORM GAMES

```
                    Player 1
         Not challenge    Challenge
            /                \
           /                  \
          /                 Player 2
        3,3              Not fight   Fight
                          /            \
                         /              \
                        4,2             1,1
```

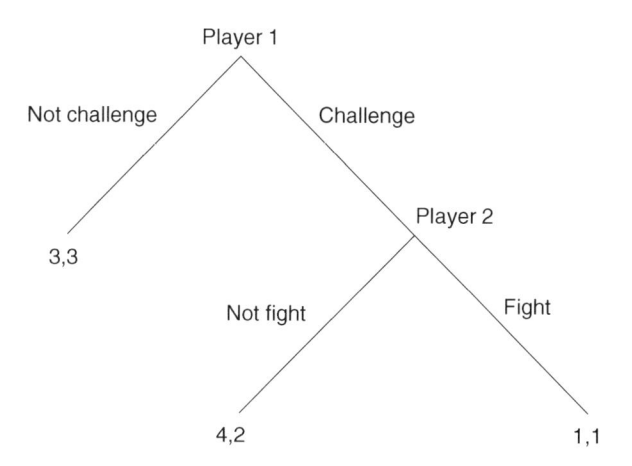

Figure 4.1 The Deterrence game

challenge, the payoffs are 3 for both players. If player 1 challenges and player 2 fights back, the payoffs are 1 for each player. If player 1 challenges and player 2 does not fight back, then player 1 gets 4 and player 1 only gets 2. Note, the payoffs are reminiscent of the Chicken game of Chapter 3. War is so bad for both players that player 2 would prefer to capitulate rather than face the prospect.

Player 1's choice is the *initial node*, the starting point of the game. Player 2's choice is a *successor* of player 1's in that it follows immediately from it. The three nodes with payoffs are the *terminal nodes*; because they have no successor nodes, they end the game. More generally, we can define an extensive form game as follows:

Definition 4.1 *An* extensive form game *has the following elements.*

1. *A set of players.*
2. *A rooted tree, consisting of a set of nodes – or decision points – and branches – sometimes called edges – that link them. One node, the initial node, has no nodes that precede it; every other node has one node that immediately precedes it. A subset of nodes, the terminal nodes, have no nodes succeeding them.*
3. *A vector of payoffs for each of the players assigned to each of the terminal nodes.*
4. *A partition of the nodes among the players and a fictitious player called "Nature," that represents chance exogenous events in the environment. Each node then represents a choice made by one player.*
5. *A probability density for each of Nature's nodes determining the likelihood that each branch is chosen.*
6. *A partition of the nodes into* information sets *such that any two nodes in the same information set must belong to the same player and have the same number of branches, or choices, available. The different nodes in the information set represent uncertainty a player might have over the state of the world when called upon to make a certain choice.*

The game tree branches out from the initial node. Each node represents a choice available to one of the players. Each branch leading out from a node leads to another node, or choice by another player, until a terminal node is reached and the game ends and payoffs are distributed. Elements 5 and 6 in the definition will become useful when we consider games featuring uncertainty. For now, we focus on a game featuring *complete information*, so all players know where they are in the game tree at all times.

The Nash equilibrium still works as a solution concept for extensive form games. For instance, the Deterrence game has two Nash equilibria. In one of them, player 1 does not challenge and player 2 fights back. If player 2 is planning to fight back, not challenging makes sense for player 1. If player 1 is not challenging, then fighting back is just as good as not fighting for player 2, since player 2's decision node is not reached in any event. In this equilibrium, player 2's choice is *off the equilibrium path*, meaning it is not reached in the equilibrium if the other players are choosing their equilibrium strategies. In the other Nash equilibrium, player 1 challenges and player 2 does not fight back. Here again, each player's strategy is a best response to what the other side is doing. In this case, player 2's decision node is reached on the equilibrium path.

While the Nash equilibrium still makes sense as a solution concept, in extensive form games some Nash equilibria seem peculiar. The first one just discussed, in which player 1 does not challenge and player 2 would fight back, is an example. The reason this seems unrealsitic is that if player 2 did have to make the choice, it would prefer to not fight back. Therefore, the expectation on player 1's part that player 2 would fight back seems unwarranted. Player 1 should put player 2 to the test and challenge; in that case player 2 would surely choose to not fight back.

This idea is formalized in the *subgame perfect Nash equilibrium* (SPNE). First, we define a subgame.

Definition 4.2 *A subgame is a subset of a game consisting of one node and all of its successors, such that no node belongs to an information set that contains a node not in the subset.*

A subgame of a game is a part of the game, starting with one node and continuing on to the terminal nodes that follow it, which could be pulled out and be a well-defined game all by itself. A game is always a subgame of itself. A proper subgame is a subgame that does not consist of the whole game. In the Deterrence game illustrated in Figure 4.1, player 2's move is a (very simple) subgame.

The subgame perfect equilibrium concept can now be defined.

Definition 4.3 *A subgame perfect Nash equilibrium (SPNE) of a game is a Nash equilibrium that is a Nash equilibrium in every subgame of the game.*

The SPNE is the main solution concept for extensive form games with complete information. The main point of insisting on subgame perfection is that it rules out actions that a player would not wish to do if it were actually put to the test by arriving at that particular node. That is, some Nash equilibria in extensive form games include behavior off the equilibrium path that would not be optimal. In the Deterrence game, player 2 might threaten to fight back with nuclear weapons if the other country challenges by invading a client state. However, this might not be rational because the other side has nuclear weapons as well, and so a nuclear war would be a disaster for both sides. But so long as the threatened state backs down, the strategy "attack if the other state invades" is rational, because it is never put to the test. Subgame perfection rules out this kind of non-credible threat. It is another important way of formalizing the general inability of states to make commitments to courses of action that they would not actually wish to carry out that is mandated by the assumption of anarchy, as discussed in Chapter 1. This will in turn become very important in Chapter 5 when we discuss preventive war, where states will wish to make promises that they would not actually abide by.

In games of complete information, in which every information set is a single node and all players know where they are in the game at all times, subgame perfection is equivalent to *backwards induction*. Backwards induction is solving the game from the terminal nodes, working backwards to the initial node. At each node, the optimal choice is made and the payoffs of the chosen successor node are implicitly substituted for the node. Then at the previous node the optimal choice is made, given the understanding of what would happen subsequently. Every complete information game will have at least one subgame perfect Nash equilibrium.

With extensive form games and subgame perfect equilibria defined, we may now proceed to begin to analyze international bargaining.

4.2 A Bargaining game

Consider two states, 1 and 2, bargaining over an issue space designated $X = [0, 1]$, as illustrated in Figure 4.2. There are a range of possible issue resolutions, from 0 to 1. Any issue resolution, x, provides a certain level of utility for both parties, $u_1(x)$ and $u_2(x)$. Assume that the players have strictly opposed preferences, such that player 1 prefers that x be higher and player 2 prefers that x be lower. I normalize the utility functions so that $u_1(0) = u_2(1) = 0$ and $u_1(1) = u_2(0) = 1$. In the case illustrated, the utility is the risk-neutral case, where $u_1(x) = x$ and $u_2(x) = 1 - x$. I will assume risk neutrality for the first pass of the analysis for two reasons. First, risk neutrality seems "neutral" as the name suggests, a midway assumption rather than assuming that states love or hate

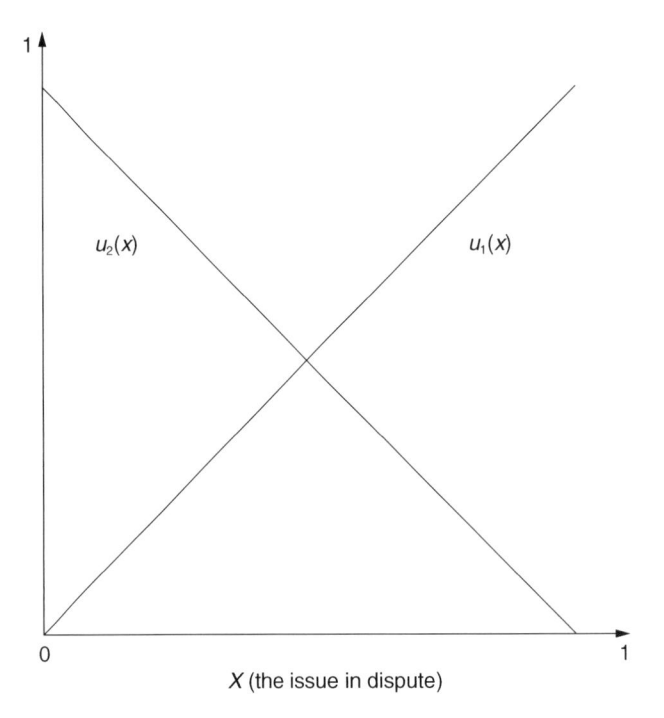

Figure 4.2 The issue space

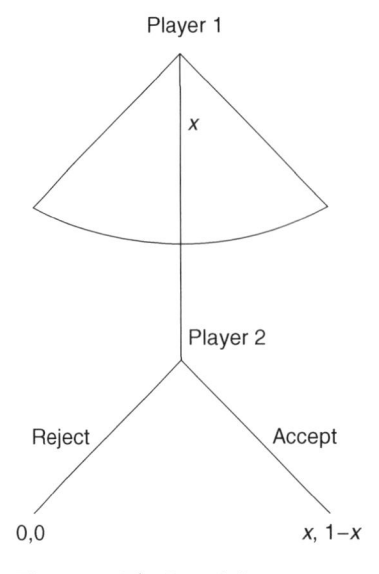

Figure 4.3 The Bargaining game

risk per se. Second, risk-neutral preferences are mathematically the simplest to work with, so the results will be easy to follow. However, the case of risk acceptance is also important and will also be discussed.

The game tree is illustrated in Figure 4.3. Player 1 moves first, proposing an issue resolution x in X to player 2. Player 2 then responds, and can either accept the new

Table 4.1 SPNE in the Bargaining game

Player 1	Offer $x = 1$
Player 2	Accept if $x \leq 1$

proposed issue resolution or reject it. If player 2 accepts the proposal, the game ends and the payoffs are x and $1-x$. If player 2 rejects the deal, then the payoffs are $0, 0$. Note, this implies that the players are negotiating over how to divide a good that is in some sense not yet allocated; so if they fail to come to an agreement, there will be no good to divide. The game is, therefore, positive sum; both players can be made better off than they would be if they fail to agree. We will modify this assumption momentarily. This game is commonly known as a "take it or leave it" bargaining game, or as the "ultimatum game" in the experimental literature.

What is the equilibrium of this game? The unique subgame perfect equilibrium can be easily found. Player 2 will accept any offer such that $1 - x \geq 0$, since player 2 gets 0 from rejecting the offer. Player 2 will be indifferent between an offer of $x = 1$, which will produce a payoff of 0, and getting 0 from rejecting the offer, and so will be willing to accept such an offer. Player 1 receives x from any offer that is accepted and so wishes to maximize x subject to the offer being accepted. Therefore, no x short of 1 can be an equilibrium offer. The only equilibrium is, therefore, for player 1 to offer $x = 1$ and for player 2 to accept it, as shown in Table 4.1.

This outcome is of course quite lopsided in favor of player 1, because player 1 gets to make the offer. It also happens to be a very poor predictor of what real people will do. Experimental studies of the ultimatum game routinely find people in player 2's role rejecting offers of less then half the good, out of a sense of fairness, or holding out for at least some positive payoff, despite the seeming irrationality (Camerer 2003, Chapter 2). However, the model serves as a basic building block of bargaining theory that can be developed further.

4.3 Adding a status quo

One modification is to introduce the notion of a status quo division of the good, $s \in [0, 1]$. In this version of the game, the good is assumed to be already divided between the players, where player 1 has s and player 2 has $1 - s$, so this payoff forms the disagreement payoff in the game, as illustrated in Figure 4.4. The bargaining then represents an effort to change the status quo, rather than divide some newly available good, or surplus over an inefficient outcome. For instance, if two adjacent states bargain over the border between their countries, the existing border will remain

Table 4.2 SPNE in the Bargaining game with a status quo

Player 1	Offer any $x \geq s$
Player 2	Accept if $x \leq s$, reject otherwise

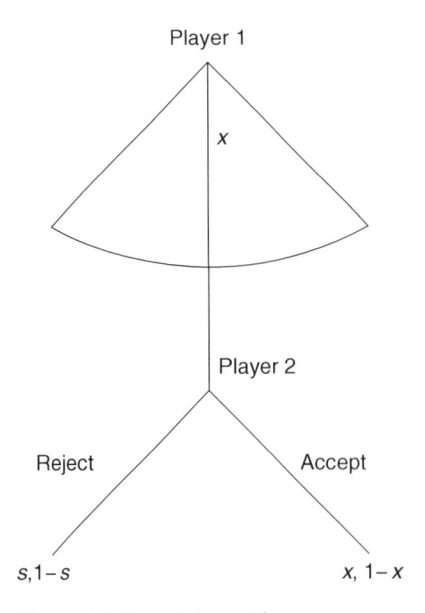

Figure 4.4 Bargaining with a status quo

in place if they fail to agree on a new one. This version of the game is, therefore, zero sum.

What are the equilibria of this modified game? There is actually a continuum of equilibria, shown in Table 4.2. Player 2 will accept any offer such that $x \leq s$ because this will produce a payoff $1 - x$ that is at least as big as $1 - s$. Player 2 will be indifferent between accepting and rejecting the status quo, $x = s$. Player 2 will reject any offer $x > s$, since this will produce a payoff $1 - x < 1 - s$. From player 1's perspective, any offer $x < s$ will be beat by offering $x = s$, since it would yield a payoff of $x < s$. Any offer $x > s$ will be rejected, leading to a payoff of s. Therefore, player 1 is indifferent between any offer $x \in [s, 1]$; they all lead to an equilibrium payoff vector $(s, 1 - s)$.

The lesson is that in bargaining over a revision of the status quo, there is no possibility for agreement to shift to a new outcome, since the bargaining is zero sum. Both players cannot be made better off in this game, so there is no agreement to change the status quo.

4.4 Bargaining and conflict

Bargaining often takes place in the shadow of some kind of conflict, be it war, economic sanctions, diplomatic pressure, etc. One or both states may be tempted to resort to conflict to improve their leverage at the bargaining table. We can model this in the simplest possible way by giving player 2 an additional option besides accepting or rejecting the offer – what economists call an outside option. In Figure 4.5, player 2 can attack, which produces a payoff vector of w_1, w_2 for war, although it need not refer explicitly to actual combat.

What should we assume, if anything, about the conflict payoffs? The fundamental assumption made almost universally in the rationalist tradition about conflict and war is that they are inefficient. Real war involves killing and destruction, trade sanctions impose economic costs by interrupting profitable trading relations, diplomatic isolation incurs less tangible but still important costs on a state's ability to achieve its goals. While certain individuals may enjoy war or conflict, we typically assume that the actors in our game do not, and so their decision to engage in it becomes something of a puzzle in need of explanation. To capture the inefficiency of conflict, we assume that the war payoffs sum to less than the good the two sides are bargaining over

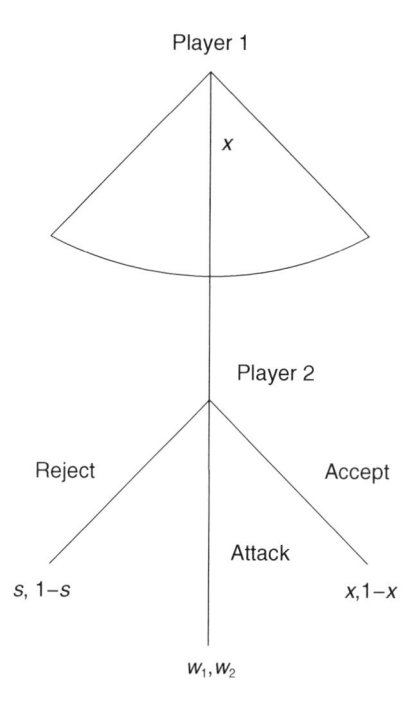

$$w_1 + w_2 < 1 \qquad (4.1)$$

Figure 4.5 Bargaining with a status quo and conflict option

```
              Deals both sides
              prefer to conflict
                    │
                    ▼
   ├──────────┼──────────┼─────────────────┤
   0          b₁         b₂                1

              X (the issue in dispute)
```

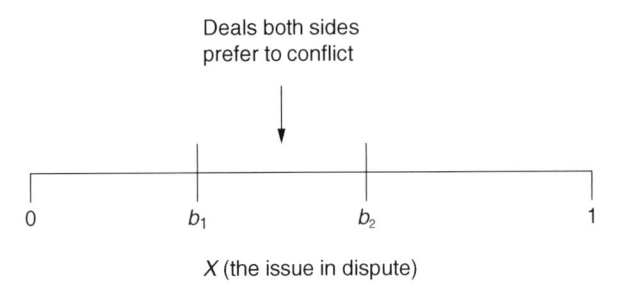

Figure 4.6 The bargaining range

In solving the game with a conflict option, a crucial piece of information is what each side would be willing to settle for rather than fight. Define a state's *bottom line*, to be the worst deal they would be willing to accept rather than fight.[2] If we denote player i's bottom line as b_i, we can define it as

$$b_i = \{x | u_i(x) = w_i\} \tag{4.2}$$

The bottom line will exist and be unique if $u_i(\cdot)$ is continuous and strictly monotonic, either increasing or decreasing. Player 1, for instance, would prefer to fight rather than receive any outcome $x < b_1$, but would be willing to accept any outcome $x \geq b_1$. Player 2 would be willing to fight rather than be forced to accept some outcome $x > b_2$, but would be willing to accept any $x \leq b_2$.

The range between the bottom lines, $[b_1, b_2]$, if it exists, is sometimes called the *bargaining range*, or more precisely, the range of agreements both sides prefer to conflict. We can easily show that if the players have linear preferences, a bargaining range will exist. With linear payoffs, player 1's bottom line is $x = w_1$, and player 2's bottom line is the x that solves $1 - x = w_2$, or $x = 1 - w_2$. Putting these together we get

$$b_1 = w_1$$
$$b_2 = 1 - w_2$$

Since we assumed that war is inefficient, we know that $w_1 + w_2 < 1$. This implies that $w_1 < 1 - w_2$, so that $b_1 < 1 - w_2$, and in turn $b_1 < b_2$, so a bargaining range of outcomes that both sides prefer to war exists, as illustrated in Figure 4.6. Any outcome below b_1 is unacceptable to player 1, any outcome above b_2 is unacceptable to player 2, but any outcome between b_1 and b_2 would be acceptable to both sides.

What are the equilibria of the new game? There are two different cases to consider, as shown in Table 4.3. First, consider the case where $s \leq b_2$, so that player 2 finds the status quo acceptable and would rather live with it than fight. In this case, player 2 will

---

[2] Another term for this concept in common usage is *reservation value*.

Table 4.3 SPNE in the Bargaining game with conflict

	Case 1, $s \leq b_2$
Player 1	Offer $x \geq s$
Player 2	Accept if $x \leq s$, reject otherwise
	Case 2, $b_2 < s$
Player 1	Offer $x = b_2$
Player 2	Accept if $x \leq b_2$, attack otherwise

prefer to reject an offer and keep the status quo rather than attack. The equilibrium is therefore just as in the previous case, player 1 offers some $x \in [s, 1]$ and player 2 accepts if $x \leq s$ and rejects if $x > s$. In this case, conflict is essentially "off the table," because it is too costly for player 2. The game proceeds as if conflict is not an option and the outcome of the bargaining is the status quo.

In the second case, $b_2 < s$, so player 2 would rather fight than accept the status quo. In this case, we say that player 2 has a *credible threat to fight*. Player 2 will never reject a deal, but instead will attack. Player 1, therefore, knows that the price of making an unacceptable offer is conflict, rather than just the status quo. In this case, there is a unique equilibrium. Player 1 offers player 2's bottom line, $x = b_2$, and player 2 accepts any offer at least as good as its bottom line, $x \leq b_2$, and attacks in response to any offer worse than it, $x > b_2$. In this case, player 1 never offers any $x > b_2$, because the outcome will be a fight, with a payoff of w_1 for player 1, which is worse than b_1 because we know that player 1's bottom line is lower than player 2's, $b_1 < b_2$, so we know player 1 prefers to live with player 2's bottom line rather than fight.

The relationship between the bargaining outcome and the status quo is illustrated in Figure 4.7. The horizontal axis is the status quo, s, which can be anywhere between 0 and 1. The vertical axis is the outcome of the Bargaining game. If the status quo is less than player 2's bottom line, $s < b_2$, then the equilibrium outcome is that the status quo is preserved. Either player 1 offers to continue it, or player 1 demands more but the demand is rejected. If the status quo is higher than player 2's bottom line, $b_2 < s$, then player 2 finds it unacceptable and would rather fight than live with it. In that case, player 1 offers player 2 its bottom line, b_2. The conflict option, therefore, imposes a ceiling on how bad things can get for player 2. Player 2 cannot be forced to accept a status quo that is worse than its bottom line.

Summing up, in this game, if player 2 has a credible threat to fight, because $b_2 < s$, the equilibrium offer is

$$x^* = b_2 \tag{4.3}$$

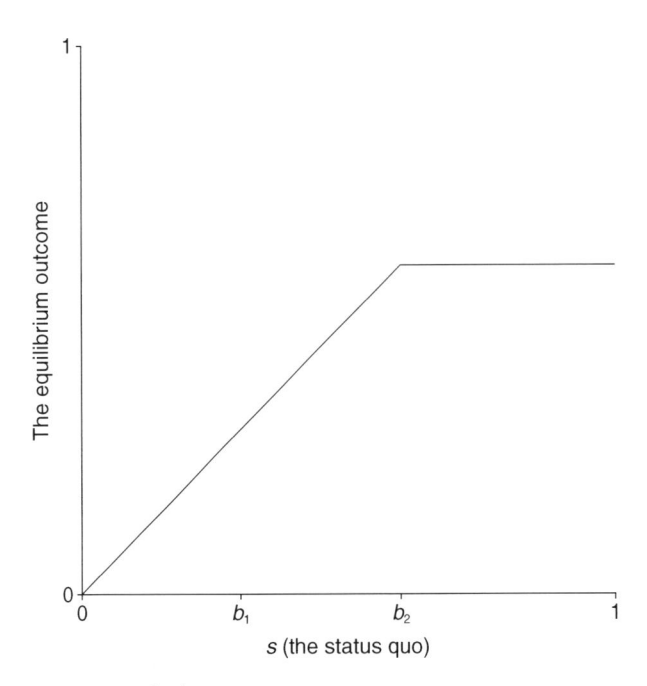

Figure 4.7 The bargaining outcome

The implication is, the better it does at conflict, the higher w_2, the lower b_2 and hence the better player 2 does in the bargaining. Having a good conflict payoff constitutes bargaining leverage. I summarize this in the following result.

Result 4.1 *If a state prefers conflict to the status quo, the higher a state's payoff for conflict, the better it does in bargaining.*

4.5 War as a binary lottery

Let's further unpack the conflict payoff, w_i. As was mentioned in Chapter 1, non-decisive wars involve the mutual infliction of costs until one side gives in. There is nothing at work in the conflict that can force any side to give in, they must decide to do so. By contrast, potentially decisive wars, particularly large-scale conventional conflicts and civil wars, embody a process that can essentially remove one actor from the game by disarming it. That is, war can end with one side winning even if the loser does not agree to lose, simply because the loser is disarmed and cannot offer further resistance. This kind of process is important enough in the international security context to be worthy of specific representation.

4.5 WAR AS A BINARY LOTTERY

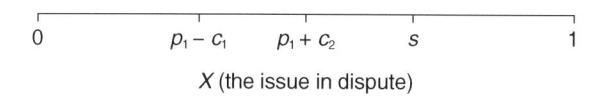

```
├─────────┼────────┼──────────┼──────────────────────────┤
0       p₁-c₁    p₁+c₂        s                          1
                X (the issue in dispute)
```

Figure 4.8 The bargaining range with war as a lottery

The simplest possible way to represent this kind of war is as a binary lottery. By choosing war, in Figure 4.5, player 2 may be thought to trigger a lottery. With probability p_1, player 1 wins, and with probability $p_2 \equiv 1 - p_1$, player 2 wins. Each side pays a cost of fighting, c_1 and c_2. We assume that if they win, they get the entire issue space, worth 1, and if they lose, they get nothing. Therefore, player 1's payoff for war is $p_1(1) + (1-p_1)(0) - c_1$ or just $p_1 - c_1$; player 2's utility for war is $p_2(1) + (1-p_2)(0) - c_2$ or just $p_2 - c_2$.

If we interpret conflict to mean war and model it as an event that can lead to victory or defeat for the players in a binary lottery, the payoffs become

$$w_i = p_i - c_i \tag{4.4}$$

and the bottom lines then become the following[3]

$$b_1 = p_1 - c_1$$
$$b_2 = p_1 + c_2$$

Substituting player 2's bottom line into Equation (4.3), we can see that the optimal offer when player 2 has a credible threat to fight is now the following

$$x^* = p_1 + c_2 \tag{4.5}$$

We can make use of this representation to think about the impact of military power on the distribution of benefits in bargaining. Bargaining power comes in two forms in this game. First, is the relative power of the two sides, p_i. This represents the likelihood of wining a war, should negotiations fail. Increasing p_2 increases player 2's payoff in this case. So the more likely player 2 is to win the war, the greater the payoff in the Bargaining game. The balance of power will determine whether the status quo is in the bargaining range or not. To see this, note that the bargaining range is $[b_1, b_2]$ or $[p_1 - c_1, p_1 + c_2]$. This range is increasing in p_1 and implicitly decreasing in p_2. If the status quo starts out in this range and player 2's power grows, then the status quo will remain in the bargaining range for a while, but then may go out of the bargaining range, $s > b_2$. In this case, player 2 will have a credible threat to fight, and player 1 will have to buy it off with a concession, moving the status quo to the new value of b_2.

---

[3] For player 2, $b_2 = 1 - w_2 = 1 - (p_2 - c_2) = p_1 + c_2$.

This dynamic is illustrated in Figure 4.8. Here, b_1 and b_2 have been replaced by $p_1 - c_1$ and $p_1 + c_2$, respectively. Player 1 must offer to shift the status quo to $p_1 + c_2$ to obtain peace, and is willing to do so. The lower p_1 and c_2 are, the more the status quo will have to be shifted. These facts can be summed up in the following results. The first concerns the balance of power between the two players.

Result 4.2 *If a state has a credible threat to fight, the more powerful it is the better it will do in the bargaining.*

The second concerns player 2's costs of fighting, c_2. Player 2's equilibrium payoff decreases in its costs of fighting. The more costly war is for player 2, the less player 1 must offer to accommodate it in equilibrium. Thus, the cost of fighting also affects the location of the ultimate bargain.

Result 4.3 *If a state has a credible threat to fight, the less costly it finds war to be, the better it will do in the bargaining.*

Thus, even with a very simple bargaining model, we can already give some tentative answers to the second question we began this chapter with: What determines how well each side does in the bargaining? The answer, broadly speaking, is bargaining leverage, which can come in several forms. If there is a status quo, unless at least one actor prefers conflict to the status quo, it will remain in place. If one actor prefers conflict to the status quo, then the other will buy it off with just enough to appease it. How much is required to do this depends on the war payoff. The more powerful the state is, the more it will get, and the less costly it finds war to be, the more it will get.

This case can shed light on an important topic in international relations: the causes of change. When is the status quo stable and when is it likely to be revised? Gilpin's analysis of change in the international system argued that powers that win systemic wars establish international systems to their liking in the aftermath of the conflicts (Gilpin 1981).[4] Then a process of differential economic growth takes place, which produces a disjuncture between the balance of power and the various states' level of satisfaction with the current system. Eventually, this disjuncture leads to some kind of change in the international system, usually accompanied by war. This model reflects this logic. In the model, the status quo will remain in place if the two sides prefer it to conflict, but will be peacefully revised if one side prefers conflict to the status quo and there are deals that both sides prefer to war. However, the model so far does not predict war as

---

[4] See also Kennedy (1987).

the mechanism by which the status quo is revised – peaceful bargaining achieves the same task with less cost.

4.6 War and intermediate outcomes

While we have gathered some preliminary answers to our second question, who gets what, we have still failed to come up with any answer to the first question: When does bargaining succeed and when does it fail? So far, bargaining has always succeeded in equilibrium. This question will be explored at length in the next few chapters, and it is the subject of many more complex models. But even with the simple model we have already developed, we can still provide one answer. In the bargaining model, war may arise if intermediate outcomes are either not sufficiently valued or not sufficiently plentiful. To show this, I will first prove that if intermediate outcomes are continuously available and sufficiently valued, then war is avoided: I will then show by example what may happen when these conditions are not met.

Theorem 4.1 *If conflict is inefficient and intermediate outcomes are continuously available and sufficiently valued, then conflict will not occur in equilibrium in the Bargaining game.*

Proof We have already seen that if player 2 does not prefer war to the status quo, then in the equilibrium player 1 makes an offer $x \in [s, 1]$, and player 2 accepts any offer $x \leq s$ and rejects any offer $x > s$. In no case does player 2 attack. In terms of player 2's bottom line, this is when $s \leq b_2$.

What if player 2 does prefer war to the status quo, so $b_2 < s$? In this case, player 2's strategy in equilibrium is to accept any offer $x \leq b_2$ and attack in response to any offer $x > b_2$. The crucial question then becomes: Does player 1 prefer to offer player 2 its bottom line, or make a more extreme demand and precipitate a war?

We have assumed that intermediate values are available and sufficiently valued. This means that $u_1(x) + u_2(x) \geq 1$, $\forall x \in X$, and, specifically, $u_1(b_2) + u_2(b_2) \geq 1$. By the definition of b_2, we know that $u_2(b_2) = w_2$; so substituting this we have $u_1(b_2) + w_2 \geq 1$. Knowing that conflict is inefficient implies that $1 > w_1 + w_2$, so we have $u_1(b_2) + w_2 > w_1 + w_2$, which implies the following result

$$u_1(b_2) > w_1 \qquad (4.6)$$

Therefore, player 1 prefers to offer player 2 its bottom line rather than make an unacceptable demand and precipitate a war. □

$u_2(x)$ $\quad\quad\quad\quad\quad\quad$ $u_1(x)$

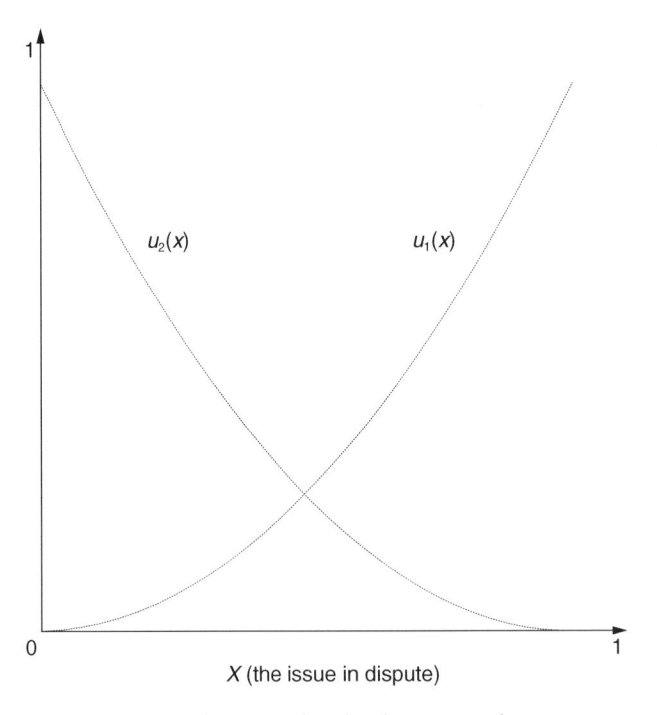

X (the issue in dispute)

Figure 4.9 Utility functions that devalue intermediate outcomes

So if war is inefficient and intermediate outcomes are continuously available and sufficiently valued, then there is no equilibrium in the game featuring war. What happens if these conditions are violated?

First, consider a case where intermediate outcomes are available but not sufficiently valued. Let the players' utility functions be $u_1(x) = x^2$ and $u_2(x) = (1-x)^2$, as illustrated in Figure 4.9. These utility functions do not sufficiently value intermediate outcomes, since for $x \in (0, 1)$ we know that $x^2 < x$ and $(1-x)^2 < 1-x$, and since $x+1-x = 1$, it must be that $x^2+(1-x)^2 < 1$. Now consider the case where the players are evenly matched, so $p_1 = p_2 = 0.5$, face costs of war equal to $c_i = 0.1$, and the status quo favors player 1 at $s = 0.8$. In this case, the players' war payoff is $0.5 - 0.1 = 0.4$. Player 2's payoff for the status quo is $(1-0.8)^2 = 0.04$, which is less than the war payoff by quite a bit; so player 2 has a credible threat to fight. Player 2's bottom line can then be found by solving $(1-x)^2 = 0.4$ or $1-x = 0.63$; so we know $b_2 = 0.27$. Player 1's valuation for this outcome is $0.27^2 = .07$, which is in turn far less than player 1's payoff for war, 0.4. Therefore, player 1 will prefer to make an unacceptable offer and precipitate a war rather than buy off player 2. So we can see by example that with utility functions that do not sufficiently value intermediate outcomes, there can be war. The less intermediate outcomes are valued and the less costly war is the more likely war is to occur.

4.6 WAR AND INTERMEDIATE OUTCOMES

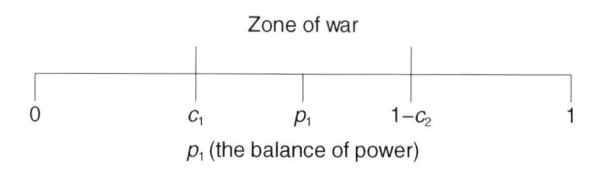

Figure 4.10 War with an indivisible good

Now consider a case where intermediate outcomes are simply not available. Consider the simplest case of indivisibility in which instead of a continuum of possible outcomes, $X = [0, 1]$, there are only two, $X = \{0, 1\}$. The analysis of war goes through as before; since these two outcomes were the only possible outcomes of war, nothing changes in that regard. Let us assume linear preferences again, so $u_1(x) = x$ and $u_2(x) = 1 - x$. The bargaining range is, therefore, still $[b_1, b_2]$, which equals $[p_1 - c_1, p_1 + c_2]$. If the status quo, now also restricted to $s \in \{0, 1\}$, is a member of this set, $s \in [p_1 - c_1, p_1 + c_2]$, then neither side will have a credible threat to fight and the status quo will remain in place.

What this implies is that if war is to be avoided, since only one side can have the good, at least one side must be content with nothing. That is, it must be the case that either player 1 is content with nothing

$$0 \geq p_1 - c_1$$

or that player 2 is content with nothing

$$0 \geq p_2 - c_2$$

or, if the costs of conflict are high enough, both sides are content with nothing. Player 1's condition can be rewritten as $p_1 \leq c_1$, and player 2's as $p_2 \leq c_2$, $1 - p_1 \leq c_2$, and finally $p_1 \geq 1 - c_2$. If either of these conditions holds, then war can be avoided by giving the good to one side. If neither of these conditions holds, then war is inevitable. That is, war is inevitable if the following condition holds

$$c_1 < p_1 < 1 - c_2 \tag{4.7}$$

This relationship is illustrated in Figure 4.10. If the chance of winning is in this middling range, where the boundaries are determined by the costs of conflict, then war is inevitable. If the costs of war are increased, the region shrinks and peace becomes easier to achieve. Imbalances of power are, therefore, conducive to peace with indivisible issues.[5] Note that if the costs of conflict are high enough, then war need not happen

---

[5] Note, the similarity to the result obtained in Smith (1998, 308), in which he considers a prolonged war over an indivisible good.

even with an indivisible good and a middling balance of power. If $1 - c_2 \leq c_1$, then war can always be avoided by allocating the good to one side or the other.

Result 4.4 *If the issue is indivisible, war will result if $c_1 < p_1 < 1 - c_2$, that is, if the power balance is middling and the costs of war are not too great. With an indivisible good, imbalanced power promotes peace.*

The indivisibility does not have to be total to cause problems. Consider a modification of the model in which the issue space is altered and there are four viable issue resolutions, and $X = \{0, \frac{1}{3}, \frac{2}{3}, 1\}$. If we consider the same game with the altered issue space, how does it change the results? As in the case of extreme indivisibility, if the costs of war are small enough and the balance of power is far enough from one of the available deals, then the bargaining space will contain no actually possible settlements, so negotiations will fail. For instance, consider a case where the preferences are risk neutral, $u_1(x) = x$ and $u_2(x) = 1 - x$. Let $p_1 = 0.5$ and $c_1 = c_2 = 0.1$. In that case, $b_1 = p_1 - c_1 = 0.4$ and $b_2 = p_1 + c_2 = 0.6$. The bargaining range is now $[0.4, 0.6]$, which unfortunately does not contain any of the feasible deals.

Note, if player 1 grew stronger, so p_1 increased to 0.6, then player 2's bottom line would increase to $b_2 = 0.7$, and the third issue resolution, two-thirds, would fall within the bargaining range, which would make it the unique equilibrium offer in the game. If player 2's costs of war increased, it could have the same result. If player 1 became weaker, it might become willing to accept one-third. But there are some combinations of power, costs, and available issue resolutions that can lead to war, even with risk-neutral or risk-averse preferences.

While some issues may be genuinely indivisible, few in international relations are intrinsically so. The Temple Mount could easily be physically partitioned, as easily as any public square. Issues that are loosely called indivisible may be better thought of as characterized by extreme undervaluing of intermediate outcomes. The most extreme such preferences, after all, are $u(x) = 0, \forall x \in [0, 1)$, and $u(x) = 1$ for $x = 1$. In this case, there is no utility to be gained from splitting the good, although this is physically possible, only for complete possession. The mathematics of such a utility function are the same as for the previous case, however, so the analysis is basically the same.

Powell has argued that this explanation of conflict with reference to undervalued or non-existent intermediate outcomes is really an example of the commitment problem in disguise, because the players should be willing to accept a costless lottery presided over by an international body rather than face the costly lottery of conflict (Powell 2006). What prevents them from doing so is their inability to commit to abide by the lottery in case they lose.

4.7 Conclusion

These bargaining games in which conflict is possible if the parties fail to come to agreement are simple but shed light on many issues in international relations. Power, understood here as the chance of prevailing in a conflict, improves the bargained outcome, but only if one side has a credible threat to fight, so the status quo will be overturned. The more costly war is, the less likely the status quo is to be vulnerable to being changed.

However, these results generate a certain puzzle, in the sense that we observe many wars and other costly instances of conflict. So far, the only explanation we have for such events is the absence of or undervaluing of intermediate outcomes. While this factor may account for some instances of conflict, it seems that other factors may also account for conflict and war. We will turn to the most popular of these explanations next.

EXERCISES

4.1 Consider a version of the game illustrated in Figure 4.5, but with an additional move in which player 1 can attack. Assume linear preferences, $u_1(x) = x$ and $u_2(x) = 1 - x$, and payoffs for conflict of w_1 and w_2, where $w_1 + w_2 < 1$.

1. Draw a new game tree with a node for player 1 after player 2's choice of Reject, in which player 1 may attack or not. If player 1 chooses not to attack, the status quo payoffs remain in place. If player 1 chooses to attack, the conflict payoffs are realized.
2. Identify the bottom lines for each player, b_1 and b_2.
3. Solve for the subgame perfect equilibrium in each of three cases:
   (a) $s \leq b_1$,
   (b) $b_1 < s \leq b_2$,
   (c) $b_2 < s$.

4.2 Consider two parties to a civil war contemplating a peace treaty that will lead to elections. They face an issue space $X = [0, 1]$ and $u_1(x)$ is monotonically increasing and $u_2(x)$ is monotonically decreasing, with $u_1(0) = u_2(1) = 0$ and $u_1(1) = u_2(0) = 1$. Player 1 moves first, choosing either to keep fighting or to opt for peace. If player 1 opts for peace, player 2 then has a decision to keep fighting or opt for peace. If either side keeps fighting, the result is a war in which player i has a chance of winning of p_i^w, where $p_1^w + p_2^w = 1$. Victory enables the winner to impose their ideal point, and each side pays costs of fighting of c_i, so the war payoff is $p_i^w - c_i$ for player i. If both sides opt for peace, the result is an election in which player i has a p_i^e chance of winning and a $1 - p_i^e$ chance of losing, where $p_1^e + p_2^e = 1$. The election is not costly. Winning the election also allows the winner to impose their ideal point.

1. Draw the game tree.
2. Under what conditions is it an equilibrium for the two parties to opt for peace? What role does the shape of their utility functions play?
3. Now assume that the electoral competition is not necessarily all or nothing. Specifically, assume that if player 1 wins, it can impose the outcome $x = 1 - a$ and if player 2 wins, it can impose the outcome $x = a$, where $a \in [0, \frac{1}{2}]$. Now under what conditions is it an equilibrium for the two parties to opt for peace? What role does the shape of their utility functions play?
4. What does this analysis imply for a conflict between a militarily weak but popular rebel group and a militarily strong but unpopular government?

4.3 Consider a model of war with three possible outcomes, victory for one side, victory for the other, and stalemate. The stalemate outcome is denoted $\sigma \in (0, 1)$. Victory is worth 1, defeat is worth 0, and stalemate is worth $u_i(\sigma)$. Player i's probability of winning is p_i^v and the probability of stalemate is p^σ. War still costs player i c_i.

1. What is each side's war payoff?
2. Assuming that the parties have linear preferences, solve for their bottom lines, b_1 and b_2. How do they respond to changes in p_1^v, p_2^v, and p^σ? Will there be a range of deals that both sides prefer to war?
3. Continue the assumption of linear preferences, and now assume the three outcomes of war are also the only three available issue resolutions for bargaining, $X = \{0, \sigma, 1\}$. Under what conditions will there be war in the Bargaining game?

5 Power change and war

THIS chapter addresses the question of how exogenous changes in relative power affect bargaining between states. Exogenous power changes may happen for a variety of reasons – for instance, states differ in their economic growth rates. States that are undergoing industrialization usually experience a period of rapid economic growth before settling down to a more normal rate. As one state grows richer because of industrialization, it will be able to devote more resources to military power. This will shift the balance of power with other states who are not industrializing, or not as quickly. This process may lead to war if the parties are not willing to come to new agreements reflecting the new balance of power.

Thucydides argued that the Peloponnesian war began because of "the growth of Athenian power and the fear which this caused in Sparta" (Thucydides 1954, 49). Since that time, the idea that war could be caused by changes in relative power has become a mainstay of international relations theory (Levy 1988). The related literature on power transitions argues that war is especially likely when rising states overtake declining states (Gilpin 1981, Organski and Kugler 1980, Kugler and Lemke 1996, DiCicco and Levy 1999, Tammen et al. 2000). Fearon (1995) considered power change to be one of two main plausible rationalist explanations for war and Powell (1996, 2006) further investigated the conditions under which it operates. Fearon (2004) argues that this kind of commitment problem helps explain why some civil wars last so long, and Powell (2004) finds a similar mechanism at work in a variety of contexts where there is shifting power.

Another manifestation of this problem is the *window of opportunity*. A window of opportunity can arise if a state is temporarily weakened but will regain its strength over time (Van Evera 1999, Chapter 4). For instance, a revolution may overthrow an established government and greatly weaken the state, but over time as the new regime consolidates the state will regain its strength, and perhaps grow even stronger if the new government enjoys more popular support. This may present external rivals with a temptation to attack just after the revolution in order to seize advantage of a fleeting opportunity while the state is temporarily weak (Walt 1996). A similar story is used to explain secessionist wars after state collapse, particularly in the Yugoslav case (Fearon 1998b). With the collapse of the central state, minorities will want to secede. Members of the former majority that are trapped in seceding regions will, therefore, want to secede themselves rather than allow the secessionist regime to consolidate power and disenfranchise them in the future.

Three cases of particular historical interest are the First World War, the Cold War, and current US–Chinese relations. One of the most plausible interpretations of the First World War is that it was deliberately launched by Germany, in part due to preventive motivations, because of its fear of the rising power of Russia (Fischer 1975, Copeland 2000, Lieber 2007). The causal role of German expansionist inclinations may remain important because it is not clear that a Germany interested solely in security would have attacked. Nonetheless, the documentary record contains many references to German fears of the future with respect to Russia.[1] The Cold War contains two large power shifts at the beginning and at the end. In the beginning, the Soviet Union was catching up to the US at least in terms of nuclear weapons acquisition. The United States considered launching a preventive war on the Soviets, but ultimately let the opportunity slip (Trachtenberg 1988/89). At the end of the Cold War, Soviet power imploded, but the Soviet Union went peacefully into the night, retreating from Eastern Europe, and eventually abandoning the Russian Empire. This led some analysts to wonder why such a massive power change took place peacefully (Schweller 1992, Lebow and Risse-Kappen 1995). Finally, the current rise of China, fueled by extraordinary economic growth and based on the largest population in the world, has led to concern about China's relationship with the currently dominant global power, the United States, as well as its regional neighbors. So far, preventive war has not been mentioned aloud as a possible policy option, but there is certainly a vigorous debate about the merits of containment vs. engagement. (Brown *et al.* 2000a).

The key question to ask about power change and war is under what conditions relative decline leads to war and when is a state willing to decline peacefully. A related question concerns the role of bargaining in preventive war: Under what conditions can peaceful deals be struck that avoid the necessity of war? Copeland (2000, 38) analyzes the effect of a number of variables. He argues that preventive war is more likely if the state starts out with a large power advantage, foresees a decline that is both likely and steep, believes that other hard-line policies such as arms racing and imperial expansion will fail to address the problem, and believes that the rising state is likely to attack in the future. Powell (1999a, 132) focuses more explicitly on bargaining and shows in a

---

[1] For the political science debate about the origins of the First World War, see Miller *et al.* (1991).

multiperiod model that if the shift in power is less than the cost of war, the declining state should be willing to buy off the rising state without fighting. In what follows, I develop a simple two period model of power change and highlight the conditions under which it leads to war. By adding opportunities for bargaining both before and after the power change, the conditions under which war occurs can be reduced, but not to 0. We will see that power changes that are too large in comparison to the costs of war and the ability of the rising state to buy off the declining state in the present will lead to war.

5.1 The problem of preventive war

Preventive war is usually defined as war initiated by a declining state against a rising challenger that will pose a greater threat in the future. The simplest representation of the preventive war problem is illustrated in Figure 5.1. First, player 1 has the option to attack or wait. If player 1 attacks, a war takes place with payoffs $2(p_1 - c_1)$ and $2(p_2 - c_2)$ where $p_i \in [0, 1]$ is player i's chance of winning the war (and $p_2 \equiv 1 - p_1$) and $c_i > 0$ are the costs of fighting. The payoffs are multiplied by two because they are incurred over two rounds, representing the present and the future. If player 1 waits, we assume some years go by during which the status quo remains in place. Denote the payoff for living with the status quo $u_i(s) \in [0, 1]$. Each player may be quite satisfied with the status quo if $u_i(s)$ is close to 1, or quite dissatisfied if it is near 0. Then the future arrives and player 2 has a chance to attack. At this point, the balance of power has changed so that player 1 has lost, and player 2 has gained, an amount of power equal to Δ_p, where $\Delta_p \in [0, p_1]$, and player 2's chance of winning does not exceed 1. The new war payoffs are $p_1 - \Delta_p - c_1$ and $p_2 + \Delta_p - c_2$. If player 2 also decides to wait, then the status

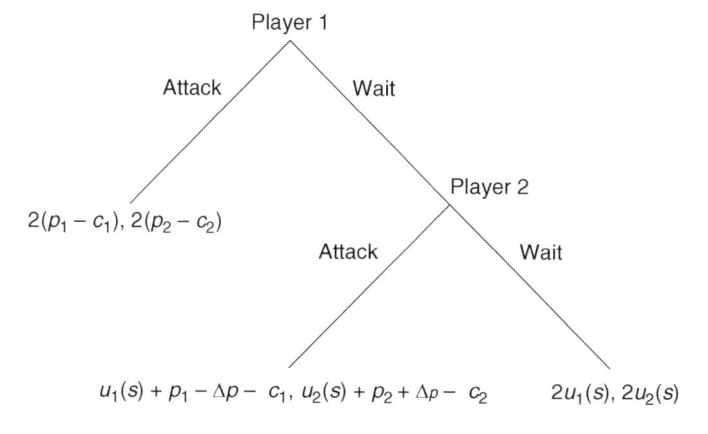

Figure 5.1 The Power Change game without bargaining

Table 5.1 Equilibria in the Power Change game without bargaining

	No war equilibrium	War in the future equilibrium	Preventive war equilibrium
Player 1	Not attack	Not attack	Attack
Player 2	Not attack	Attack	Attack
Conditions	$u_2(s) \geq p_2 + \Delta_p - c_2$	$u_2(s) < p_2 + \Delta_p - c_2$	$u_2(s) < p_2 + \Delta_p - c_2$
		$u_1(s) \geq p_1 + \Delta_p - c_1$	$u_1(s) < p_1 + \Delta_p - c_1$

quo remains in place, so the players get another round at $u_i(s)$. In order to focus on the effect of the power shift, I assume that the status quo would be acceptable to both sides if power was stable, so that the following holds

$$u_i(s) \geq p_i - c_i \tag{5.1}$$

How should the players play the game? Backwards induction enables us to identify three subgame perfect equilibria in the game, shown in Table 5.1. First, consider player 2's choice. If the status quo is still satisfactory to player 2 in the future, that is, if the following condition holds

$$u_2(s) \geq p_2 + \Delta_p - c_2 \tag{5.2}$$

then player 2 will not attack in the future. If this is the case, player 1 will not attack in the present, since not attacking gives a payoff of $2u_1(s)$ and attacking gives $2(p_1 - c_1)$, which is worse, by the assumption embodied in Equation (5.1). Thus, in this equilibrium neither side attacks, despite the shift in power, as shown in the first column of Table 5.1.

Conversely, if the status quo will not be acceptable to player 2 in the future, then player 2 will attack. Player 1 will then compare war now, with payoff $2(p_1 - c_1)$, with war in the future, with payoff $u_1(s) + p_1 - \Delta_p - c_1$, and will not attack if $2(p_1 - c_1) \leq u_1(s) + p_1 - \Delta_p - c_1$ or if

$$u_1(s) \geq p_1 + \Delta_p - c_1 \tag{5.3}$$

If this condition is satisfied, then player 1 will not attack, despite knowing that player 2 will attack in the future. The equilibrium in which player 2 attacks but player 1 does not is shown in the second column of Table 5.1. In this case, the power shift is enough to cause player 2 to attack in the future. However, player 1 still does not attack in the present, because the shift in power is not sufficient to outweigh the loss that would be incurred by attacking in the present rather than living with the status quo and postponing the war.

Only in the third equilibrium, shown in the last column of Table 5.1, does preventive war occur. The shift in power renders player 2 dissatisfied, so it attacks in the future.

5.1 THE PROBLEM OF PREVENTIVE WAR

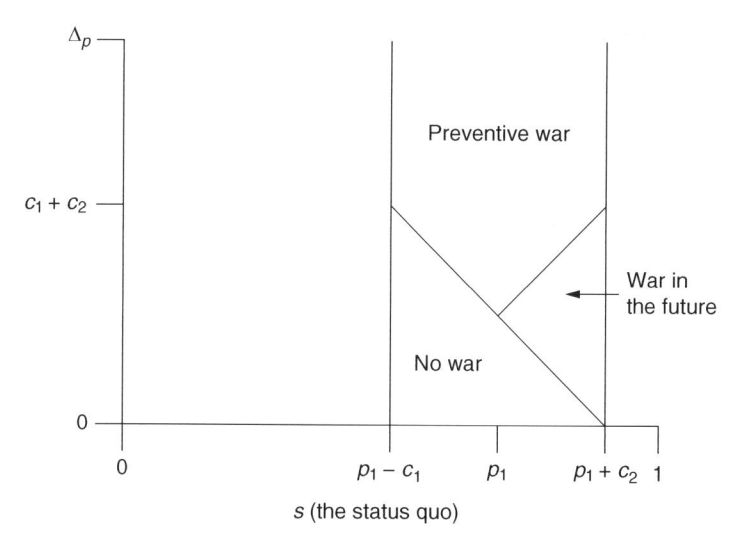

[Figure 5.2: graph with vertical axis Δ_p (marked at $c_1 + c_2$) and horizontal axis s (the status quo), with marks at $p_1 - c_1$, p_1, $p_1 + c_2$, and 1. Regions labeled "Preventive war," "No war," and "War in the future."]

Figure 5.2 Power change equilibria without bargaining

The shift in power is also large enough to make up for the loss incurred by fighting in the present, so player 1 chooses to fight as well. This refines and makes more precise Copeland's hypothesis that the likelihood of preventive war is greater the "deeper" the decline of the currently dominant power (Copeland 2000, 39).

The three equilibria in the game are illustrated in Figure 5.2. Here I assume linear utility functions, so $u_1(s) = s$ and $u_2(s) = 1 - s$. The horizontal axis is the status quo, s, and the vertical axis is the change in relative power, or Δ_p. Note, player 1's power can only decline to 0, so the maximum that Δ_p can attain is p_1, set at 0.7 in the figure. The costs of war are set at 0.2. If the status quo is relatively favorable to player 2 (that is, between $p_1 - c_1$ and p_1), increasing Δ_p will at first have no effect, since player 2 will not have a credible threat to fight in the second round. Eventually, if Δ_p grows large enough, however, player 2 will attack later and player 1 will fight a preventive war. If the status quo starts out favorable to player 1 (larger than p_1), then increasing Δ_p will at first have no effect, but if it grows too large, it will cause a war in the future, because player 2 will become dissatisfied but player 1 will prefer to postpone the war and enjoy the status quo for the present rather than fight now. Only if Δ_p becomes larger still will player 1 launch a preventive war. Note, the width of the interval is determined by the cost of fighting. As the costs of war shrink, the interval narrows, and the slanted lines move downward, making the preventive war equilibrium more common in comparison to the other two. As war becomes cheap, player 2 is quicker to attack in the future and player 1 in the present.

What can such a simple model teach us about preventive war? By comparing the three equilibria and examining the conditions that underlie them, we can deduce several results. First, the higher the states' satisfaction with the status quo, $u_i(s)$, the more likely Equations (5.2) and (5.3) are to be satisfied leading to the no war equilibrium. It is perfectly possible for both sides to be relatively satisfied with the status quo, that is, for $u_1(s)$ and $u_2(s)$ to both be close to 1. In this case, power shifts are relatively harmless. In the extreme case, if the rising player 2 is fully satiated, so that $u_2(s) = 1$, then Equation (5.2) will automatically be satisfied, because $p_2 + \Delta_p \leq 1$, so the right-hand side cannot possibly equal 1. In that case, the no war equilibrium will obtain regardless of the level of power shift. With linear preferences, making one side more satisfied will make the other less so. However, as Figure 5.2 shows, the happier player 2 is with the status quo, the larger the power shift that can be accommodated peacefully.

Result 5.1 *The more satisfied with the status quo the states are, the less likely preventive war is. If the rising power is satiated, preventive war will not occur.*

While this result may seem obvious, it bears remembering when considering the many power transitions that have passed peacefully. For instance, in the late nineteenth century the US surpassed Great Britain as the leading industrial power and hegemon in the western hemisphere. The disparity deepened in the twentieth century as the US took over the reins of global hegemony. Yet this process was peaceful, between the US and Britain at least, in part because the US had no serious conflicts of interest with Britain. In contrast, Britain perceived Germany to be a very unsatisfied power that would make revisionist demands as its power grew. This helped draw Britain into the wars that Germany initiated in the twentieth century, for fear of letting Germany become predominant on the continent (Kennedy 1980). In the case of Germany and Russia before the First World War, this also helps illuminate the debate between those who emphasize preventive motivations and fear of Russian military programs on Germany's part (Copeland 2000), and those who emphasize German expansionist motivations, in part driven by internal pressures (Kehr 1965). The model shows that the less satisfied a declining state is with the status quo, the smaller the decline in power it will be willing to tolerate before deciding to attack. So German expansionist motivations may have tipped it over the brink into preventive war, when a more satisfied Germany would have been willing to ride out the power fluctuation. From this reading, both the power change and the expansionist motivations were necessary to cause the war.

If player 2 is not entirely satiated, so $u_2(s) < 1$, then the other factors come into play. The larger the shift in power, Δ_p, the more incentive both players have to attack, as a larger Δ_p makes both Equations (5.2) and (5.3) harder to satisfy. If the rising power is rising by leaps and bounds, this poses more of a problem for the declining power. For this reason, nuclear proliferation has been a focus of preventive war analysis. The 2003 US invasion of Iraq is often thought of as a preventive war that was designed to stop

Iraq from developing nuclear weapons. This has led to a number of papers modeling this problem and attempting to understand when preventive wars may be "mistaken" in the sense of being launched, despite the fact that no actual weapons program exists (Bas and Coe 2012, Debs and Monteiro 2014).

Result 5.2 *The larger the rising state's rate of increase in power, the more incentive there is for preventive war.*

Finally, the higher the costs of conflict, c_i, the less likely the rising power will attack in the future, and so the less need to attack now. For instance, some analysts argue that the advent of nuclear weapons raised the cost of war between great powers enormously and that this explains why the enormous power shift that took place at the end of the Cold War between the United States and the Soviet Union transpired without major war (Oye 1995). Since the Soviets retained nuclear weapons, they could be assured that the US would continue to find war prohibitively costly into the future, even as Soviet power declined. Therefore, there was no need for the Soviets to lash out.

Result 5.3 *The higher the cost of war, the less likely preventive war is.*

5.2 Power change with bargaining in the future

The preceding model already sheds some light on preventive war, but it raises the question: What would happen if the parties were able to adjust the status quo, in particular to give player 2 more of the good in the dispute in the second round, reflecting its newfound power? That is, preventive war is often thought to be motivated by the anticipation of a future attack. But what if in the future the players bargain rationally? Should they not come up with a deal that both prefer to war? If so, what does this do to the motivation for preventive war in the present?

Consider a modified version of the preventive war game with bargaining, depicted in Figure 5.3. As in the first game, player 1 starts the game considering an attack on player 2. If player 1 decides to not attack, then time passes and player 2 grows stronger. In the future, player 1 makes an offer x to player 2 to potentially revise the status quo. Player 2 can then either accept the offer, reject it and maintain the current status quo, or attack. Note, this is the same bargaining model as discussed in Chapter 4. I assume linear utility functions, so $u_1(x) = x$ and $u_2(x) = 1 - x$.

As before, reflecting the two-round structure, the payoffs are a combination of what happens in the present and what will happen in the future. If player 1 attacks, a war

POWER CHANGE AND WAR

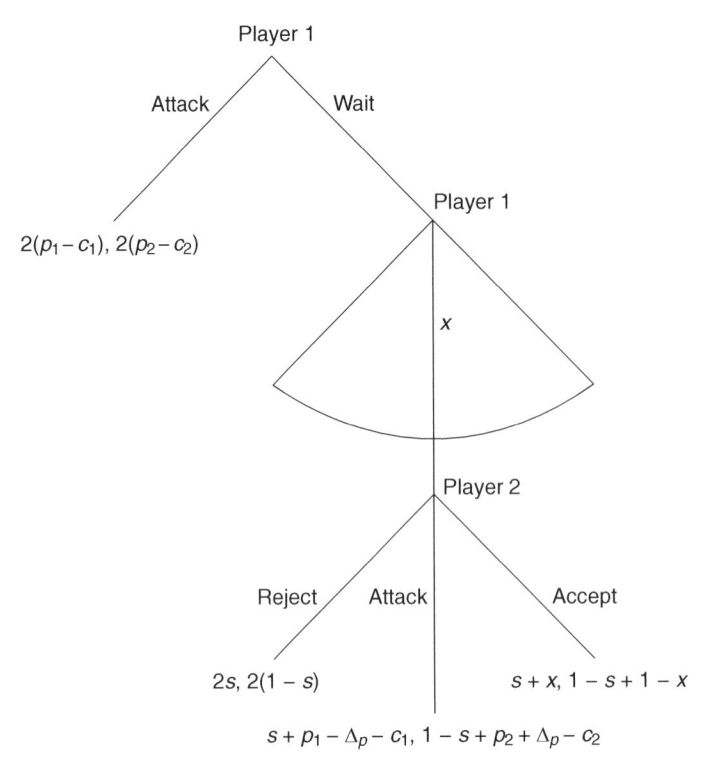

```
                        Player 1
              Attack  /        \  Wait
                     /          \
                    /            \
                   /           Player 1
   2(p₁-c₁), 2(p₂-c₂)           / \
                               /   \
                              /  x  \
                             /       \
                            /         \
                           /       Player 2
                          /        /  |  \
                    Reject      Attack   Accept
                    /             |          \
                  2s, 2(1-s)      |        s+x, 1-s+1-x
                                  |
                      s+p₁-Δₚ-c₁, 1-s+p₂+Δₚ-c₂
```

Figure 5.3 The Power Change game with bargaining in the future

takes place and its outcome is assumed to last for both rounds, hence the payoffs are multiplied by 2. If player 1 decides to wait, then the first round is assumed to pass without conflict and the two sides receive the status quo payoffs, s and $1-s$. Thus, these quantities are added to the payoffs at the end of the game tree. In addition, there are payoffs reflecting what happens in that round.

In solving the game, we start by considering player 2's decision. As in Chapter 4, the first question is whether player 2 has a credible threat to fight in the second round. First, consider the case where player 2 has no credible threat to fight. Player 2 will live with the status quo rather than fight if $1-s+p_2+\Delta_p-c_2 \leq 2(1-s)$, or $\Delta_p \leq p_1+c_2-s$. This is the same condition as before in Equation (5.2) (slightly rewritten to bring the power shift to the left-hand side). If player 2 has no credible threat to fight in the second round, then there is no reason to offer it more in the second round, nor to attack in the first round. Therefore, in the modified game there is an equilibrium with no war and no change to the status quo, much as in the previous version shown in the first column of Table 5.2. Player 2 does not fight in the future, so player 1 makes no concessions, nor does player 1 fight in the first round, so the status quo remains in place.

If player 2 has a credible threat to fight in the second round, $\Delta_p \geq p_1 + c_2 - s$, then player 1 must buy it off if it wishes to avoid war. Just as in Chapter 4, player 1's optimal offer is player 2's bottom line, which in this case equals

5.2 POWER CHANGE WITH BARGAINING IN THE FUTURE

Table 5.2 Equilibria in the Power Change game with bargaining in the future

	No revision equilibrium	Future revision equilibrium	Preventive war equilibrium
Player 1's attack choice	Not attack	Not attack	Attack
Player 1's offer	$x \geq s$	$x = b'_2$	$x = b'_2$
Player 2's response	Accept if $x \leq s$, reject otherwise	Accept if $x \leq b'_2$, attack otherwise	Accept if $x \leq b'_2$, attack otherwise
Conditions	$\Delta_p \leq p_1 + c_2 - s$	$\Delta_p > p_1 + c_2 - s$, $\Delta_p \leq s - (p_1 - c_1) + c_1 + c_2$	$\Delta_p > p_1 + c_2 - s$, $\Delta_p > s - (p_1 - c_1) + c_1 + c_2$

$$b'_2 \equiv p_1 + c_2 - \Delta_p \tag{5.4}$$

Anything more will be rejected and lead to war, which is worse for player 1, and anything less is needlessly generous. But will player 1 prefer to make this concession in the future or attack in the present? Attacking now is not as good as moving to the second round and buying off player 2 if $2(p_1 - c_1) \leq s + p_1 + c_2 - \Delta_p$, so war will be avoided despite the power shift if

$$\Delta_p \leq s - (p_1 - c_1) + c_1 + c_2 \tag{5.5}$$

A little algebra will show that this expression is quite similar to that in Equation (5.3) (if that equation is rewritten to isolate Δ_p). However, now the sum of the costs of war, $c_1 + c_2$, sometimes known as the "bargaining surplus," are added to the right-hand side, making the condition easier to satisfy. Adding bargaining to the second round makes preventive war easier to avoid, because it makes the future better than it otherwise would be for both players, in the case that player 2 will be dissatisfied. Instead of a war, there is peaceful bargaining, so the costs of war are saved.

If player 2 has a credible threat to fight in the future, revision will take place in the future and there may or may not be preventive war. One equilibrium, illustrated in the second column of Table 5.2, features revision in the future in player 2's favor, but no preventive war. The shift in power is enough to give player 2 a credible threat to fight, but player 1 will buy it off in the future, thereby preventing a future war. Furthermore, player 1 prefers to face this future loss rather than attack now, because the shift in power is sufficiently small.

Finally, there is a preventive war equilibrium, shown in the third column of Table 5.2. Here player 2 will have a credible threat to fight, and player 1 will be forced to appease it in the future. However, the anticipated loss is too great for player 1 to bear, given its

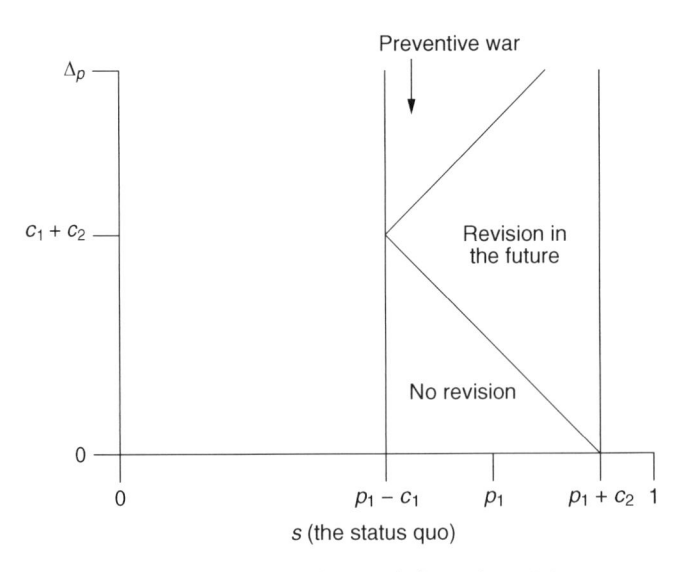

Figure 5.4 Power change equilibria with future bargaining

current strength. It, therefore, decides to fight in the present rather than live with the future loss in bargaining power, even though, unlike in the first model, war does not take place in the future, merely a peaceful concession.

These equilibria are illustrated in Figure 5.4. The parameter values are the same as in Figure 5.2. The downward-sloping line is the border where player 2 is indifferent between fighting and not in the future, so this constraint is the same as before in Figure 5.2. Below it, there is no revision; the status quo remains in place. Above it, however, instead of the war in the future equilibrium we have the revision in the future equilibrium. Thus, where there would have been war, there is now peace because of the bargaining that will take place in the future. The upper boundary of this equilibrium is higher than in the previous case, by the amount $c_1 + c_2$, or 0.4 in this case. Note, where the status quo is particularly favorable to player 1, for $s > p_1$, the revision in the future equilibrium occupies much of the parameter space. Very large power shifts can be dealt with by peaceful transfers in the future. Finally, in the remaining upper-left-hand corner there is the preventive war equilibrium, greatly reduced in size from the previous case with no bargaining. Bargaining has made preventive war not worthwhile for most of its previous range in the parameter space. Only if the status quo is currently quite favorable to player 2 and the shift in power likely to be extreme, will player 1 decide to attack in the present.

Result 5.4 *The prospect of bargaining in the future increases the size of the power shift that can be peacefully accommodated. If states anticipate concessions in the future rather than war, the incentive for preventive war diminishes.*

5.3 Power change with bargaining in the present and future

Bargaining in the future lessened the preventive war problem, because player 1 was able to buy off player 2 in the future, making the future better than it otherwise would be because war is avoided. This raises the question: Could the preventive war problem be solved by allowing player 2 to buy off player 1 in the present? This would make the present better for player 1 in the case that player 1 is contemplating preventive war. To answer this, we consider a preventive war game with bargaining in both the present and the future.

Consider a game consisting of the Bargaining game from Chapter 4 repeated once. In the first round, player 2 starts the game making an offer, x, to player 1. Player 1 can accept the offer, reject it, or attack. Attacking gives the same payoffs as before, $2(p_1-c_1)$, and $2(p_2 - c_2)$. Rejecting the offer leaves the current status quo, s, in place, and moves the game to the next round. Accepting the offer shifts the status quo to x, and moves the game to the next round. Call the status quo going into the second round s', so if player 2's offer was accepted, then $s' = x$, and if it was rejected, then $s' = s$. In the second round, player 2 has grown more powerful, as before, so player 1's new power level is $p_1 - \Delta_p$. The game then proceeds as in the previous game with player 1 making an offer x' and player 2 either accepting, rejecting, or attacking.

The game is solved by backward induction as before. The second round of strategies of the players are the same in all equilibria, and are conditional on the status quo going into the second round. As before, if player 2 has a credible threat to fight given s', then player 1 will buy it off by offering it its bottom line. Otherwise, player 1 will make no concessions and player 2 will not attack. Whether the status quo gets revised depends on the equilibrium.

Equilibria are similar to the previous game, but with one additional case. First, there is a no war, no revision equilibrium as before if player 2 does not have a credible threat

Table 5.3 Power Change game with present and future bargaining: no revision equilibrium

Player 2's offer	$x \leq s$
Player 1's response	Accept if $x \geq s$, reject otherwise
Player 1's offer	if $s' \leq b'_2$, then $x' \geq s'$
	if $b'_2 < s'$, then $x' = b'_2$
Player 2's response	if $s' \leq b'_2$, then accept if $x' \leq s'$, reject otherwise
	if $b'_2 < s'$, then accept if $x' \leq b'_2$, attack otherwise
Condition	$\Delta_p \leq p_1 + c_2 - s$

Table 5.4 Power Change game with present and future bargaining: revision in the future equilibrium

Player 2's offer	$x \leq s$
Player 1's response	Accept if $x \geq s$, reject otherwise
Player 1's offer	if $s' \leq b'_2$, then $x' \geq s'$
	if $b'_2 < s'$, then $x' = b'_2$
Player 2's response	if $s' \leq b'_2$, then accept if $x' \leq s'$, reject otherwise
	if $b'_2 < s'$, then accept if $x' \leq b'_2$, attack otherwise
Conditions	$\Delta_p > p_1 + c_2 - s$
	$\Delta_p \leq s - (p_1 - c_1) + c_1 + c_2$

to fight in the future if the status quo is left in place, shown in Table 5.3. In this case, player 1 also has no credible threat to fight because if it rejects player 2's first round offer, the equilibrium payoff will be $2s$, which beats the war payoff. Therefore, neither side has any incentive to fight, and hence neither side need make a concession. The equilibrium payoff vector is, therefore, the status quo in both rounds, $(2s, 2(1-s))$.

The second case features revision in the second round only, shown in Table 5.4. Here player 2 has a credible threat to fight in the second round if the status quo is left in place, $b'_2 < s$. Consider player 1's decision in the present about whether to accept or reject player 2's offer, or whether to attack. There is no need for player 1 to accept anything worse that the status quo, since player 2 can always be bought off in the next round. Compare attacking and rejecting. Attacking yields $2(p_1 - c_1)$, rejecting yields $s + p_1 + c_2 - \Delta_p$, which is the same comparison as in Equation (5.5). If player 1 will not attack, then, turning to player 2, there is no need to appease it, so the equilibrium offer will be some $x \leq s$.

Third, we have a new case in which player 2 has a credible threat to fight and player 1 has a credible threat to wage preventive war, but can be bought off in the present, shown in Table 5.5. In this case, war is avoided once again. In the first round, player 2 makes a concession to player 1 that just suffices to buy it off, so it does not launch a preventive war. In the second round, player 1 makes a concession to player 2 that just suffices to buy it off from launching a simple revisionist war. These concessions keep the two sides happy and suffice to keep the power transition peaceful.

When does this case obtain? Player 1 must prefer to launch a preventive war, $\Delta_p > s - (p_1 - c_1) + c_1 + c_2$, and must also accept a deal that makes it at least as well off as its payoff for preventive war, bearing in mind that it will have to buy off player 2 in the next round, $x + p_1 + c_2 - \Delta_p \geq 2(p_1 - c_1)$, and fight otherwise. The deal that would just buy it off is

5.3 POWER CHANGE WITH BARGAINING: PRESENT AND FUTURE

Table 5.5 Power Change game with bargaining in the present and future: double revision equilibrium

Player 2's offer	$x = x^*$
Player 1's response	Accept if $x \geq x^*$, attack otherwise
Player 1's offer	if $s' \leq b_2'$, $x' \geq s'$
	if $b_2' < s'$, $x' = b_2'$
Player 2's response	if $s' \leq b_2'$, then accept if $x' \leq s'$, reject otherwise
	if $b_2' < s'$, then accept if $x' \leq b_2'$, attack otherwise
Conditions	$\Delta_p > p_1 + c_2 - s$
	$\Delta_p \in (s - (p_1 - c_1) + c_1 + c_2, 1 - (p_1 - c_1) + c_1 + c_2]$

$$x^* \equiv p_1 - c_1 + \Delta_p - (c_1 + c_2) \tag{5.6}$$

Player 2 must also be willing to make this offer, rather than make an unacceptable offer and precipitate a war. Player 2's payoff for making the offer, $1 - (p_1 - c_1 + \Delta_p - (c_1 + c_2)) + 1 - (p_1 + c_2 - \Delta_p)$, beats its war payoff, $2(p_2 - c_2)$, if

$$1 - (p_1 - c_1 + \Delta_p - (c_1 + c_2)) + 1 - (p_1 + c_2 - \Delta_p) \geq 2(p_2 - c_2)$$

$$c_1 - \Delta_p + c_1 + c_2 - c_2 + \Delta_p \geq -2c_2$$

$$2(c_1 + c_2) \geq 0$$

This condition is always satisfied – because of the inefficiency of war, the joint costs of war are positive. Therefore, player 2 will always prefer to buy off player 1 if it can.

The final question to ask is whether it is feasible to buy off player 1 in the present. This question arises because the necessary offer could be greater than 1, and hence it would take more than all of the available good to prevent player 1 from initiating a preventive war. The offer is feasible if $p_1 - c_1 + \Delta_p - (c_1 + c_2) \leq 1$, or if

$$\Delta_p \leq 1 - (p_1 - c_1) + c_1 + c_2 \tag{5.7}$$

Note, this is the same as the condition stated in Equation (5.5), except that 1 is substituted for s, making it even easier to satisfy. If the change in power is small enough, then player 1 can be bought off, otherwise preventive war is inevitable.

Summing up, for this equilibrium to hold the shift in power must be great enough that player 1 would prefer to wage a preventive war if unappeased, but not so large that player 1 cannot be bought off in the present.

Finally, we have the preventive war equilibrium, shown in Table 5.6. In this case, although player 2 would like to buy off player 1 in the first round, it cannot do so because even giving player 1 all of the disputed good would not suffice to

Table 5.6 Power Change game with bargaining in the present and future: preventive war equilibrium

Player 2's offer	$x \in [0, 1]$
Player 1's response	Attack
Player 1's offer	if $s' \leq b'_2, x' \geq s'$
	if $b'_2 < s', x' = b'_2$
Player 2's response	if $s' \leq b'_2$, then accept if $x' \leq s'$, reject otherwise
	if $b'_2 < s'$, then accept if $x' \leq b'_2$, attack otherwise
Conditions	$\Delta p > p_1 + c_2 - s$
	$\Delta p > 1 - (p_1 - c_1) + c_1 + c_2$

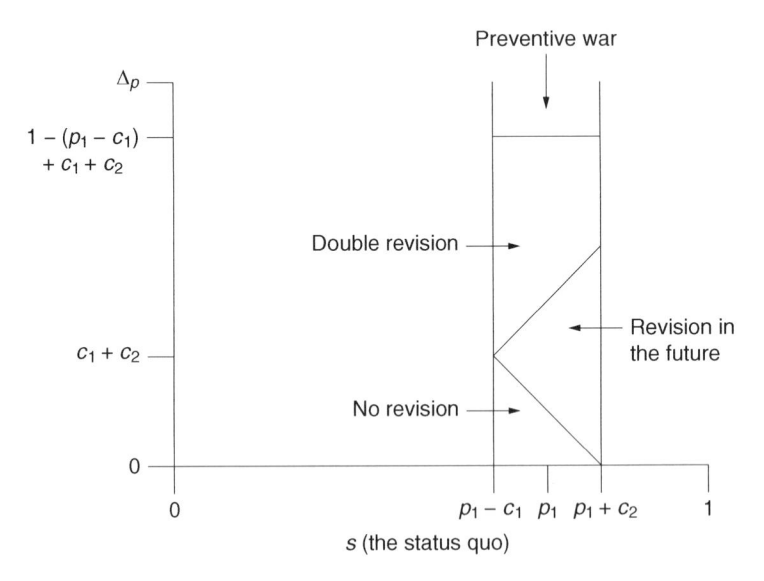

Figure 5.5 Power change equilibria with present and future bargaining

convince player 1 not to attack. The fall in power will be so precipitous that player 1 would prefer to attack even if it had the whole good in the first round. Note, the condition determining whether player 1 can be bought off can be made easier to meet if the costs of conflict increase. If they are high enough, any shift in relative power can be accommodated, since Δp cannot exceed 1 and $1 - (p_1 - c_1) + c_1 + c_2$ certainly can.

These equilibria are illustrated in Figure 5.5. With the old parameters, $p_1 = 0.7$ and $c_i = 0.2$, the preventive war equilibrium is no longer feasible in the game. To illustrate it, therefore, I shrink the cost of war to $c_i = 0.1$. The result is the narrower band around p_1 shown in Figure 5.5. With these lower costs, the no revision and revision in the future equilibria are possible for lower levels of Δ_p than before. Above them, however, is the new band occupied by the double revision equilibrium, in which an exchange of concessions keeps the peace. Only above the horizontal line is the preventive war equilibrium possible, that is, for very high levels of Δ_p. With the parameters illustrated, if the costs of war are a tenth of the good at stake, preventive war is only rational if the decline in power is anticipated to be from a 70% probability of victory to a less than 10% chance of winning. This precipitous decline is too large to be negotiated successfully.

The game with bargaining in the present and future further reduces the likelihood of preventive war. Concessions made in the present by the rising power can buy off the declining power, overcoming the incentive to attack preventively.

Result 5.5 *Rising powers can reduce the likelihood of preventive war by making concessions in the present to declining powers. These concessions will be reversed in the future, but serve to tip the balance against preventive war in the present.*

5.4 Bargaining over power

A logical next question is: What if it is possible to bargain over power itself? Chadefaux (2011) shows that if the states are allowed to bargain over power, and do not care directly about it, then they will avoid power shifts that could cause war. Fearon (1996) looks at an infinitely repeated model and argues that states could rationally allow themselves to be eaten away to nothing in small bites, in order to avoid the cost of conflict. A growing literature motivated by the US war against Iraq in 2003 looks at the question of when preventive war is rational against an aspiring nuclear power, and focuses on whether bargaining can solve the problem (Debs and Monteiro 2014). Empirically, the US negotiates about power with rogue states, such as Iran and North Korea, and the superpowers negotiated about their arsenals in the latter half of the Cold War. However, aside from these examples, negotiations about military power per se seem relatively rare. Germany refused to negotiate with Britain over its growing battleship fleet before the First World War, and the superpowers did not negotiate about their nuclear arsenals until the Soviets had reached relative parity with the US. It is an interesting question why states involved in power shifts seem to rarely negotiate about power in an effort to head off preventive war. One reason is that in the case of differential economic growth, the fundamental cause of the shift in power is itself intrinsically valuable. It is hard to imagine the US and China negotiating over the growth rate of Chinese GDP. Any rising power would be very reluctant to reduce its economic growth rate. This leaves military forces in being, and indeed it seems more reasonable for a state to accept verifiable limits on its military forces to allay the concerns of its neighbors. China has been reluctant to do so, however, possibly viewing the threat of preventive war as unlikely, and hence concessions as unnecessary. Indeed, it is hard to think of an example of a state that rose in economic power but restrained its growth in military power to reassure declining powers.

5.5 Conclusion

What have we learned about preventive war? Preventive war is likely when the anticipated drop in power is large, the current relative power or chance of winning is also large, and the costs of war, or bargaining surplus, are relatively small. When these conditions are met, the inequality in Equation (5.7) is likely to fail and preventive war will be inevitable. Note that a fear of future war is not necessary for preventive war. In the versions of the game with bargaining in the second round, war does not occur in the future. Bargaining in the first round is also sufficient to head off some potential preventive wars. Preventive war is only inevitable in the third game when there is simply not enough of the good available to compensate player 1 to forgo its temporary advantage in power. If even giving player 1 all there is to have in the present is not enough to make it prefer peace to war, then a preventive war is inevitable. The greater the costs of conflict are, the easier it is to address the problem through negotiation.

EXERCISES

5.1 Consider the model of preventive war without bargaining, illustrated in Figure 5.1. Modify the game so that if player 1 waits, there is a decision by Nature with two possibilities. In the first, there is no decline (*ND*), so the relative power remains the same as in the first round. In the second, the decline (*D*) happens as before, so player 1 loses Δ_p and player 2 gains it. Let the probability of decline be $P(D)$. Assume that the players know if the decline happens or not, so when Player 2 moves, it knows the relative balance of power.

1. Draw the game tree.
2. Solve for all subgame perfect equilibria in the game.
3. Interpret the results. What is the effect of the likelihood of decline on the incentive for preventive war?

5.2 Consider again the preventive war model without bargaining. Now modify the game so that player 1 has an additional option, which is to purchase power. To make things simple, assume it can purchase an amount of power sufficient to avert decline for a cost γ. If player 1 chooses this option, the relative power between the two sides remains unchanged at p_i, and player 2 has an option to attack, as it does if player 1 chooses to do nothing and allow itself to decline.

1. Draw the game tree.
2. Solve for all subgame perfect equilibria.
3. When will player 1 prefer to launch a preventive war rather than increase its power?

6 Private information and war

UNCERTAINTY has long been viewed as a central cause of conflict. Geoffrey Blainey famously argued that "wars usually end when the fighting nations *agree* on their relative strength, and wars usually begin when fighting nations *disagree* on their relative strength" (Blainey 1988, 122). Early crisis bargaining models pointed out that there would be no war with complete information but war was possible with incomplete information (Morrow 1989, Powell 1990). Fearon (1995) made it one of the three rationalist causes of war, and indeed the subsequent literature for a decade focused largely on this cause. This chapter will introduce the topic of how uncertainty can cause war.

Uncertainty is usually thought of as affecting one of three factors: the utility functions over the issue in dispute, the parties' relative power, and their costs of conflict. Some models, such as those by Fearon (1997) and Sartori (2002) (as well as the Bargaining model in Chapter 9), feature uncertainty about the states' valuations for the objects in contention. States value the (indivisible) good along a continuum, some not very much and some more so. States with a low valuation for the good are less likely to threaten or fight for it than states with a high valuation for it. Models of mistrust also usually focus on the states' utility functions, differentiating between status quo states and revisionists, where status quo states are satisfied with what they have and prefer to live in peace, while revisionists want more and may start a war to get it (Kydd 2005). Fear that the other state is a revisionist may lead even status quo states to engage in conflictual behavior and even fight a war.

Other models restrict the uncertainty to the war payoff (Powell 1999a) and focus on the likelihood of winning and the cost of conflict (Fey and Ramsay 2011). The majority of models focus on the costs of conflict, and interpret this as a privately felt cost, unrelated to the likelihood of winning. Therefore, there can be uncertainty about the costs of conflict that does not affect estimates of the probability of victory. Sometimes this is conceived of as a state's *resolve*, where states with low costs for fighting are said to have high resolve. The technical convenience of this avenue is that uncertainty about the other side's war payoff has no impact on one's own costs, which makes the game easier to solve.

Conversely, there may be uncertainty about the balance of power. Blainey's argument focuses on this factor. Uncertainty about power has the additional complication that it intertwines the two parties. Learning about one side's military capabilities informs about the balance of power, which affects the other side's war payoff as well. The resulting models are, therefore, somewhat more complex. An interesting debate has arisen recently in this context over whether mutual optimism can generate war between rational actors, as Blainey argued (Fey and Ramsay 2007).

In this chapter, I will first briefly discuss how uncertainty is modeled in game theory and the equilibrium concept used in the context of games with uncertainty. I then discuss how uncertainty over the costs of conflict can lead to bargaining failure and war. Next, I consider a simple model of mistrust, and show that sufficient mistrust can cause conflict even between status quo states. Finally, I discuss whether mutual optimism about the balance of power can lead to war between rational states.

6.1 Modeling uncertainty

In game theory, uncertainty is represented by the *information set*. An information set is a set of nodes that are conceived of as indistinguishable to a player. All the nodes in an information set must, therefore, belong to the same player and have the same number of choices available, otherwise they could be distinguished. The nodes in the information set must also not be preceded by a choice by the same actor that would lead to different nodes within the set, otherwise the actor, remembering its previous choice, would know which node it is at.

In games featuring *perfect information*, players know where they are in the game tree at every node, so there are no information sets with multiple nodes. The shifting power games of the last chapter featured perfect information. In games with *complete information*, the players are assumed to know their own and each other's utility functions, although they may not know what the other side has done previously in the game. A game with complete but imperfect information may have information sets that link nodes for a player that follow an unobserved choice by another player. For instance, an extensive form representation of the 2 × 2 normal form games in Chapter 3 would have one arbitrarily selected player moving first and the second one following with two nodes linked by an information set, indicating that the second player does not know what the first player did. In games of *incomplete information*, there is uncertainty over the players' utility functions. The fictional player "Nature" is assumed to "select" a type of player from a set of possible types that player could be, usually at the outset of the game. Other players may not know which type was selected, but they will know the probability distribution that governed Nature's choice, so they will have beliefs about the likelihood that they are facing each type (Harsanyi 1967).

The simplest solution concept usually employed with games of incomplete information is the *perfect Bayesian equilibrium* (McCarty and Meirowitz 2006, 208, Mas-Colell et al. 1995, 253).

Definition 6.1 *A perfect Bayesian equilibrium is a Nash equilibrium in which every player chooses the best action at each information set, given the other players' strategies, and given their beliefs at that information set. In turn, these beliefs are updated in response to observed behavior via Bayes' Rule, wherever possible.*

The perfect Bayesian equilibrium is a generalization of subgame perfection to games with information sets that have more than one node. At any such information set, the actors will have beliefs about which node they are at, and will choose their strategy accordingly. These beliefs must be rational in accordance with the laws of probability, in this case, Bayes' Rule, which governs how beliefs should be updated in response to new information. In the games of this chapter, Bayes' Rule will not be employed in all its glory, so I will postpone discussion of it until Chapter 9 when we discuss signaling.

When two different types of player face a choice, they can either do the same thing, which is called *pooling*, or they can do different things, called *separating*. By extension, a *pooling equilibrium* is one in which the different types pool, so that there is no way to tell from their actions what type they are. In a *separating equilibrium*, the types separate, making it possible to tell from their actions which type is being dealt with. In some cases with more than two types, or when some types play mixed strategies, the types do not pool, but they do not separate cleanly either. These equilibria are sometimes called *semi-separating* equilibria.

To make this method concrete, we turn to an example of uncertainty over the cost of conflict in a bargaining context.

6.2 Bargaining with uncertainty over the cost of conflict

Let us return to the bargaining model of Chapter 4. The players bargain over an issue space $X = [0, 1]$, and have linear preferences, $u_1(x) = x$ and $u_2(x) = 1 - x$. Player 1 makes an offer and player 2 can then accept it, reject it, or attack. This time, however, consider a version featuring incomplete information, in that player 2's costs for fighting may be either high or low. The resulting game is illustrated in Figure 6.1. Nature first chooses whether player 2 has high or low costs for fighting. There is a low cost type with costs equal to c_2^l and a high cost type with costs equal to c_2^h, where $0 < c_2^l < c_2^h$.

6.2 BARGAINING WITH UNCERTAINTY OVER THE COST OF CONFLICT

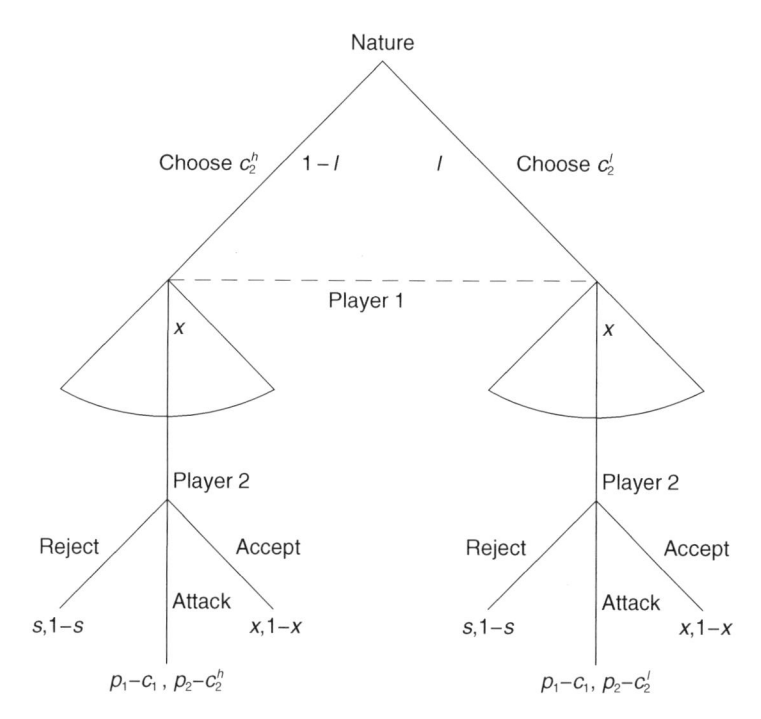

Figure 6.1 Bargaining with private information over costs

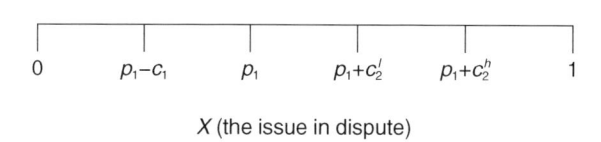

Figure 6.2 The bargaining range with incomplete information

The likelihood that player 2 has low costs is denoted l; so the likelihood that player 2 has high costs is $1 - l$. Then player 1 has a move, but it chooses its move at an information set denoted by the dotted line. This indicates that it does not know whether it is at the left-hand node where player 2 has high costs, or at the right-hand node where player 2 has low costs. Player 1 must make a decision based on its beliefs, which are just l and $1-l$. After player 1 makes its offer, player 2 chooses to accept, reject, or attack, as before. Each type of player 2 will have a strategy for every possible offer from player 1.

The two different types of player 2 will have different war payoffs. We denote the low cost type's war payoff $w_2^l = p_2 - c_2^l$ and the high cost type's war payoff $w_2^h = p_2 - c_2^h$. Obviously, the low cost type has a higher war payoff, $w_2^h < w_2^l$. As a result of their differing war payoffs, the two different types will have different bottom lines. For the low cost type, the bottom line solves $1 - x = w_2^l$, so that $b_2^l = p_1 + c_2^l$. Similarly, for the high cost type, the bottom line is $b_2^h = p_1 + c_2^h$. Note the high cost type has a weaker bottom line, $b_2^l < b_2^h$. These bottom lines are illustrated in Figure 6.2.

Table 6.1 No war, no revision equilibrium

Player 1's offer	$x \geq s$
Player 2's response (low cost type)	Accept if $x \leq s$, reject otherwise
Player 2's response (high cost type)	Accept if $x \leq s$, reject otherwise
Conditions	$s \leq b_2^l$

In the complete information version of the game that we examined in Chapter 4, we saw that there were two subgame perfect equilibria. In one case, player 2 did not have a credible threat to fight, $s \leq b_2$. In that case, player 1 made no concessions and player 2 rejected any demands but did not attack. In the second case, player 2 had a credible threat to fight, $b_2 < s$, player 1 offers player 2 its bottom line, $x^* = b_2$, and player 2 accepts any $x \leq b_2$ and fights in response to any $x > b_2$.

What are the equilibria in the incomplete information version of the game? We can distinguish three scenarios to investigate: one where neither type has a credible threat to fight, $s \leq b_2^l$, one where only the low cost type has a credible threat to fight, $s \in (b_2^l, b_2^h]$, and one where both types have a credible threat to fight, $b_2^h < s$.

Consider the first scenario in which neither type has a credible threat to fight. In this case, the uncertainty turns out to be of no interest. Player 2 will accept any offer better than the status quo and reject otherwise. Player 1, therefore, can offer any $x \geq s$ and the result will be the same in terms of the equilibrium payoff; the status quo will remain in place. This equilibrium is effectively the same as the no war equilibrium from Chapter 4, and is described in Table 6.1.

Next, consider the case where both types have a credible threat to fight, so $b_2^h < s$. In this case, player 2's strategy is to fight if the offer does not meet or exceed its bottom line, which depends on its type. So the low cost type will fight if $x > b_2^l$ and accept otherwise, and the high cost type will fight if $x > b_2^h$, and accept otherwise.

For player 1's offer, any $x < b_2^l$ is beaten by $x = b_2^l$ since all such offers will be accepted by both types, and the higher the better for player 1. Any offer $x \in (b_2^l, b_2^h)$ is beaten by $x = b_2^h$ since the outcome will be war if player 1 faces the low cost type and the offer will be accepted if player 2 is the high cost type. Finally, the payoff for any offer $x \in (b_2^h, 1]$ is the same since the result is war for certain.

The payoff for offering $x = b_2^l$ is just b_2^l, since peace is obtained for sure. The payoff for offering b_2^h is

$$lw_1 + (1-l)b_2^h$$

where l is the chance that player 2 is the low cost type and so rejects the offer. We know that both b_2^l and b_2^h are better than w_1, because they are both higher than player 1's bottom line, b_1. Therefore, player 1 will prefer to make one of these offers, rather than precipitate a war.

Player 1 will prefer to make the smaller offer if

$$b_2^l < lw_1 + (1-l)b_2^h$$

$$l < \frac{b_2^h - b_2^l}{b_2^h - w_1}$$

By noting that p_1 appears in all of the bottom lines on the right-hand side and can, therefore, be subtracted out, we get the following condition

$$l < \frac{c_2^h - c_2^l}{c_2^h + c_1} \tag{6.1}$$

Thus, if the likelihood that player 2 has low costs for fighting is low enough, then player 1 will take a risk and make a low offer, realizing that if player 2 has low costs for fighting it will reject the offer and attack. This is what Powell (1999a) calls the "risk–return tradeoff." Conversely, if the likelihood of facing the low cost type is high enough, then player 1 will choose to buy off the low cost type and war will once again be avoided. This is an equilibrium featuring peaceful revision, despite the uncertainty and the possibility that player 1 is being needlessly generous. The equilibria when both types have a credible threat to fight are shown in Table 6.2.

Finally, consider the case where the low cost type has a credible threat to fight but the high cost type does not, $s \in (b_2^l, b_2^h]$. This case is similar to the last case with one difference. The low cost type will accept any offer better than its bottom line and fight otherwise, as before. The high cost type will reject any offer worse than the status quo

Table 6.2 Equilibria when both types have a credible threat to fight

	Peaceful revision equilibrium
Player 1's offer	$x = b_2^l$
Player 2's response (low cost type)	Accept if $x \leq b_2^l$, attack otherwise
Player 2's response (high cost type)	Accept if $x \leq b_2^h$, attack otherwise
Conditions	$b_2^h < s, l \geq \frac{c_2^h - c_2^l}{c_2^h + c_1}$

	Risk of war equilibrium
Player 1's offer	$x = b_2^h$
Player 2's response (low cost type)	Accept if $x \leq b_2^l$, attack otherwise
Player 2's response (high cost type)	Accept if $x \leq b_2^h$, attack otherwise
Conditions	$b_2^h < s, l < \frac{c_2^h - c_2^l}{c_2^h + c_1}$

Table 6.3 Equilibria when only low cost type has credible threat to fight

Peaceful revision equilibrium	
Player 1's offer	$x = b_2^l$
Player 2's response (low cost type)	Accept if $x \leq b_2^l$, attack otherwise
Player 2's response (high cost type)	Accept if $x \leq s$, reject otherwise
Conditions	$s \in (b_2^l, b_2^h], l \geq \frac{s-b_2^l}{s-w_1}$

Risk of war equilibrium	
Player 1's offer	$x = s$
Player 2's response (low cost type)	Accept if $x \leq b_2^l$, attack otherwise
Player 2's response (high cost type)	Accept if $x \leq s$, reject otherwise
Conditions	$s \in (b_2^l, b_2^h], l < \frac{s-b_2^l}{s-w_1}$

and accept any offer better. Player 1, therefore, needs only consider offering the status quo, s, which will buy off the low cost type but not the high cost type, or the low cost type's bottom line, which will buy off both types. Player 1 will offer the status quo if $lw_1 + (1-l)s > b_2^l$, or if

$$l < \frac{s-b_2^l}{s-w_1} \tag{6.2}$$

There will be a risk of war equilibrium if this condition is true and a peaceful revision equilibrium if it is false. These equilibria are described in Table 6.3.

The equilibria in the game are illustrated in Figure 6.3. If the status quo is already fairly good for player 2, such that no type of player 2 has a credible threat to fight, ($s \leq p_1 + c_2^l$), then the no war, no revision equilibrium holds. In the middling range, where the low cost type has a credible threat to fight but the high cost type does not, there will be a peaceful revision equilibrium if player 2 is likely to be low cost, and a risk of war equilibrium if it is unlikely to have low costs. The boundary increases here as a function of s, because $\frac{s-b_2^l}{s-w_1}$ is increasing in s, and the equilibrium offer if there is a risk of war is s. Finally, for s above b_2^h, both types have a credible threat to fight. There is a peaceful revision equilibrium if player 2 is likely to have low costs, and a chance of war equilibrium if not. In the latter case, the offer will be b_2^h and only the high cost types will accept it.

Let's think about the comparative statics of these thresholds, that is, how they depend on the underlying factors. First, increasing c_1 reduces the threshold since it appears positively in the denominator. Therefore, increasing the costs of war for player 1 lowers the threshold, making the marginal player 1 switch from the risk of war equilibrium to the peaceful revision equilibrium. This makes sense, as war becomes more

6.2 BARGAINING WITH UNCERTAINTY OVER THE COST OF CONFLICT

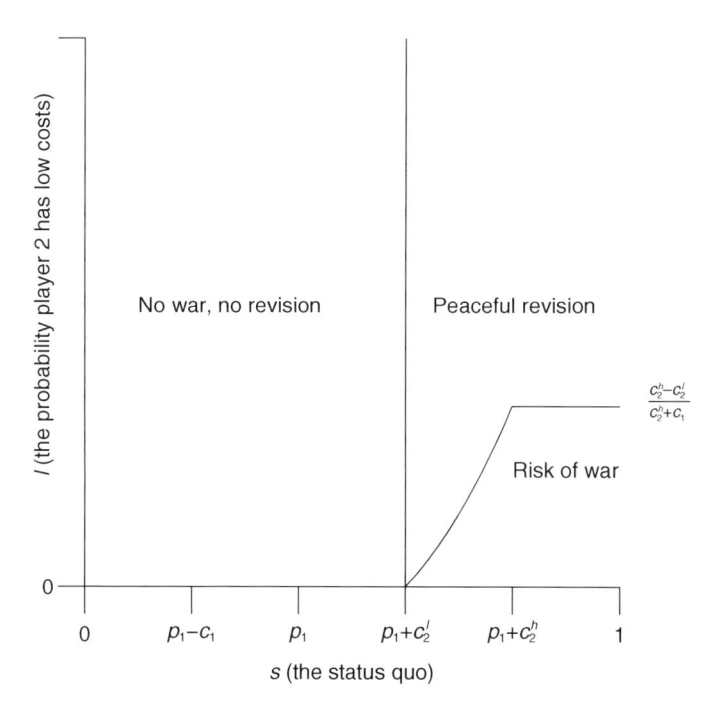

Figure 6.3 Equilibria in the Bargaining game with incomplete information

expensive for player 1, there is more incentive to avoid it. Second, increasing c_2^h increases the threshold (you can verify this by taking the derivative). As the high cost type of player 2 has higher costs, this means their bottom line is weaker, which increases the payoff for risking war, in comparison with buying off the low cost type as well. As the high cost type has even higher costs, the equilibrium offer in the risk of war equilibrium is even more favorable for player 1, making it better for the marginal player than the no risk equilibrium. Third, increasing c_2^l reduces the threshold, making war less likely. This is because increasing the costs paid by the low cost type worsens their bottom line and so improves the payoff for offering the low cost type's bottom line, which happens in the peaceful revision equilibrium. It, therefore, makes buying off both types cheaper than it was, and so more attractive. Finally, in the zone where only the low cost type has a credible threat to fight, s and p_1 also appear in the condition. Increasing s increases the cutoff point because it makes the risk of war equilibrium more attractive, since the equilibrium offer in that case is s, which will be accepted if player 2 has low costs. Increasing p_1 lowers the threshold, reducing the risk of war. While it increases the payoff for war, it also increases the payoff for offering the low cost type of player 2's bottom line, and this effect dominates because war is not certain if the low offer is made.

Thus, even in this very simple incomplete information game, we can see how private information about the cost of fighting a war can generate a risk of war. If the status quo is favorable to player 1, so much so that player 2 has or may have a credible threat to fight, and if player 1 thinks player 2 unlikely to be the low cost type who will attack unless it receives a large concession, then player 1 will make a low offer that will result in war if player 2 has a high war payoff. Note, this can happen even with linear preferences, unlike in the model in Chapter 4, in which we saw that with complete information there was no war if the players sufficiently valued intermediate outcomes. Here war can arise, driven by the fact that player 2 knows its war payoff and player 1 does not. This insight is summarized in the following result:

Result 6.1 *Bargaining may break down if there is uncertainty about the states' cost of conflict. In that case, one side will be tempted to make an offer that they know will be rejected if the other side has low costs for fighting, because the payoff is greater if the offer is accepted. This produces a tradeoff between the risk of war and the return from making an offer.*

6.3 Game forms and game free results

Powell (1999b, Chapter 3) develops an infinite horizon version of this model with the same basic equilibrium, in that the satisfied player makes an offer that is either accepted by the dissatisfied player or war occurs. Somewhat counterintuitively, the dissatisfied player never rejects the offer to make a counteroffer. The reason is essentially that the satisfied player has all the bargaining leverage and the dissatisfied player can only look forward to receiving its war payoff in the future if it rejects an offer, so it would prefer to get the war payoff now by attacking. Leventoğlu and Tarar (2008) point out that this is not empirically accurate, in that bargaining often lasts a fair length of time before war breaks out. Powell's model has some additional peculiarities, most notably that the dissatisfied state offers less than its war payoff, because it is constrained from attacking until after the other side's offer. Leventoğlu and Tarar modify the model so that the dissatisfied player can attack in any round, and find an equilibrium in which bargaining lasts two rounds, with the low cost type of dissatisfied state, and war is avoided altogether, so there is no risk–return tradeoff, aside from the risk of bargaining delay. This raises the interesting question of what makes costly bargaining break down into even more costly and risky war. Leventoğlu and Tarar's answer has to do with impatience; they argue that players that heavily discount the future may attack rather than continue to bargain.

However, Leventoğlu and Tarar's model has its own quirks. For instance, they make much of the fact that their model improves on Powell's by giving the dissatisfied state some of the bargaining leverage. However, given that the satisfied state prefers the status quo to the eventual bargain, and war outcomes, it is not clear why the satisfied state should not have all the leverage. In their model, the dissatisfied state obtains some bargaining leverage because it can make a proposal and then attack in the current round unless the satisfied state accepts. This allows it to propose more than its bottom line, but less than the satisfied state's bottom line with some prospect of success since it has a credible threat to attack if the satisfied state rejects the offer. However, this in turn depends on preventing the satisfied state from making a lower counteroffer before the dissatisfied state has a chance to attack. If the satisfied state can simply say that the dissatisfied state's bottom line is always on the table, then the dissatisfied state would seem to have no bargaining leverage beyond its bottom line.

Fey and Ramsay (2011) present some "game free" results based on the theory of mechanism design (Myerson 1979). They make two points with respect to bargaining with uncertainty over costs. First, there will always be a bargaining protocol, or game tree, in which war is avoided with certainty. For instance, one bargaining protocol involves having a mediator propose a division of the good and then both sides must accept or fight. If the mediator proposes to divide the good in proportion to the relative power of the two sides, so that player 1 gets p_1 and player 2 gets p_2, both sides will prefer this deal to war and so the result will be peace for sure, no matter what the cost of conflict is or what the player's beliefs are. In this case, it does not matter what the costs for conflict are, the deal is the same. Conversely, in any game form and equilibrium in which different types with different costs get different payoffs in the game, as in the example presented above, there will be some chance of war, as there is in the example of the risk of war equilibrium.

6.4 The problem of mistrust

Another prominent literature that links uncertainty to conflict is that focusing on the spiral model and the problem of mistrust (Jervis 1976, Kydd 2005, Glaser 2010). Here the uncertainty is usually thought to center on the extent of a state's ambitions. Revisionist states want to overturn the status quo, take territory from other states, and expand. Status quo states are content with what they have and are defensively motivated. Two status quo states that knew each other to be status quo states could easily get along, since neither one would have any reason to expand or attack the other (Schweller 1996). The problem arises when they are uncertain about each other's motivations, because fear of a revisionist state could cause status quo states to act more aggressively (Kydd 1997b).

Consider two states that face a Pre-emptive War game similar to the one in Chapter 3, illustrated in Table 6.8. If both sides do not attack, the status quo remains

Table 6.4 The Preventive War game with mistrust

		Player 2	
		Not attack	Attack
Player 1	Not attack	s_1, s_2	$p_1^s - c_1, p_2^f - c_2$
	Attack	$p_1^f - c_1, p_2^s - c_2$	$p_1 - c_1, p_2 - c_2$

in place, with payoffs s_1, s_2. If both sides attack, a war takes place, and player i's payoff is $p_i - c_i$, where p_i is player i's chance of winning, and c_i is player i's cost for fighting. If one side attacks while the other side does not, its chance of winning is p_i^f, reflecting that it has a first strike advantage, while the other side's chance of winning is p_i^s for a second strike. To reflect the first strike advantage, I assume the following

$$p_i^s < p_i < p_i^f \qquad (6.3)$$

With complete information, peace could be preserved if the both sides like the status quo better than a first strike, $s_i \geq p_i - c_i$. If this condition is violated for either player (or both), then mutual attack is the only equilibrium in the game.

Let's now add uncertainty to the game by positing that each side can be one of two types. Status quo types value the status quo at 1, so $s_i^S = 1$. Greedy types value the status quo at $s_i^G < 1$. This implies that status quo types gain nothing that they do not have already from a successful war, whereas greedy types can be made better off if they fight and win. To make the game interesting, assume that status quo types prefer to not attack if certain the other side will not attack, while greedy types have the opposite preference, summed up in the following condition[1]

$$s_i^G < p_i^f - c_i < 1 \qquad (6.4)$$

Let the likelihood that player i is the status quo type be q_i, so the likelihood that it is the greedy type is $1 - q_i$.

How should the different types play the game now? Greedy types have a dominant strategy to attack. If the other side is expected to attack, attacking is the best response, since $p_i > p_i^s$. If the other is expected to not attack, then attacking is still the best response, as reflected in Equation (6.4). Therefore, regardless of what the other side is expected to do, greedy types prefer to attack.

Status quo types could be willing to not attack if they are sure enough that the other side is a status quo type. Posit an equilibrium in which the status quo types do not attack and the greedy types do. The payoff for not attacking for the status quo type is $q_j + (1 - q_j)(p_i^s - c_i)$, while the payoff for attacking is $q_j(p_i^f - c_i) + (1 - q_j)(p_i - c_i)$.

---

[1] That is, status quo types have Assurance game preferences, while greedy types do not.

6.4 THE PROBLEM OF MISTRUST

Not attacking beats attacking for the status quo types if the following holds

$$q_j + (1 - q_j)(p_i^s - c_i) \geq q_j(p_i^f - c_i) + (1 - q_j)(p_i - c_i)$$

$$q_j(1 - p_i^f + c_i - p_i^s + c_i + p_i - c_i) \geq p_i - c_i - p_i^s + c_i$$

$$q_j(1 - p_i^f + c_i - p_i^s + p_i) \geq p_i - p_i^s$$

$$q_j \left(\frac{1 - (p_i^f - c_i)}{p_i - p_i^s} + 1 \right) \geq 1$$

which yields the following condition

$$q_j \geq \frac{1}{\frac{1-(p_i^f-c_i)}{p_i-p_i^s} + 1} \qquad (6.5)$$

This means that if the likelihood that the other side is the status quo type is high enough, the status quo types will be willing to take a chance and not attack, realizing that if the other side is the greedy type, the outcome will be war on worse terms.

If we examine Equation (6.5), we can see how the parameters in the game affect the necessary degree of trust. Increasing p_i^f, the first strike advantage, raises the threshold, meaning that as first strikes are more militarily successful, the players need to be more trusting of each other to exercise restraint. The higher the second strike's chance of winning, p_i^s, the lower the threshold is, so if being struck first is not so disadvantageous, less is needed to avoid war. Note, as p_i^s approaches p_i, the denominator expands without limit, so the threshold goes to 0. This means that if there is no disadvantage to striking second, then no trust is required for status quo types to refrain from attacking. Finally, if the costs of fighting increase, then the threshold also decreases, lowering the level of trust necessary for not attacking.

The simple Trust game leads to the following result:

Result 6.2 *Mistrust between states can cause conflict if the level of trust falls below a critical threshold. That threshold depends on the payoffs being exploited. In the preemptive war case, the larger the likelihood of winning with a first strike and the smaller the likelihood of winning with the second, the greater the degree of trust needed to avoid war.*

The fact that mistrust can cause conflict has led to research on the topic of reassurance, or how trust can be built through cooperative gestures. The main insight is that the parties must start small, with limited but not too limited reassuring gestures that put the state at some risk but convey some benefit on the other side (Watson 1999, Kydd 2000). Schultz analyzes the classic case of "Nixon going to China," to clarify

Table 6.5 Four types of state

		Utility for more	
		Status quo	Greedy
Resolve	High	Lions	Wolves
	Low	Lambs	Jackals

the conditions under which more hawkish actors are more readily able to make peace (Schultz 2005). There is also a small but growing literature that combines uncertainty about the costs of fighting, discussed in the previous section, with uncertainty about motivations in the sense of the trust model just covered (Kydd and McManus 2014, Kurizaki 2014, Schultz and Goemans 2014). This can produce models with (at least) four types, illustrated in Table 6.5. The top row is highly resolved states, who have low costs for fighting, while the bottom row has low resolve. The left column has status quo motivations, and hence gets little or no utility from getting more, while the right-hand column has revisionist motivations, and so benefits from conquest. I fill in the boxes with the animal names conferred by Schweller (1996), although he focused on power as the distinction between the top row and the bottom rather than resolve. Models that conceive of stakes along these lines are typically concerned with the role of signaling, often looking at the role of threats and assurances. Threats can signal low costs for fighting, but also may convey revisionist intentions, which may be provocative rather than a deterrent. Assurances can signal status quo intentions but also high costs for fighting, making a state look weak, and so easily pushed around. Threats and assurances combined may signal that a state is a lion, highly resolved but moderate in its motivations, which may be ideal in the sense of deterring challenges while not provoking resistance. How and when threats and assurances should be combined is a subject of current research.

6.5 Uncertainty over the balance of power

While uncertainty about the costs of conflict has been extensively studied in the formal literature, much of the pre-existing non-game theoretic literature has focused on uncertainty about relative power. An interesting question concerning the relationship between information and war is whether *mutual optimism* can cause war. Mutual optimism has been featured in many prominent explanations of war, particularly of the First World War (Blainey 1988, Van Evera 1999). Mutual optimism is defined variously, but one fairly restrictive but somewhat plausible interpretation is that mutual optimism causes war when two states essentially agree to fight a war because they both

6.5 UNCERTAINTY OVER THE BALANCE OF POWER

Table 6.6 The Mutual Optimism game, version 1

		Player 2	
		Decline to fight	Agree to fight
Player 1	Decline to fight	$s, 1-s$	$s, 1-s$
	Agree to fight	$s, 1-s$	$p_1 - c_1, p_2 - c_2$

think they will do better in the war than the status quo. Fey and Ramsay (2007) present an argument that this is impossible in equilibrium, while Slantchev and Tarar (2011) counter that they have misrepresented the argument. Let us consider a highly simplified version of this debate, through the lens of the game in Table 6.6.

This game represents a situation in which the players must agree to fight a war. If either side declines to fight the other side, then the status quo payoffs, $s, 1 - s$, remain in place. If both sides agree to fight, they have a war with payoffs $p_1 - c_1, p_2 - c_2$.

There are no conditions under which agreeing to fight is a pure strategy equilibrium of this game. If it were, then it would have to be the case that $p_1 - c_1 \geq s$ and $p_2 - c_2 \geq 1 - s$. The second condition implies that $s \geq p_1 + c_2$, which contradicts the first condition. As in any similar game with complete information, if one side wants to fight, the other side will not because the costs of war render war inefficient. If $p_1 < s - c_2$, then player 2 will want to fight and player 1 will not; if $s - c_2 < p_1 < s + c_1$, then neither side will wish to fight; and if $s + c_1 < p_1$, then player 1 will want to fight and player 2 will not. Conversely, both sides declining to fight is a Nash equilibrium, regardless of the value of the parameters. The off diagonal outcomes may be Nash equilibria if the side declining to fight actually prefers the status quo to war.

What happens if we add uncertainty to the picture? Let there be three possible levels of player 1's power, such that $p_1^l < p_1^m < p_1^h$. To make the problem interesting, let's assume that $p_1^l < s - c_2$, $p_1^m \in (s - c_2, s + c_1)$, and $p_1^h > s + c_1$. Therefore, at p_1^l player 2 will want to fight, at p_1^m neither side will want to fight, and at p_1^h player 1 will want to fight. Let the probability that each level of relative power obtains be q_l, q_m, and q_h, respectively, so $q_l + q_m + q_h = 1$. We can now ask the question: Is there any possible level of uncertainty about relative power that would cause war in this game?

First, we need to figure out the new war payoffs. There is a q_l chance that the payoff is $p_1^l - c_1$, a q_m chance that the payoff is $p_1^m - c_1$, and a q_h chance that the payoff is $p_1^h - c_1$. This implies that the war payoff is

$$q_l(p_1^l - c_1) + q_m(p_1^m - c_1) + q_h(p_1^h - c_1)$$

or

$$q_l p_1^l + q_m p_1^m + q_h p_1^h - c_1$$

Player 1 will prefer to fight rather than decline if

$$q_l p_1^l + q_m p_1^m + q_h p_1^h - c_1 > s$$

or

$$q_l p_1^l + q_m p_1^m + q_h p_1^h > s + c_1$$

Player 2 will prefer to fight if

$$q_l(1 - p_1^l) + q_m(1 - p_1^m) + q_h(1 - p_1^h) - c_2 > 1 - s$$

$$q_l p_1^l + q_m p_1^m + q_h p_1^h < s - c_2$$

This is much like the previous result, and indeed once again the two conditions cannot be reconciled, because if one side wants to fight, the other side will not. Thus, merely adding shared uncertainty over the balance of power does not induce an agreement to fight.

However, so far we have considered uncertainty about power, but not mutual optimism about power. How can we incorporate this concept? Imagine that each side is attempting a technological breakthrough in its military forces, such as the development of the dreadnought battleship or nuclear weapons (Horowitz 2010). Each side's baseline level of absolute military power is m_i. The military innovation would act as a "force multiplier" by increasing each side's absolute military power to βm_i, where $\beta > 1$. There are, therefore, three possible levels of relative power depending on which side successfully develops the innovation

$$p_1^l = \frac{m_1}{m_1 + \beta m_2}$$

$$p_1^m = \frac{m_1}{m_1 + m_2} = \frac{\beta m_1}{\beta m_1 + \beta m_2}$$

$$p_1^h = \frac{\beta m_1}{\beta m_1 + m_2}$$

Let these three probabilities of victory take on the values that they did before, so that player 1 prefers to fight at p_1^h, player 2 wants to fight at p_1^l, and neither side wants to fight at p_1^m.

Let the ex ante chance of success for each side's innovation be r_i. Therefore, we have for the ex ante probabilities

$$q_l = (1 - r_1)r_2$$

$$q_m = (1 - r_1)(1 - r_2) + r_1 r_2$$

$$q_h = r_1(1 - r_2)$$

Now let each side observe whether its innovation has succeeded or not, by testing the innovation in a way that the other side cannot see. Each side now knows whether it has succeeded but is uncertain about whether the other side has or not. We can now really consider mutual optimism, which would be a case where both sides observed that their innovation succeeded.

In this game, each side must choose a strategy for each condition, whether it succeeds or fails. Let us consider whether it is possible to have a separating equilibrium in which each side agrees to fight if it succeeds in developing the military innovation, and declines to fight if it fails. The answer is once again no. If player 1 succeeds, it knows its level of absolute power is βm_1. In equilibrium, if player 2 fails, it will decline to fight, and player 1's payoff for agreeing to fight in that case is just s. If player 2 succeeds, it will agree to fight, and player 1's chance of winning will be

$$\frac{\beta m_1}{\beta m_1 + \beta m_2} = \frac{m_1}{m_1 + m_2} = p_1^m$$

The overall payoff for agreeing to fight is, therefore, $(1 - r_2)s + r_2(p_1^m - c_1)$, which will beat the payoff for declining to fight if

$$(1 - r_2)s + r_2(p_1^m - c_1) > s$$
$$r_2(p_1^m - c_1) > r_2 s$$
$$p_1^m - c_1 > s$$

But this condition is not true; this would imply that player 1 wishes to fight with a middling level of power, which is not the case by assumption.

The problem is that even though player 1 has succeeded in developing the new technology, it understands that player 2 would not agree to fight unless it too had developed the new technology. Since neither side would want to fight unless it had an advantage, neither side is willing to fight even if it knows that it has scored a breakthrough and cannot observe whether the other side has done so as well. Fey and Ramsay (2007) make this point in a much more general technical setting involving a model of common knowledge.

Fey and Ramsay's point is well taken as a fairly abstract but plausible interpretation of some versions of the mutual optimism argument. A thoroughgoing attempt to explain the First World War would hold that the governments truly agreed that war was better than the status quo, and so both sides went willingly to the trenches to try their luck. This model does invalidate the argument that both sides could prefer war to the status quo because of mutual optimism about their chances of winning. As such, it is an important clarification of the non-formal theoretical literature.

One possible critique of this argument, however, is that it assumes that the weaker side can prevent a war by simply declining to fight, and that this will keep the status quo in place. This seems unrealistic in the anarchic world of international politics in that, if one side attacks, the other side must either fight, producing a war, or capitulate,

Table 6.7 The Mutual Optimism game, version 2

		Player 2	
		Capitulate	Attack
Player 1	Capitulate	$s, 1-s$	$s-t, 1-s+t$
	Attack	$s+t, 1-s-t$	p_1-c_1, p_2-c_2

resulting in some loss in comparison with the status quo (Slantchev and Tarar 2011). That is, states cannot just opt for the status quo when another state wants to attack. To reflect this reality, consider the alternative game in Table 6.7.

In the new version, mutual attack produces a war and mutual capitulation leaves the status quo in place, just as before. However, if one side attacks and the other side capitulates, there is a transfer of $t > 0$ from the side that capitulates to the side that attacks. This reflects an assumption that declining to fight involves making a concession that shifts the status quo in favor of the attacker. Declining to fight when the other side wants to fight is, therefore, not free.

Can there be a war in this game? In the complete information version, the answer is no so long as the transfer, t, is not so large that either side prefers war to capitulation, which is true if the following holds

$$t \leq \min\{s - (p_1 - c_1), p_1 + c_2 - s\} \tag{6.6}$$

If this is true, then with a mutual attack, both sides would have an incentive to deviate to capitulation, as in the Chicken game. Mutual capitulation is also not an equilibrium because both sides will prefer to deviate to attack and get the transfer. The Nash equilibria of the game, therefore, involve one side attacking and the other side capitulating, as in Chicken.

Now consider an incomplete information version of the game. If a war occurs, the payoffs are $q_l p_1^l + q_m p_1^m + q_h p_1^h - c_1, 1 - (q_l p_1^l + q_m p_1^m + q_h p_1^h) - c_2$, as before.

Let each side pursue a military innovation that would multiply its military effectiveness by a. Now we ask: Is there an equilibrium in which types that succeed in developing the innovation attack, and those that do not capitulate. Consider player 1, in the case where their innovation has failed. The payoff for capitulation is

$$(1-r_2)s + r_2(s-t) \tag{6.7}$$

and the payoff for attack is

$$(1-r_2)(s+t) + r_2(p_1^l - c_1) \tag{6.8}$$

6.5 UNCERTAINTY OVER THE BALANCE OF POWER

Capitulation beats attack as long as

$$(1 - r_2)s + r_2(s - t) \geq (1 - r_2)(s + t) + r_2(p_1^l - c_1)$$
$$r_2(s - t) \geq (1 - r_2)t + r_2(p_1^l - c_1)$$
$$r_2 s \geq t + r_2(p_1^l - c_1)$$
$$r_2 \geq \frac{t}{s - (p_1^l - c_1)}$$

So if the innovation fails, player 1 would prefer to capitulate so long as the likelihood that player 2 succeeds is high enough.

Now consider the case where the innovation has succeeded. The payoff for capitulation is the same as before

$$(1 - r_2)s + r_2(s - t) \tag{6.9}$$

and the payoff for attack is

$$(1 - r_2)(s + t) + r_2(p_1^m - c_1) \tag{6.10}$$

which is higher than before because the chance of winning the war, if it happens, is p_1^m rather than p_1^l.

Attack beats capitulation if

$$(1 - r_2)(s + t) + r_2(p_1^m - c_1) \geq (1 - r_2)s + r_2(s - t)$$
$$(1 - r_2)t + r_2(p_1^m - c_1) \geq r_2(s - t)$$
$$t + r_2(p_1^m - c_1) \geq r_2 s$$
$$r_2 \leq \frac{t}{s - (p_1^m - c_1)}$$

That is, if the likelihood that the other side will succeed is not too great, then attack makes sense for player 1 if they succeed.

The final question is: Can these two conditions be satisfied simultaneously? They can be if

$$\frac{t}{s - (p_1^l - c_1)} \leq \frac{t}{s - (p_1^m - c_1)}$$
$$s - (p_1^l - c_1) \geq s - (p_1^m - c_1)$$
$$p_1^l \leq p_1^m$$

This latter condition is, of course, true by assumption. Therefore, there will always be a range of r_2 that will make player 1 willing to follow its strategy of capitulating in response to bad news and attacking in response to good news. A similar analysis shows that the same is true for player 2.

Therefore, in a model in which the side declining war because of bad news about its military program must actually make a concession rather than simply maintain the status quo by fiat, we have shown that mutual optimism can indeed produce a war. Each side, thinking that the other side will capitulate in response to force if its weapons program failed, attacks when its own program succeeds. War occurs when both sides succeed in their innovation, and so are mutually optimistic about their chances of prevailing. Both sides realize that war, if it occurs, will be on even terms and will, therefore, be undesired by both sides. However, there is no way to avoid war without also passing up the gains associated with coercing a concession out of the other side if the latter is weak. The prospect of coercing gains out of the other side if it is weak makes it worthwhile to run the risk of an unwanted war on even terms.

Result 6.3 *Mutual optimism may cause war if declining to fight comes at a price and there is no way to coerce concessions from the other side without running the risk of war. In that case, strong states will be willing to attack in equilibrium, and can end up in war with each other.*

Note, this model may still not quite capture Blainey's argument and that of those who focus on the First World War as the paradigmatic case of mutual optimism. In this model, it would not be the case that both sides would go to war "cheerfully," expecting it to be over by Christmas. Both sides would realize that if it comes to war, it will not be a walkover. However, they are willing to take that risk, and that willingness produces a positive chance of war.

This model is obviously very simplified; in particular it does not feature any explicit bargaining. Fey and Ramsay (2011) provide more general results, showing that in any game with uncertainty over relative power, if the costs are sufficiently low, there is no equilibrium in which war is avoided for certain.

6.6 Conclusion

Private information is one of the primary rationalist explanations of war. When each side knows something about its resolve, preferences, or military capabilities that is not known to the adversary, there may be a tendency to demand more than the other side will concede, to attack out of fear that the other side will attack, or to attack in the hope that the other side will capitulate. Private information, therefore, provides a powerful explanation of inefficient conflict. In Chapter 9, we will investigate the extent to which communication can overcome private information and lower the likelihood of war.

EXERCISES

6.1 Consider the first model with uncertainty over the costs of conflict. Now assume that player 2's costs for conflict are uniformly distributed over an interval from 0 to an upper bound, $c_2 \in [0, C]$. Assume that $s > p_1$ and $C = s - p_1$.

1. Plot the status quo, relative power, and the bottom line of the highest cost type on the x axis.
2. Derive the equilibrium strategy for each type of player 2, depending on the costs.
3. What is the chance of war for each offer x that player 1 might make? Graph this.
4. What is player 1's utility for making each offer x? Graph this.
5. What is the equilibrium offer for player 1?

6.2 Two states face a Trust game depicted in Table 6.8, where t_i and e_i are greater than 0. The payoff t_i corresponds to the "temptation" to defect, and e_i is the payoff for being exploited by cooperating unilaterally. Assume that Nature starts the game by selecting types for each player. Each player's temptation payoff, t_i, is drawn from a uniform distribution on the interval $[0, 2]$.

Table 6.8 The Trust game

		Player 2 Cooperate	Player 2 Defect
Player 1	Cooperate	1, 1	$-e_1, t_2$
	Defect	$t_1, -e_2$	0, 0

1. Under what condition is mutual defection by both players and all types a Nash equilibrium?
2. Is there an equilibrium in which some types on each side cooperate? Posit a threshold for t_j under which types cooperate and over which types defect. What is the payoff for cooperation and defection? For what types would cooperation be preferred to defection? How does this threshold depend on e_i?

7 Arms competition and war

STATES spend a great deal of money on their armed forces, and on other things designed to increase their power and military capabilities. Models of arms competition seek to explain this level of spending. Theories of international relations also link military spending to conflict and war in a variety of ways. Arms competition, therefore, can be considered as both a dependent and an independent variable.

Arms competition was first studied using formal theory by Lewis Fry Richardson in the wake of the First World War (Richardson 1960). He used a pair of linked differential equations to model the arms spending of two competing powers, in which each side's spending was a function of the other side's, as well as its own existing stock of weapons. Richardson's models did not assume that states are rational, but the principal results of his models can be replicated in the currently more conventional rational choice framework (Lichbach 1989, 1990). In particular, arms choices can look like a Prisoner's Dilemma, as discussed in Chapter 3. Downs and Rocke applied a continuous strategy space version of the repeated Prisoner's Dilemma model to the arms race context, to analyze when arms control agreements can be sustained (Downs et al. 1985, Downs and Rocke 1990).[1]

The link between arms races and war has also been widely analyzed. (Kennedy 1984, Intrilligator and Brito 1984, Brito and Intrilligator 1985, Siverson and Diehl 1989, Downs 1991). There are three principal explanations of war that have to do with arms competition. First, is the simple idea that arms are expensive, and, more generally, deterrence is expensive. The tradeoff between "guns and butter" is well known, and is the foundation of all arms race analyses (Powell 1999a, Chapter 2). In judging war to be inefficient, as we did in Chapter 4, we compared it to an idealized version of peace in which there are no costs associated with deterring predation or revisionist demands from other states. In reality, there may be such costs and they may outweigh the costs of war. This has led to a growing literature on "costly peace" as an explanation for war,

---

[1] See also Garfinkel (1990).

although I prefer to think of it as costly deterrence, since peace per se is not costly (Coe 2011, Willard-Foster 2011).

The second and closely related mechanism is the idea that military spending for the purposes of deterrence suffers from a risk–return tradeoff much as the crisis bargaining context explored in the last chapter does. In crisis bargaining, states will sometimes make an offer that fails to buy off the most resolved type of adversary, realizing that if the adversary turns out to be this type, the result will be war. The reason for running the risk is that a more generous offer comes at the expense of the state's own payoff. The same mechanism can be seen to operate in the arms race context. If a state wishes to deter another state, it will wish to do so as cheaply as possible. As a result, it may set military spending at a level that will not produce enough power to deter all possible types of adversary, but will leave some wealth available for domestic uses if the adversary is deterred. It will, therefore, accept a risk of war in exchange for greater consumption. For instance, Britain and France were widely criticized, in retrospect, for not building up their armed forces sufficiently in the 1930s to deter Germany, or at least fight more effectively in case deterrence failed. At the time, however, they hoped that the buildups they did engage in would be sufficient. This phenomenon is widespread in society. People in civilized countries generally go unarmed even though, if they meet a criminal or psychopath, this may result in their being robbed or killed. Merchant vessels go unarmed or lightly armed though this means that if they encounter pirates, they will be captured and held for ransom. People put locks on their doors but also have windows that can be kicked in by a determined intruder, etc. In general, people do not prepare to successfully cope with the worst possible contingency, they balance preparedness against cost and convenience, taking into account probabilities.[2]

The third mechanism linking arms to war is the "spiral model," developed by theorists of the security dilemma. Herbert Butterfield and John Hertz developed the concept of the security dilemma in the early Cold War, to describe a situation in which a state's efforts to be secure were provocative to other states and could cause war (Butterfield 1951, Herz 1950). Robert Jervis developed these ideas further in the security dilemma and the spiral model (Jervis 1976, 1978). A security dilemma is a situation in which each side's efforts to make itself more secure make the other side less secure, and so both parties end up worse off than they started because of their efforts to increase their security. The spiral model develops this logic further and explains how it may lead to war. Essentially, arms increases make states rationally more suspicious of each other, fearful of each other's intentions, and hence lead to pre-emptive or preventive war (Kydd 1997a). Slantchev develops a mechanism that is related to the spiral model and also to the bargaining models of the previous chapter

---

[2] Brooks (1997) argues that offensive realism assumes such worst case thinking.

(Slantchev 2005, 2011). He argues that military increases serve as signals of resolve in crisis bargaining contexts (as will be discussed in Chapter 9) and so help deter adversaries. However, they also have the effect of increasing a state's military power and hence committing it to fight in contingencies that it would not have fought before by raising its bottom line. This latter effect of committing a state to fight when it would not have may lock a state into a war that it would have preferred to avoid.

With such a large literature discussing so many distinct mechanisms, a single chapter cannot hope to be fully representative of all the work on arms competition and conflict. This chapter will limit itself to introducing a simple model connecting arms racing and war and then examining the costly deterrence argument and the risk–return tradeoff mechanism.

7.1 Costly deterrence

Consider an Arms–War game with a two player game with three simultaneous decisions in sequence. First, there is a decision whether to attack the other side or defend. Second, there is a decision to engage in a military buildup or not. Finally, there is a second opportunity to attack the other side. The first two decisions constitute the first "round" and the second attack decision corresponds to the second round, much as in the preventive war models of Chapter 5. The two rounds can be thought of as representing the present and future, now and later. The game tree would be fairly large if drawn out in full, with 19 terminal nodes; however, we will see that the game can still be easily analyzed.

If either side attacks in the first round, a war takes place and the game ends, the results of the war being assumed to last for both rounds. The first round level of relative power for player 1, p_1, is determined by the two sides' first round (exogenous) levels of absolute military power, m_1 and m_2, in the usual ratio formula, $p_1 = \frac{m_1}{m_1+m_2}$. Player 2's chance of winning is just $p_2 \equiv 1-p_1$. If neither side attacks in the first round, they move to the arms choice. Here each side has an opportunity to multiply its absolute military power by a factor $\beta > 1$, at a cost $\gamma_i > 0$.[3] After the arms choice, the two players have a second opportunity to attack each other. If neither side does, the game ends with the status quo payoffs $2s, 2(1-s)$, minus the cost of the buildup, if they undertook one. If either side attacks, a war takes place with payoffs reflecting any arms buildups that may have happened. I assume no first (or second) strike advantage. There are three possible levels of military power after the arms buildup, as in the Mutual Optimism game of the previous chapter. If neither or both sides increased their arms, the level

---

[3] Assuming β is common across the players simplifies the analysis.

7.1 COSTLY DETERRENCE

Table 7.1 Payoffs in the Arms–War game

Outcome	Player 1's payoff	Player 2's payoff
War in the first round	$2(p_1^m - c_1)$	$2(1 - p_1^m - c_2)$
No war in either round and		
Neither side builds	$2s$	$2(1-s)$
Only player 1 builds	$2s - \gamma_1$	$2(1-s)$
Only player 2 builds	$2s$	$2(1-s) - \gamma_2$
Both players build	$2s - \gamma_1$	$2(1-s) - \gamma_2$
No war in the first round, war in the second round and		
Neither side builds	$s + p_1^m - c_1$	$1 - s + 1 - p_1^m - c_2$
Only player 1 builds	$s + p_1^h - c_1 - \gamma_1$	$1 - s + 1 - p_1^h - c_2$
Only player 2 builds	$s + p_1^l - c_1$	$1 - s + 1 - p_1^l - c_2 - \gamma_2$
Both players build	$s + p_1^m - c_1 - \gamma_1$	$1 - s + 1 - p_1^m - c_2 - \gamma_2$

of power is $p_1^m = \frac{m_1}{m_1 + m_2}$. If player 1 built up and player 2 did not, the level of power is $p_1^h = \frac{\beta m_1}{\beta m_1 + m_2}$. Finally, if player 2 armed and player 1 did not, the relative power is $p_1^l = \frac{m_1}{m_1 + \beta m_2}$. Payoffs in the game are listed in Table 7.1.

I will assume that both players prefer the status quo to war with the prior level of military power, which is equal to the posterior level if neither side or both sides build up. This means that war in the model is not a result of immediate dissatisfaction with the status quo; if it occurs, it must have something to do with the arms decisions and their influence on war choices. This is captured in the following condition

$$p_1^m - c_1 < s < p_1^m + c_2 \tag{7.1}$$

This can easily be satisfied if s is close enough to p_1^m. It also implies *a fortiori* that neither side prefers war to the status quo if it has a power disadvantage.

7.1.1 Equilibria in the Arms–War game with complete information

There are many equilibria in the game, depending on the parameters, and in some cases on equilibrium expectations. I will consider a subset of equilibria that illustrate the range of possibilities. Since war is precipitated whenever one side attacks, mutual attack will always be an equilibrium in the model. If one side is attacking, the other side receives the war payoff regardless of what it does, so it might as well attack too. However, the concern here is on how arms buildups are related to war, so I will focus on equilibria in which countries only attack if they prefer war to the status quo because

Table 7.2 The Arms–War game: no build equilibrium 1

First attack choice	Defend
Build choice	Not build
Second attack choice	Defend for any balance of power
Conditions	$p_1^h - c_1 < s < p_1^l + c_2$

of the arms buildups. The same result could be achieved by adding a small cost to striking first, perhaps motivated by the diplomatic costs of looking like an aggressor. I also focus on symmetrical equilibria, in which the players adopt similar strategies.

First, consider an equilibrium in which the players would not attack even if they had a military advantage in the second round. For player 1, this implies $s > p_1^h - c_1$, and for player 2, $1 - s > 1 - p_1^l - c_2$, or $s < p_1^l + c_2$. Combining these, neither side will prefer to attack with a military advantage if the following holds

$$p_1^h - c_1 < s < p_1^l + c_2 \tag{7.2}$$

This will be true if the military advantage of building weapons, β, is small enough, so that p_1^h and p_1^l are close to p_1^m, and if the costs of war are high enough. In this case, it will be an equilibrium for neither side to attack in the first round, neither side to build, and then neither side to attack in the second, as shown in Table 7.2. Attacking in either round would produce a worse payoff than defending, and building weapons would be a waste of money given the strategy of not attacking in the second round no matter what the balance of power.

Now let's consider the case where both players would prefer war to the status quo if they have a military advantage. This will be true if Equation (7.2) is reversed. Does this mean that an arms buildup is inevitable? Consider the build choice. Both sides not building will be (part of) an equilibrium if each side prefers not to build and live with the status quo, rather than build and fight with an advantage in the next round. This will be the case for player 1 if $s - \gamma_1 + p_1^h - c_1 \leq 2s$, and for player 2 if $1 - s - \gamma_2 + 1 - p_1^l - c_2 \leq 2(1 - s)$. These equations can be combined and reexpressed as follows

$$p_1^h - c_1 - \gamma_1 < s < p_1^l + c_2 + \gamma_2 \tag{7.3}$$

This is possible so long as the costs of the buildup, γ_1 and γ_2, are large enough to make the buildup too costly in comparison to the benefits of the prospective war. Basically, the cost of the buildup makes it preferable to live with the status quo rather than build military forces sufficient to make war seem an option. This equilibrium is described in Table 7.3. The result on the equilibrium path is the same as in the previous case, but off the equilibrium path, if one side were to build, there would be war.

Table 7.3 The Arms–War game: no build equilibrium 2

First attack choice	Defend
Build choice	Not build
Second attack choice	Attack only with favorable balance of power
Conditions	$p_1^l + c_2 < s < p_1^h - c_1$
	$p_1^h - c_1 - \gamma_1 < s < p_1^l + c_2 + \gamma_2$

This leads naturally to a consideration of what happens when the costs of the buildup are not so great as to be prohibitive, so Equation (7.3) is reversed. In this case, there will no longer be a pure strategy equilibrium in which neither side builds, since each side would like to take advantage of the other's weakness, build up its forces, and attack with an advantage. Will there be a pure strategy equilibrium in which both sides build and do not fight in the second round, deterring each other? There will be if neither side wishes to accept inferiority and be attacked in the second round, which will be the case for player 1 if $s - \gamma_1 + s \geq s + p_1^l - c_1$, and for player 2 if $1 - s - \gamma_2 + 1 - s \geq 1 - s + 1 - p_1^h - c_2$. These conditions can be rewritten as follows

$$p_1^l - c_1 + \gamma_1 < s < p_1^h + c_2 - \gamma_2 \tag{7.4}$$

If this condition holds, then (at least one) equilibrium exists in which both sides build up their forces, and peace prevails on the equilibrium path in the second round.

Now consider the first attack choice. First, consider if there is an equilibrium in which both sides anticipate that they will build up their forces and deter each other, and yet neither side attacks in the first round. For player 1 to prefer not to attack, it must prefer the payoff for engaging in the buildup and making it to the second round, $2s - \gamma_1$ to the payoff for attacking now, $2(p_1^m - c_1)$. For player 2, deterrence will be preferable to war if $2(1 - s) - \gamma_2 \geq 2(1 - p_1^m - c_2)$. These conditions can be combined in the following expression

$$p_1^m - c_1 + \frac{\gamma_1}{2} < s < p_1^m + c_2 - \frac{\gamma_2}{2} \tag{7.5}$$

If this condition holds, a deterrence equilibrium, as illustrated in Table 7.4, will hold. The key factor making this equilibrium possible is that the costs of the buildup, γ_1 and γ_2, are not too high. If γ_i gets too high, then the players will either prefer not to build up and fight on poor terms in the second round, or to attack in the first round to forestall that eventuality. Thus, deterrence cannot be too expensive in comparison to war for the deterrence equilibrium to hold.

Finally, consider an equilibrium in which the last condition, Equation (7.5), is reversed. In this case, there will be war in the first round. Such an equilibrium is described in Table 7.5. Here, in contrast to the previous case, there is a lower bound

Table 7.4 The Arms–War game: deterrence equilibrium

First attack choice	Defend
Build choice	Build
Second attack choice	Attack only with favorable balance of power
Conditions	$p_1^l + c_2 < s < p_1^h - c_1$
	$p_1^l - c_1 + \gamma_1 < s < p_1^h + c_2 - \gamma_2$
	$p_1^m - c_1 + \frac{\gamma_1}{2} < s < p_1^m + c_2 - \frac{\gamma_2}{2}$

Table 7.5 The Arms–War game: war equilibrium

First attack choice	Attack
Build choice	Build
Second attack choice	Attack only with favorable balance of power
Conditions	$p_1^l + c_2 < s < p_1^h - c_1$
	$p_1^l - c_1 + \gamma_1 < s < p_1^h + c_2 - \gamma_2$
	$p_1^m + c_2 - \frac{\gamma_2}{2} < s < p_1^m - c_1 + \frac{\gamma_1}{2}$

on how costly the arms buildup can be. If γ_i gets too low, then the players will not wish to attack in the first round, but rather to go to the second round and simply deter the other side. There still remains the upper bound on γ_i, however, associated with the fact that the players must be willing to build the forces if they get to the second round, rather than not build them and invite attack. Therefore, for war to break out due to costly deterrence, it must be the case that deterrence is costly enough to be worse than war, but not so costly that it would be avoided altogether in equilibrium.

The equilibria in the game are illustrated in Figure 7.1. For the sake of simplicity, I illustrate the symmetrical case in which $m_1 = m_2$, $c_1 = c_2$, and $\gamma_1 = \gamma_2$, and in which the status quo perfectly reflects the initial balance of power, so $s = p_1^m = 0.5$. This implies that p_1^h ranges between $\frac{1}{2}$ and 1. In the figure, the horizontal axis is γ, the cost of the military buildup. The vertical axis is p_h, which is a way of measuring the military advantage of the buildup. If the level of power with a buildup is too low, below the cost of war, then the first no build equilibrium is possible. Neither side will attack even with a power advantage, so there is no point in building up forces, or of attacking. If the level of power with a buildup is high enough so that the states would fight with an advantage, the second no build equilibrium is possible so long as the costs of the buildup are high enough. If the advantage is higher still, but the costs of a buildup are low, the deterrence equilibrium is possible, where both sides will refrain

7.1 COSTLY DETERRENCE

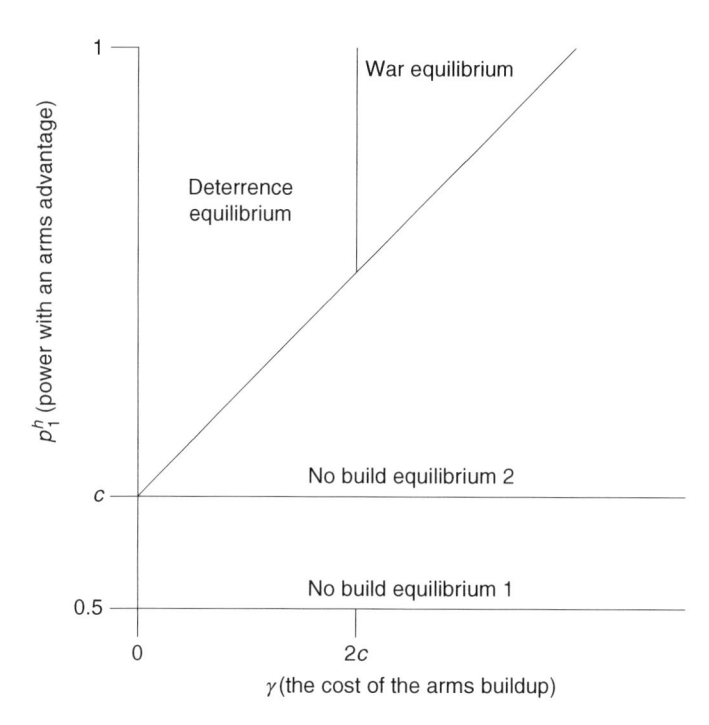

Figure 7.1 Arms race equilibria: complete information

[Figure shows a graph with p_1^h (power with an arms advantage) on the y-axis ranging from 0.5 to 1, and γ (the cost of the arms buildup) on the x-axis. Regions labeled: War equilibrium, Deterrence equilibrium, No build equilibrium 2, No build equilibrium 1. Key values marked: c on y-axis, $2c$ on x-axis.]

from attacking, build, and then refrain from attacking again. Finally, if the buildup is very effective but the cost of the buildup is middling, then both sides will be willing to attack in the present, rather than have to build up their forces to achieve mutual deterrence.[4]

The Arms–War game, simple as it is, helps clarify when costly deterrence will lead to war. The most interesting finding is that there is a non-monotonic relationship between the costs of the buildup and the occurrence of war. If the buildup is cheap, then states will prefer to pursue the arms race and deter each other. If the buildup is prohibitively expensive, states will not attack, assured that the other side will also prefer to avoid the costly weapons system, and the arms race will be avoided altogether. It is only in a middling range of buildup costs, and when the advantage of the weapons system is great, that an anticipated costly arms race will be an incentive to wage war in the present.

---

[4] Note, the upward sloping line starting at c_i when $\gamma = 0$ is the upper bound of the No Build Equilibrium 2, derived from Equation (7.3), rather than the lower bounds of the deterrence and war equilibria, which are given by Equation (7.4). Equation (7.4) produces a lower parallel upward sloping line starting at $0.5 - c$. This implies that there is a region between the two lines in which multiple equilibria are possible for the same set of parameter values. I have chosen to focus on and illustrate the Pareto superior equilibria in which the parties refrain from arming and/or war, since both sides are better off than at the deterrence and war equilibria.

Result 7.1 *If an arms buildup would be very effective militarily and is expensive but not prohibitively so, states may fight a war rather than build up their armed forces to deter each other. The more costly war is in comparison to the arms buildup, the less likely such a war is.*

7.2 The risk–return tradeoff and deterrence

The fact that power is expensive, the guns vs. butter tradeoff, motivates the war equilibrium in the costly deterrence model. It also can motivate a decision to skimp on guns in favor of butter if war is not certain in the future. This kind of dynamic arises even in games with complete information, so long as they have continuous and simultaneous arms choices.

To see why this is so, consider the arms choice game of Chapter 3. There each side maximized the utility function

$$u_i(m_i) = \frac{m_i}{m_1 + m_2} - \gamma_i m_i$$

where m_i is player i's military power and γ_i is their cost for a unit of military power. There we derived reaction functions and an equilibrium in the level of armaments. Interestingly, we can reinterpret this game as an Arms–War game without changing the analysis. Posit a game in which the two sides first choose a level of arms and then face a bargaining round in which player 1 makes an offer and player 2 either accepts or attacks. In the bargaining round, the players will bargain based on the realized balance of power, so player 1 will offer player 2's bottom line, which is $x = \frac{m_1}{m_2 + m_2} + c_2$, where c_2 is player 2's cost for war. Player 2 will accept this, since it is as good as fighting. In the arms choice, therefore, player 1 maximizes $x - \gamma_1 m_1$ and player 2 maximizes $1 - x - \gamma_2 m_2$, which is the same maximization problem we solved in Chapter 3 (the constant, c_2, drops out). The equilibrium is the same, and there will be a pure strategy allocation of military spending followed by peaceful bargaining based on the realized level of power.

In this case, there is no risk–return tradeoff, because arms levels translate smoothly into bargained results in the next round. Powell's arms–war model also exhibits no risk–return tradeoff because the alternating structure of the game means that players can observe and respond to the other side's military spending, and decide to spend more and attack, or spend enough to deter the other side in the next round and not attack (Powell 1999a, Chapter 2).

Things change if we stick with a simultaneous move setup and posit a status quo. Jackson and Morelli (2009) analyze a model much as I have just described, but they

7.2 THE RISK–RETURN TRADEOFF AND DETERRENCE

essentially posit a status quo division of resources, which can be altered by war. With a status quo, there is no pure strategy equilibrium that results in peace with certainty. To see why, posit a level of spending for player 1. Player 2's best response to that level of spending, assuming peace, is the level that will just suffice to deter player 1 from attacking. For there to be an equilibrium, player 1's best response to player 2's level of spending would have to be the same as player 1's initial level of spending. Unfortunately, under general conditions, it is less than that, which sets up a dynamic in which each player's best response to the other, assuming peace, is less than their previous level of spending until one or both sides prefer to increase their spending and attack.

This generates an equilibrium in which the players mix between a low level of spending that would not deter the other side if they arm at a high level, but will save money if they don't; a higher level of spending that will deter the other side if they arm at a high level; and a highest level of spending at which a player will attack the other side if they spend the low amount. Meirowitz and Sartori (2008) get a similar result by assuming that the arms choices are not observable. They rightly point out that states often take great pains to keep their military spending secret. If we posit that the arms choices are not observable, then there is an obvious incentive to skimp in the deterrence context. If the other side is expected to not attack, and they cannot observe a state's arms level, the best response is to spend nothing at all. This induces a mixed strategy dynamic once again; the players randomize over their military spending. They use this as an explanation for the existence of uncertainty about relative power, which then in turn causes war in the manner outlined in the previous chapter.

While these mixed strategy equilibria are unavoidable in these models, they seem implausible in empirical contexts. It seems unlikely that the US government picks its level of military spending at random from year to year just to keep adversaries guessing. More plausible is that each side may be one of several types, and that each type plays a pure strategy, which generates the same kind of uncertainty from the other side's perspective. This is indeed one of the justifications of mixed strategy equilibria in general (Harsanyi 1973). Under this interpretation, different types of actors spend different amounts on the military, and some types consciously spend less than it takes to deter the highest spending, most expansionist, type on the other side. This generates the familiar risk–return tradeoff in a new guise.

We can model the risk–return tradeoff with an incomplete information version of the Arms–War game. Consider a version of the game where each side has two types. The *status quo* types value the status quo at 1, so $u_i^S(s) = 1$. Because they value the status quo at 1, they have nothing to gain from even a successful war, which would also produce a payoff of 1. They will, therefore, be motivated to build weapons only for deterrence purposes. The *greedy* types value the status quo at its previous value, so $u_1^G(s) = s$ and $u_2^G(s) = 1 - s$. Greedy states value victory in war more than the

Table 7.6 The Arms–War game with uncertainty: risk–return equilibrium

	Status quo types
First attack choice	Defend
Build choice	Not build
Second attack choice	Defend for any balance of power

	Greedy types
First attack choice	Defend
Build choice	Build
Second attack choice	Attack only with a favorable balance of power
Conditions	$t_2 \geq 1 - \frac{\gamma_1}{1-(p_1^l - c_1)}, t_1 \geq 1 - \frac{\gamma_2}{p_1^h + c_2}$
	$t_2 \geq \frac{2p_1^m - c_1 - 1 - p_1^l}{1-(p_1^l - c_1)}, t_1 \geq \frac{p_1^h - 2p_1^m - c_2}{p_1^h + c_2}$
	$p_1^l + c_2 < s < p_1^h - c_1$
	$p_1^m - c_1 < s < p_1^m + c_2$
	$\gamma_1 \leq t_2(p_1^h - c_1 - s) + (1 - t_2)(s - (p_1^l - c_1))$
	$\gamma_2 \leq t_1(1 - p_1^l - c_2 - s) + (1 - t_1)(s - (1 - p_1^h - c_2))$
	$t_2 \geq \frac{2(p_1^m - c_1 - s) + \gamma_1}{p_1^h - c_1 - s}, t_1 \geq \frac{2(s - p_1^m - c_2) + \gamma_2}{s - p_1^l - c_2}$

status quo, so they may wish to attack for offensive reasons. There is a prior probability t_i (t for trust) that player i is the status quo type, and so has no real interest in expansion, and a corresponding $1 - t_i$ chance the player i is greedy.

A risk–return equilibrium in this modified game is illustrated in Table 7.6. The status quo and greedy types pool on defending in the first round, so there is no updating of beliefs there. Then the types separate, the status quo types do not build, while the greedy types build. Then in the final round, the status quo types do not attack regardless of the balance of power, while the greedy types attack if they have a military advantage, but not otherwise. The greedy types are, therefore, deterrable, but status quo types choose not to deter them.

When is this an equilibrium? First, consider the status quo types. At the final attack choice, if the other side did not build, they are identified as a status quo type who will defend. Defending, therefore, gives a payoff of 1, the status quo payoff for the status quo types, while attacking will give a war payoff, which is lower regardless of the balance of power. If the other side build up their forces, they are identified as greedy and are anticipated to attack. Whether the state attacks or not, therefore, the payoff is the same. Therefore, the status quo type is willing to defend in the final round, as specified. The absence of any first strike advantage means the status quo types are willing to defend, even if they think they will be attacked.

Consider the buildup choice. The status quo type must not build, realizing that if they do not build and the other side turns out to be greedy, the result will be war in the next round on poor terms. Building, however, will suffice to deter both types, and so will yield the status quo. The payoff for not building for the status quo type of player 1 is, therefore, $t_2(1) + (1-t_2)(p_l - c_1)$ and the payoff from building is $-\gamma_1 + 1$ (omitting the first round payoffs which are fixed by this point). Not building beats building if the following holds

$$t_2 \geq 1 - \frac{\gamma_1}{1 - (p_1^l - c_1)} \tag{7.6}$$

For player 2, the condition is

$$t_1 \geq 1 - \frac{\gamma_2}{p_1^h + c_2} \tag{7.7}$$

Finally, consider the first attack choice. Since the other side is expected to not attack regardless of what type they are, the payoff for not attacking is $1 + t_2(1) + (1-t_2)(p_1^l - c_1))$, which beats the payoff for attacking in the first round, $2(p_1^m - c_1)$, if the following holds

$$t_2 \geq \frac{2p_1^m - c_1 - 1 - p_1^l}{1 - (p_1^l - c_1)} \tag{7.8}$$

and for player 2

$$t_1 \geq \frac{p_1^h - 2p_1^m - c_2}{p_1^h + c_2} \tag{7.9}$$

Both of these conditions must hold for the status quo type of player 1 to fulfill their strategy. In sum, the satiated types must be trusting enough of the other side to not build in the second round, thereby running the risk of war at a disadvantage, and also to not attack in the first round, which would obviate the need to build.

Now turn to the greedy types. In the second round, they must prefer to attack only with an advantage. The payoff for attacking (for player 1) with an advantage is $p_1^h - c_1$, while the payoff for not attacking will be s, because, having not built, player 2 is identified as the satiated type and will not attack. Thus, the first condition for the greedy types is $p_1^l + c_2 \leq s \leq p_1^h - c_1$, which is the reverse of Equation (7.2). If, off the equilibrium path, they do not build, they must prefer to not attack. If the other side has built, they will attack, and so not attacking is the same as attacking. If the other side has not built, the power is equal and not attacking gives s, which must beat the war payoff, $p_1^m - c_1$. This leads to the condition, $p_1^m - c_1 \leq s \leq p_1^m + c_2$, which as assumed from the outset is the same as Equation (7.1) that no player wants to attack unless it has a military advantage. These conditions ensure the greedy types will attack only with an advantage.

Turn now to the build choice. The greedy type of player 1 must prefer to build, for a payoff of $-\gamma_1 + t_2(p_1^h - c_1) + (1 - t_2)s$, rather than not build, for a payoff of $t_2 s + (1 - t_2)(p_1^l - c_1)$, which leads to the following constraint on γ_1

$$\gamma_1 \leq t_2(p_1^h - c_1 - s) + (1 - t_2)(s - (p_1^l - c_1)) \tag{7.10}$$

So if the buildup is not too costly, the greedy type will be willing to build up. The corresponding condition for player 2 is

$$\gamma_2 \leq t_1(1 - p_1^l - c_2 - s) + (1 - t_1)(s - (1 - p_1^h - c_2)) \tag{7.11}$$

Finally, consider the first attack choice. Not attacking, which gives $s - \gamma_1 + t_2(p_1^h - c_1) + (1 - t_2)s$, must beat attacking, which gives $2(p_m - c_1)$

$$t_2 \geq \frac{2(p_1^m - c_1 - s) + \gamma_1}{p_1^h - c_1 - s} \tag{7.12}$$

For player 2, the condition is

$$t_1 \geq \frac{2(s - p_1^m - c_2) + \gamma_2}{s - p_1^l - c_2} \tag{7.13}$$

Note, the numerator might be negative in which case the greedy type would be willing to not attack regardless of the level of trust. Only if the cost of the buildup is high will there be any level of trust at which the greedy type would attack rather than wait and build up forces later.

This equilibrium is illustrated in Figure 7.2. The parameters underlying the illustrations are symmetrical, $p_1^m = s = .5$, $p_1^h = .7$, $p_1^l = .3$, and $c_i = .1$. The first constraint on the status quo types, from Equations (7.6) and (7.7), is the downward sloping line starting at (0,1). The level of trust must be above this line for the equilibrium to work. This means that the cheaper the weapons (lower γ_i), the more trusting the status quo players need to be to forgo acquiring them. The second constraint needed to ensure that status quo types do not attack in the first round is negative for these parameter values, and hence not binding. The constraint on the greedy type to get them to build, from Equations (7.10) and (7.11), amounts to $\gamma_1 < 0.3 - 0.2 t_2$. The constraint that prevents them from attacking in the first round reduces to $t_i > 10\gamma_i - 2$, and so is not binding. The two binding constraints, therefore, govern the build choices, the status quo types must be trusting enough to not build, and the greedy types must find the cost of weapons not too great. If these two conditions are satisfied, in the upper triangle of the figure, the risk–return equilibrium is possible, and the status quo types will forgo building while the greedy types build, and attack if they get an advantage in the second round.

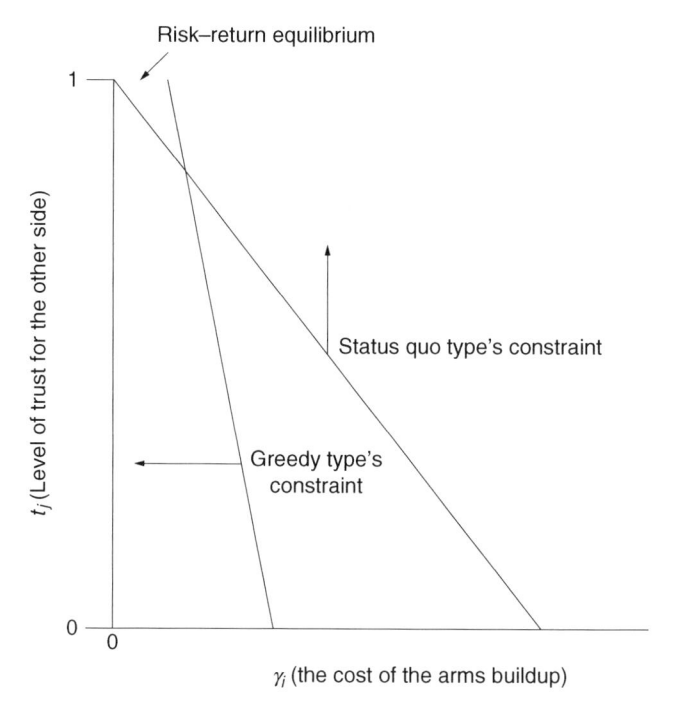

Figure 7.2 Arms–War game with uncertainty: risk–return equilibrium

Result 7.2 *States may rationally arm at levels insufficient to deter all possible types of adversary. Crises and wars may arise because states run the risk that their preparations will not be sufficient for the worst possible contingency.*

7.3 Conclusion

We have explored two mechanisms linking arms choices, or, more broadly, endogenous power and war. First, states may find deterrence too costly, and so decide to fight a war to eliminate the threat rather than live with the military spending level required to deter it. Second, states may decide to skimp on military spending in the sense of consciously spending less than would be required to deter all possible types of adversary, engaging in a risk–return tradeoff. These are not the only mechanisms linking arms decisions and war: the spiral model and the issue of endogenous asymmetrical power changes leading to preventive war are especially salient (Debs and Monteiro 2014). Models that combine endogenous power choices, bargaining, and war choices are increasingly common as researchers seek to understand the links between these central processes in international security.

EXERCISES

7.1 Consider a modification of the Arms–War game. The first two decisions on attacking and building weapons are the same. In the second round, however, there is a standard Bargaining game from Chapter 4. If player 1 builds and player 2 does not, then player 2 makes the offer, otherwise player 1 makes the proposal. What are the equilibria in the modified model? How do they compare with the version in which the only option in the second round is to attack?

7.2 Consider a modification of the Arms–War Game with uncertainty. Instead of the greedy type having a status quo payoff of s or $1 - s$, posit a type with a status quo payoff of 0. Consider the case where the costs of war are such that the greedy types are undeterable even if they have a power disadvantage, that is $p_1^l - c_1 > 0$, and similarly for player 2. How does this modify the risk–return equilibrium in the game?

8 Cooperation theory

IN strategic settings where all out war is too costly or ineffective to be a live option, states face the prospect that they must live together for the indefinite future. Taking war off the table certainly makes life more civilized, but peace can be made better or worse, depending on the strategies states pursue and the level of cooperation they attain. The literature on international cooperation has developed to analyze such situations.

Cooperation theory arose in the 1980s and marked the first time game theory made a major impact on central debates in international relations theory. Prior to that point, the 2×2 normal form games of Chapter 3 had been widely applied to various strategic issues, such as nuclear deterrence and the security dilemma, and had served to clarify the logic involved. However, they had not posed a serious challenge to any extant international relations theory. In 1979, Waltz's *Theory of International Politics* reformulated and reinvigorated realism as a paradigmatic approach, and its pessimistic view of conflict as an inevitable consequence of anarchy was bolstered by the return to confrontation between the United States and the Soviet Union in that period. Scholars who viewed realism as unduly pessimistic, and the trend of world affairs with alarm, sought for ways to undermine or at least qualify the realist logic Waltz had laid out.

Fortuitously, applied game theorists had recently begun studying the Repeated Prisoner's Dilemma (RPD) game, which offers an explanation of how cooperation can be sustained without centralized enforcement.[1] In the early 1980s, Robert Axelrod conducted a series of computer experiments to determine what strategy would fare best in an evolutionary setting based on the RPD and published a widely read book on the results (Axelrod 1984). This framework was seized upon by critics of Waltzian realism, who applied it to a variety of settings in both security and economic affairs (Oye 1986). Keohane made it a cornerstone of his liberal institutionalist challenge to realism, despite the absence of any formal institutions in the RPD model (Keohane 1984, 1986). The RPD based attack on realism was lent additional force by the mathematical

---

[1] For a technical introduction, see Abreu (1988).

and hence scientific nature of game theory, and the widespread application of the RPD model in other social scientific disciplines, such as economics and sociology.

Realists quickly developed a counterattack centered on the concept of "relative gains." Grieco (1988) argued, drawing on Waltz, that states seek relative gains because international anarchy and the threats posed by other states force them to be concerned with their relative power, rather than the "absolute gains" posited by the RPD. Relative gains seekers find cooperation more difficult because, in the limit, it is impossible to cooperate in a zero sum interaction if there are only two actors. This critique was particularly important because liberal institutionalists had made much of the claim that they were adopting realism's own assumptions, and proving that the conclusions did not follow from them. Grieco could argue with some justice that they had misunderstood realist assumptions and that properly understood realism implied that cooperation was much more difficult to attain than the RPD framework would lead us to believe. In response to this critique, game theorists stepped once more into the breach. Snidal argued that relative gains seeking should not prevent cooperation except in the two person zero sum case (Snidal 1991a, 1991b). Powell argued that we should model states as absolute gain seekers who sometimes, for security reasons, must acquire relative power to defend their absolute gains (Powell 1991).[2] In the end, realists had a point that the RPD framework was not a good model of international bargaining in the shadow of a potentially game-ending war, and this became a primary focus of work in the 1990s, as reflected in the preceding several chapters. Cooperation theorists, for their part, also had a point in that in the many international settings where game-ending war is off the table, the RPD can provide a good model for analyzing the prospects for international cooperation without centralized enforcement. Subsequent models have mixed bargaining and RPD elements without attaching paradigmatic significance to the exercise (Fearon 1998a, Schultz 2010).

The core of cooperation theory is the RPD model, in which two players play the Prisoner's Dilemma over time indefinitely. The central question to be addressed is when states are able to sustain mutual cooperation and when they cannot. As discussed in Chapter 1, mutual cooperation is a Pareto improvement over mutual defection, so mutual defection is regarded as inefficient behavior that is in need of explanation. The usual explanation of inefficiency in this context is the fourth one discussed in the introduction, *impatience*. The more states value future payoffs, the easier cooperation is to achieve because the more states care about the future, the less temptation there is to pursue immediate gains at the expense of long-term relationships. The *shadow of the future*, therefore, promotes cooperation. Another explanation of inefficiency in this

---

[2] Baldwin (1993) gathers contributions to the debate, see also Mearsheimer (1994/5) and Niou and Ordeshook (1994).

context, and in a sense a more fundamental one, is *monitoring problems*. If states could perfectly monitor each other's behavior, they would be able to reduce or eliminate the risk of being exploited by the other side. It is this risk that patience is required to run, so the less risk, the less patience is required for cooperation. This chapter will lay out the basic analysis of the RPD and highlight these results. I conclude with a brief discussion of some related empirical questions.

8.1 The problem of cooperation

As discussed in Chapter 3, the Prisoner's Dilemma game has come to be regarded as representative of a broad class of cooperation problems. The game is illustrated in Table 8.1 with the conventional notation for the payoffs. The payoff ordering for a Prisoner's Dilemma is $T > R > P > S$.

As we discovered earlier, the only Nash equilibrium in the Prisoner's Dilemma is mutual defection. That outcome can also be arrived at through the elimination of dominated strategies. Mutual defection would, therefore, seem to be a very solid prediction for this model. However, defection is individually rational, but collectively sub-optimal, in that both players could be made better off if they switched to mutual cooperation. Mutual cooperation Pareto dominates mutual defection. It would be nice if there was a way to sustain mutual cooperation, but in the game as specified so far, it cannot be done.

Yet, thinking about it from another angle, does the Prisoner's Dilemma as specified really make sense as a model of many political situations? Consider the trade context and the question of whether to protect an import-competing industry. The Prisoner's Dilemma might fairly well describe the payoffs states experience in a single decision about imposing non-tariff barriers. However, these decisions do not crop up once and only once, they are repeated every time trade policy is considered, which could be once an election cycle, once a year, or even more frequently. When a state considers imposing a non-tariff barrier, it recognizes that the game will continue, time marches on, and the other state may decide to retaliate. This generates an additional disincentive to defect

Table 8.1 The Prisoner's Dilemma

		Player 2 Cooperate	Player 2 Defect
Player 1	Cooperate	R, R	S, T
	Defect	T, S	P, P

not captured in the Prisoner's Dilemma as so far examined. To analyze this incentive properly, we must look at a repeated version of the game.

8.2 Discounting future payoffs

In analyzing repeated games, the first thing we need to think about is how actors value future payoffs. People tend to value future payoffs less than present ones. Given a choice between receiving a payoff $u(x)$ today and a year from today, most people will prefer getting it today. If the payoff derives from money, then if you really want it a year from now, you can just save it and spend it later, possibly with interest. If it is a durable good, like a house or a car, getting it now rather than a year from now gives you a year's additional enjoyment from possessing it.

One way to measure time preference is to ask people to compare their utility for the same good at different times. For instance, compare receiving x today, denoted x^0, with x a year from now, denoted x^1, where the superscript denotes the time. Presumably x^0 is better than x^1, and this should be reflected in the utility function, such that we can posit a discount factor, $\delta \in [0, 1]$, and that $u(x^1) = \delta u(x^0)$. In money terms, getting $100 a year from now might be equivalent in value to getting $80 today, so it would be worth 80% of what it would be if it were available immediately. The bigger δ is, the more you care about future payoffs; the lower δ is, the less you care about future payoffs. Note, as applied to money, δ is related to the interest rate, usually denoted r. An amount of money x invested at interest rate r will be worth $(1 + r)x$ in a year, so that if these are equivalent in value, $x^0 = (1 + r)x^1$, or $\frac{1}{1+r}x^0 = x^1$, so $\delta = \frac{1}{1+r}$.

Having a discount rate for one period, the question then arises what about two periods from now, three periods, etc.? We could go through the same procedure and come up with an independent discount factor for each time interval. However, we typically make the stronger assumption that we can use the one period discount factor to cover all these cases. For instance, consider a good x^2 that will become available in two years. We assume that the utility of this good one year from now will be $\delta u(x_1)$ and that the utility of this in the present can be expressed as $\delta \times \delta u(x^0)$ or just $\delta^2 u(x^0)$. This is known as *exponential discounting* because the discount factor is raised to the exponent of the period in the future under consideration.[3]

Making this assumption, we can place a value on indefinite payoff streams. If an actor receives x every year from pursuing some strategy, how much should this income stream be valued? We can write the infinite series as follows

$$V_\infty = u(x) + \delta u(x) + \delta^2 u(x) + \delta^3 u(x) \ldots$$

[3] An alternative is hyperbolic discounting (Frederick *et al.* 2002).

8.2 DISCOUNTING FUTURE PAYOFFS

A very nice fact about this sequence is that it is easy to solve for a finite expression. If we multiply both sides of the above by δ, we get

$$\delta V_\infty = \delta u(x) + \delta^2 u(x) + \delta^3 u(x) + \delta^4 u(x) \ldots$$

We can then subtract the second equation from the first, which nicely gets rid of the infinite sequence because every term in the bottom right-hand side is also on the right-hand side of the top equation

$$V_\infty - \delta V_\infty = u(x)$$

and solve for the value of the stream of payoff:

$$V_\infty = \frac{1}{1-\delta} u(x) \qquad (8.1)$$

Notice that since δ is less than 1, $V(S)$ is greater than $u(x)$, which it should be since you get $u(x)$ today, plus more to come in the future. Also, the greater your discount factor, the greater the value of the income stream. As δ approaches 1, the value of the payoff stream gets very large. Sometimes Δ is defined as $\Delta \equiv \frac{1}{1-\delta}$ and thought of as the present value of the income stream.

This trick can be used to generate a neat expression for long but finite payoff streams as well. Consider the payoff for n rounds of $u(x)$

$$V_n = u(x) + \delta u(x) + \delta^2 u(x) + \ldots + \delta^{n-1} u(x)$$

We can think of this as the infinite sequence, minus the infinite sequence that starts at round $n+1$, as follows

$$V_n = \frac{1}{1-\delta} u(x) - \delta^n u(x) - \delta^{n+1} u(x) - \ldots$$

The infinite sequence starting at round $n+1$ in turn is just δ^n times the original infinite sequence

$$V_n = \frac{1}{1-\delta} u(x) - \delta^n \frac{1}{1-\delta} u(x)$$

which can be reexpressed more simply as the following

$$V_n = \frac{1-\delta^n}{1-\delta} u(x)$$

Note, if $n = 1$, this is just equal to $u(x)$, as it should be since it would be for a single round. As $n \to \infty$, this expression converges on $\frac{1}{1-\delta}$, the expression for the infinite case. This formula comes in handy for calculating the payoff for punishment rounds of length n.

8.3 Finitely repeated games

A repeated game consists of playing a game, in this context called the *stage game*, more than once in succession. Consider a game consisting of playing a Coordination game, illustrated in Table 8.2, twice in a row. First, we need to consider what the strategy space is. Each player must decide whether to choose their first or second option in the first round. Then, conditional on what happened in the first round, each player must decide whether to choose the first or second option in the second round. A useful concept here is the *history* of the game, which is a way the game can be played up to a certain round.

Definition 8.1 *A history, h^t, of a repeated game in round t is a set of choices for each player for each round $0 \ldots t - 1$.*

In each round, each player must have a strategy which tells them what to do for each possible history h^t in the set of possible histories H^t up to that point in the game. In this game, there are four possible outcomes in the first round, $\{A, A\}$, $\{A, B\}$, $\{B, A\}$, and $\{B, B\}$, so there are four possible histories in the second round to cover. Each player's strategy must, therefore, cover five decisions, the first round, plus what to do after each of the four possible histories in the second round.

One possible equilibrium is for the players to alternate, so that player 1 gets her preferred outcome in the first round and player 2 gets his preferred outcome in the second round. A strategy that reflects this is the following:

- play A in the first round,
- play B in the second round no matter what happened in the first round.

Is it an equilibrium for both sides to play this strategy? In the second round, after each of the four histories, no player can deviate profitably given the other side's strategy – to change would only yield 0 instead of 1 for player 1 or 2 for player 2. In the first round, deviation is unprofitable immediately, and has no effect on future play. Hence, this forms a Nash equilibrium of the game. If we assume discounting, then player 1's payoff

Table 8.2 A Coordination game

		Player 2 A	Player 2 B
Player 1	A	2, 1	0, 0
	B	0, 0	1, 2

8.3 FINITELY REPEATED GAMES

Table 8.3 A Modified Prisoner's Dilemma

		Player 2		
		C	D	W
Player 1	C	3, 3	1, 4	0, 0
	D	4, 1	2, 2	0, 0
	W	0, 0	0, 0	0, 0

is $2 + \delta 1$ and player 2's payoff is $1 + \delta 2$. Note, player 1 still does better than player 2 because they coordinated on player 1's favorite outcome first, but the difference in payoff is smaller in the repeated game, and diminishes to 0 as the players value future payoffs more as δ increases.

As another example, consider a game consisting of playing the Modified Prisoner's Dilemma in Table 8.3 twice. This game, based on Powell (1991), is like the Prisoner's Dilemma but with an additional strategy of withdrawing from the interaction, which yields a payoff of 0 for both parties. There are two Nash equilibria in the Stage game, $\{D, D\}$ and $\{W, W\}$. What equilibria are sustainable in the version that is played twice? In particular, is it possible to attain the mutually cooperative outcome?

In this game, since there are three strategies for each of two players, there are $3^2 = 9$ histories in the second round. A complete strategy consists of a choice for the first round and a choice for the second round for each of the nine histories. We can simplify things by partitioning the histories into sets, and specifying a strategy for each set of histories. For instance, consider the strategy:

- play C in the first round,
- play D after CC, otherwise play W.

This strategy partitions the histories into two sets, the first in which the players both selected C and the other eight possibilities, and an action is specified in each case. When is this strategy an equilibrium? The payoff for playing the strategy, given that the other side also plays it, is 3 in the first round and 2 in the second, for a total of $3 + \delta 2$. The payoff for defecting to D in the first round is 4 in the first round and 0 in the second, since the other side will shift to playing W. The equilibrium strategy beats the defection if $3 + \delta 2 \geq 4$ or if

$$\delta > \frac{1}{2}$$

Thus, repetition has generated an equilibrium in which the two players play strategies that would not form a Nash equilibrium in the Stage game, provided that the actors care enough about the future. This has enabled a greater degree of cooperation than was possible in the one-shot game.[4]

We might wonder if repetition will help get cooperation going in a game like the standard Prisoner's Dilemma. Consider a game consisting of repeating the Prisoner's Dilemma n times. What Nash equilibria might such a game have? Backwards induction yields an unequivocal answer: the only equilibrium in the game is for both sides to defect in every round no matter what the history of the game. In the final round, the only Nash equilibrium is mutual defection. In the next to last round, anticipating certain mutual defection, each side is rational to defect. The defection zips back to the beginning of the game. In general, a finitely repeated game with a unique Nash equilibrium in the Stage game will have a unique Nash equilibrium consisting of playing those strategies in every round.[5] Note, the modified Prisoner's Dilemma had two equilibria in the Stage game, which made the contrary result possible.

8.4 Indefinitely repeated games

A finitely repeated game might seem unrealistic in some cases because the players do not know when the game will end. In the current international system, states exist for a long time and, may not know when any given interaction will end. We can easily represent such situations with a Prisoner's Dilemma of indefinite duration. Define the Repeated Prisoner's Dilemma (RPD) as a game with the Prisoner's Dilemma as a Stage game repeated forever. Payoffs are calculated as we just discussed, with a common discount factor δ.

What kind of strategies are possible in a game that lasts forever? As with the finitely repeated game, the strategy must provide a choice for every round for every history of the game up to that point. With infinite repetition, however, strategies that radically simplify the set of histories are usually considered. For instance: one simple strategy can be called All Defect.

Definition 8.2 *The strategy* All Defect *plays D in every period, for every history of the game.*

---

[4] Other deviations are never profitable. Deviating to W in the first round produces a payoff of 0 for the whole game. Playing C and then deviating to C in the second round produces a payoff of $3 + \delta 1$ and deviating to W in the second round produces a payoff of $3 + \delta 0$, both of which are worse than the equilibrium payoff.

[5] The same result holds in the "centipede" game. For a philosophical discussion of the rationality of such results, see Hollis (1998).

8.4 INDEFINITELY REPEATED GAMES

It turns out that All Defect is a Nash equilibrium with itself. The payoff for two players playing All Defect is

$$P + \delta P + \delta^2 P + \delta^3 P \ldots = \frac{P}{1-\delta}$$

Cooperating at any round will simply lower the payoff in that round to S_i and produce no other effects. Hence, cooperating in any round or subset of rounds lowers the payoff, so All Defect is a Nash equilibrium with itself.

All Defect is simply playing the Nash equilibrium of the Stage game forever. The point of considering a repeated version of the game, however, was the hope that the players could do better than that. The simplest possible strategy in which they do is often called "Grim Trigger" (GT) for reasons that will become clear.

Definition 8.3 *The strategy* Grim Trigger

- *Cooperate in the first round.*
- *In all subsequent rounds:*

    if no one has ever defected previously in the game, then cooperate;

    if anyone has ever defected in the game, then defect.

Note, this is a complete rule for playing the game. It gives a strategy for the first round and then partitions the set of histories of the game for subsequent rounds into two groups: ones in which someone has defected, and the (unique) one in which no one has yet defected, and specifies an action in each case.

When is Grim Trigger a Nash equilibrium with itself? The equilibrium payoff is

$$R + \delta R + \delta^2 R \ldots = R + \frac{\delta R}{1-\delta}$$

The payoff for defection is

$$T + \delta P + \delta^2 P \ldots = T + \frac{\delta P}{1-\delta}$$

When does the equilibrium payoff beat defection?

$$R + \frac{\delta R}{1-\delta} > T + \frac{\delta P}{1-\delta}$$

$$(R-P)\frac{\delta}{1-\delta} > T - R$$

$$(R-P)\delta > (T-R) - (T-R)\delta$$

$$(T-P)\delta > (T-R)$$

$$\delta > \frac{T-R}{T-P} \qquad (8.2)$$

Note, given the preference ranking $T > R > P > S$, we can easily show that $\frac{T-R}{T-P} \in (0, 1)$, which means that since $\delta \in [0, 1]$ cooperation will be possible for high enough discount rates, but impossible if the discount rate falls below the threshold. With the 4, 3, 2, 1 payoffs of the usual game matrix $\frac{T-R}{T-P} = \frac{4-3}{4-2} = \frac{1}{2}$, so the critical threshold is one half, as it was for the two round Modified Prisoner's Dilemma game. If the discount factor is bigger than this critical value, the Grim Trigger strategy will be a Nash equilibrium with itself. This makes sense – caring about the future leads to cooperation because future payoffs will be lower because of retaliation in the future. If you care about them, you will be willing to cooperate in the present.

Note that this analysis indicates that there is not just one Nash equilibrium in the RPD. In fact, there are many. This makes the search for good strategies for playing the RPD particularly interesting. Ideally, a strategy would be a Nash equilibrium with itself and also not do too badly against other strategies that might be encountered.

8.5 Tit for Tat and Contrite Tit for Tat

Axelrod (1984) conducted a series of computer tournaments in pursuit of such a strategy and the winner was one of the simplest entrants, called Tit for Tat (TFT).

Definition 8.4 *The strategy TFT is defined as follows:*

- *Cooperate on the first round.*
- *In any subsequent round t:*

    if the other side cooperated in round $t - 1$, then cooperate;

    If the other side defected in round $t - 1$, then defect.

Note, TFT provides a complete set of instructions for playing the game at every round, just like Grim Trigger. Unlike Grim Trigger, however, TFT bases those instructions solely on what happened in the last round. Ancient history is of no interest to TFT, only the most recent behavior matters.

Is it a Nash equilibrium for both players to play TFT? The payoff for following TFT in this case is the payoff for mutual cooperation in every round

$$R + \delta R + \delta^2 R + \delta^3 R \ldots$$

For TFT to be a Nash equilibrium, this payoff must beat that of any deviation. First, consider a single deviation in the first round. The subsequent pattern of behavior is illustrated in Table 8.4. In the first round, player 1 cooperates but player 2 deviates by

Table 8.4 A one-round deviation from Tit for Tat

Round	1	2	3	4	5	6
Player 1	C	D	C	D	C	...
Player 2	D	C	D	C	D	...

defecting. After that, both sides return to TFT. This implies that in round 2, the initial defection by player 2, is punished by player 1, while player 2 cooperates, because that is what player 1 did in the first round. In round 3, the roles reverse, and player 2 defects, while player 1 cooperates. This sets up an endless cycle of cooperation and defection. The payoff for single defection is, therefore, the following

$$T + \delta S + \delta^2 T + \delta^3 S \ldots$$

Cooperation beats the single defection if

$$R + \delta R + \delta^2 R + \delta^3 R \ldots \geq T + \delta S + \delta^2 T + \delta^3 S \ldots$$

$$\frac{R + \delta R}{1 - \delta^2} > \frac{T + \delta S}{1 - \delta^2}$$

$$\delta > \frac{T - R}{R - S} \tag{8.3}$$

Once again, if you care enough about the future, it is in your interest to cooperate. The threshold in this case is greater than 0, and will be less than 1 if $T - R < R - S$, or

$$\frac{T + S}{2} < R \tag{8.4}$$

If Equation (8.4) is true, then if the players are sufficiently patient, they will prefer to play TFT rather than deviate for one round. If Equation (8.4) is not true, however, then even maximally patient players would not be able to sustain cooperation because the temptation to defect would be too great. Basically, the players would prefer to alternate between the temptation to defect and the sucker's payoff rather than receive a steady diet of the reward for mutual cooperation.

If Equation (8.4) holds, then TFT will be stable against a one-round deviation. Another deviation to check is permanent defection, which produces a payoff of $T + \frac{\delta P}{1-\delta}$. This is the same comparison as the one we made for the Grim Trigger strategy, and Tit for Tat will beat this deviation if Equation (8.2) holds.[6]

Tit for Tat has four desirable properties according to Axelrod.

1. It is *nice* because it is defined as not being the first to defect.
2. It is *retaliatory*, in that it retaliates without fail against any defection.

---

[6] It is possible to show that if a one-round deviation and a permanent defection are both unprofitable, then any finite length deviation is also unprofitable.

3. It is *forgiving*, in that after it retaliates, it lets bygones be bygones.
4. It is *clear*, or easy to understand, so other players will be able to interpret it correctly and anticipate its behavior.

These features enable TFT to do well in a variety of settings. It does well against other nice, cooperative strategies, but it does not get exploited badly by mean, defection prone strategies. In the computer tournaments organized by Axelrod, TFT proved able to invade environments populated by less cooperative strategies if it was able to move in as a cluster of like-minded individuals. Cooperators did very well with each other, and their payoffs with non-cooperators were not much lower than the natives".[7]

One serious defect of TFT is that it is not subgame perfect with itself. The problem is that if one side defects, the other side actually has an incentive to skip the punishment rather than carry it out. Imagine two players playing TFT, where player 2 cooperates in round 1, as it should, but player 1 deviates to defect instead. In the subgame that follows in the second round, player 1 should cooperate, since it is playing TFT and player 2 cooperated, but player 2 should defect, since player 1 defected in round 1 and TFT specifies that player 2 should punish this defection with a defection. Since both sides are playing TFT, this will set up a perpetual cycle of alternating defection and cooperation, as first one side, then the other, punishes the other side's defection and then rewards the other side's cooperation. Player 2's payoff for defecting in round 2, to punish player 1's defection in round 1, is, therefore, the following

$$T + \delta S + \delta^2 T + \delta^3 S \ldots$$

To deviate and "forgive" the defection puts the players back on the cooperative path, since the other side has returned to playing TFT, and so yields the following

$$R + \delta R + \delta^2 R + \delta^3 R \ldots$$

Deviating by skipping the punishment beats the payoff for TFT when

$$R + \delta R + \delta^2 R + \delta^3 R \ldots > T + \delta S + \delta^2 T + \delta^3 S \ldots$$

$$\frac{R + \delta R}{1 - \delta^2} > \frac{T + \delta S}{1 - \delta^2}$$

$$\delta > \frac{T - R}{R - S}$$

This is just the condition which was needed to make TFT safe against the one-round deviation, as shown in Equation (8.3)! Thus, if TFT is a Nash equilibrium, it is automatically not subgame perfect. The players do not have an incentive to carry out the punishments that they need to in order to enforce cooperation. This might seem like

---

[7] The literature on "agent-based modeling" has developed this mode of analysis further (Axelrod 1997, Cederman 1997).

8.5 TIT FOR TAT AND CONTRITE TIT FOR TAT

a gigantic hole in cooperation theory, but it turns out there are other similar strategies that are subgame perfect.

For instance, consider Contrite Tit for Tat (CTFT) (Signorino 1996).

Definition 8.5 *The strategy* CTFT

- *Good and bad standing are defined as follows:*

  in round 1, both players are in good standing;
  in any round $t > 1$, player i is in good standing if in round $t - 1$ it cooperated, or if it defected and player j was in bad standing. Otherwise, player i is in bad standing.

- *Cooperate, unless only the other side is in bad standing, in which case defect.*

The great advantage of CTFT is that it short circuits the infinite punishment cycles that plague TFT. If player 1 defects in the first round, for instance, it enters bad standing. Player 2 will, therefore, punish it by defecting in the second round. Since player 2 is still in good standing, player 1 will cooperate in the second round, getting the S payoff, but effectively apologizing for the defection, and returning to good standing. At the end of round 2, both players will be in good standing, and so will cooperate subsequently, where TFT would have had them enter a cycle of defection and cooperation.

Is CTFT a Nash equilibrium with itself? The equilibrium path of play produces mutual cooperation, for a payoff of

$$R + \delta R + \delta^2 R + \delta^3 R \ldots$$

A one-round deviation from Contrite Tit for Tat is illustrated in Table 8.5. In the first round, player 2 deviates to defect, landing itself in bad standing. Player 1 then punishes player 2 in round 2, while player 2 cooperates. In round 3, both players are once again in good standing, and so they both cooperate. Mutual cooperation then persists into the future. A one-round deviation, therefore, produces a payoff of

$$T + \delta S + \delta^2 R + \delta^3 R \ldots$$

Table 8.5 A one-round deviation from Contrite Tit for Tat

Round	1	2	3	4	5	6
Player 1	C	D	C	C	C	...
Player 2	D	C	C	C	C	...

We can easily see that the condition for CTFT to beat the one-round deviation is the same as that for TFT

$$\delta \geq \frac{T-R}{R-S} \tag{8.5}$$

To verify that CTFT does not suffer from the same problem as TFT, in which the players do not have an incentive to punish defection, consider a round where the other side has entered bad standing. The payoff for punishing in the correct fashion is

$$T + \delta R + \delta^2 R + \delta^3 R \ldots$$

The payoff for forgiving the defection is

$$R + \delta R + \delta^2 R + \delta^3 R \ldots$$

which is clearly less because in the first round punishing gives T as opposed to R, and in subsequent rounds the payoff is the same.

Finally, CTFT requires the party who deviates to apologize for the deviation by cooperating, while the other side defects for one round. Under what conditions do they have an incentive to so this? If the other player is in good standing, playing CTFT beats one more defection if

$$S + \delta R + \delta^2 R \ldots \geq P + \delta S + \delta^2 R \ldots$$
$$\delta(R - S) \geq P - S$$
$$\delta \geq \frac{P-S}{R-S}$$

If the other side is also in bad standing, then returning to CTFT by cooperating beats deviation if the original condition in Equation (8.5) is satisfied. Therefore, if this last condition and Equation (8.5) are satisfied, the players will prefer to play CTFT rather than deviate for one round, will prefer to punish a one round deviation, and will prefer to apologize for a one-round deviation.

The fact that CTFT does not get trapped in cycles of retaliation makes it particularly suitable to environments featuring noise, or uncertainty, over what the players have done. Signorino (1996) compares a number of different strategies in environments featuring different kinds of noise. Positive noise is defined as intended defections that come out as cooperation, negative noise as intended cooperations that turn into defections, and neutral noise is a mixture of the two. He looks at how the strategies fare against each other for varying intensities of noise, and how they replicate in an evolutionary setting where population is determined by performance in the previous round. CTFT ends up doing especially well in environments of negative noise, which seems particularly realistic in international settings where suspicion is more likely to turn intended cooperation into perceived defection than vice versa.[8]

Result 8.1 *States that value future payoffs sufficiently can cooperate with each other in the Prisoner's Dilemma like settings by threatening punishment for unprovoked defections. Impatience, or insufficiently valuing the future, may cause cooperation to break down into conflict.*

8.6 Monitoring

We have seen that players with sufficient patience, or value for future payoffs, will be able to cooperate in the RPD framework using strategies such as CTFT, despite the risk of short-term exploitation. This provides a plausible rationale for cooperation between actors who have repeated interactions and long time horizons. However, there are situations where the risk is too great or the time horizons too short, and cooperation will not be possible under the preceding analysis. This raises the question, however, of whether anything can be done to reduce the risk of exploitation if the players are unwilling to run a high risk of exploitation.

Monitoring is the usual way in which the risk of exploitation is directly addressed. In the peacekeeping context, monitors are used to help provide information about what the other side is doing, so that the players are not surprised by sudden buildups or truce violations (Lindley 2007, Fortna 2008). In the arms control context, verification procedures allow the parties to an arms control treaty to know that the other side is abiding by its provisions rather than cheating (Bailey 1995, Lacey 1996, O'Neill Jr. 2009). This may cause the difference between a successful treaty and preventive war to be motivated by uncertainty about the weapons programs of the other side (Debs and Monteiro 2014).

Monitoring can be modeled in a variety of ways. Some posit that defections by the other side are only detected probabilistically and monitoring can increase the chance that a defection is detected, or more generally sharpen an estimate of what the other side is doing (Bednar 2006, Schultz 2010). A simple alternative is to vary the time it takes to discover a move by the other side. If it takes a long time to discover what the other side has done, this means that cooperation is risky because it will take a long time to react to a defection. If a defection by the other side can be discovered quickly, then the risk of cooperation is less. For instance, in the arms control context, consider an agreement such as the 2010 New Start treaty between the US and Russia limiting

---

[8] Bendor also analyzes the noisy RPD (Bendor *et al.* 1991, Bendor 1993, Bendor and Swistak 1997).

deployed nuclear weapons. If a deviation from the agreement can only be detected a year after it happens, each side will be able to deploy many missiles in that period of time, placing the other side at a great disadvantage. Conversely, if a deviation can be detected in a day, then each side will run very little risk because not many missiles can be constructed or even deployed in a day. International institutions like peacekeepers or the International Atomic Energy Agency may help to provide this kind of information, so institutions are sometimes modeled as helping to "speed up time" (Stone et al. 2008).

The simplest way to see this comparison is to consider an alternative version of the game in which it takes two rounds to discover what the other side has done, and then compare it to the previous case in which it only took one round. That is, we will consider the game described so far as the "fast" game with international monitoring institutions providing information on what the parties are doing. Now we will investigate the conditions required for cooperation in the "slow" game without this kind of information, and in which it takes two periods to figure out what the other side has done. If cooperation is harder to sustain in the slow game, it will be evidence for the utility of monitoring institutions.

Assume the players are playing CTFT. Mutual cooperation gives a payoff of $\frac{R}{1-\delta}$ as before. A one-time deviation to defect gives a payoff of

$$T + \delta T + \delta^2 S + \delta^3 S + \delta^4 R + \ldots$$

where the temptation to defect and the punishment last two rounds – twice as long as before. Playing CTFT beats the deviation if

$$R + \delta R + \delta^2 R + \delta^3 R + \delta^4 R \ldots \geq T + \delta T + \delta^2 S + \delta^3 S + \delta^4 R + \ldots$$

$$R + \delta R + \delta^2 R + \delta^3 R \geq T + \delta T + \delta^2 S + \delta^3 S$$

$$(1+\delta)R + \delta^2(1+\delta)R \geq (1+\delta)T + \delta^2(1+\delta)S$$

$$R + \delta^2 R \geq T + \delta^2 S$$

$$\delta^2 \geq \frac{T-R}{R-S}$$

which yields the following condition

$$\delta \geq \sqrt{\frac{T-R}{R-S}} \tag{8.6}$$

This condition is quite similar in appearance to the parallel condition in the "fast time" game, shown in Equation (8.5), with the exception that the right-hand side has the square root sign. Since the fraction is less than one (if the condition can be satisfied at all), this means that the right-hand side in slow time is larger than in fast time, which means that the players must be *more patient* in the slow game than in the fast one to be willing to cooperate.[9] Speeding up the game, as monitors can do by providing more timely information on defections by the other side, makes cooperation possible for less patient players. Therefore, one potentially fruitful avenue for promoting cooperation is to have improved monitoring of the parties' behavior, so that they may detect deviations quickly and are able to respond to them.

Result 8.2 *Better monitoring that enables states to more quickly detect defections by the other side can foster cooperation by reducing the amount of patience needed to sustain cooperation. The inability to monitor the other side can prevent cooperation, even between patient states.*

8.7 A Tariff Barrier game

The RPD model generates many insights on international cooperation. One problem with it, however, is that it presents the decision to cooperate or defect as a binary choice. In the real world, states often have the option to cooperate partially, with the degree of cooperation quite flexible. This may make it hard to apply the RPD empirically, since the sharp distinction between cooperation and defection in the model may be difficult to discern in reality. One way to capture this theoretically is to model the decision space as a continuous variable rather than a discrete choice.

For instance, consider a Tariff Barrier game. Each side can impose a tariff t_i on the other side's goods. Each side has an ideal tariff that they would like to impose on imports from the other side, t_i^*, and would like the other side's tariff to be 0. For simplicity, let's assume that the utility functions are a simple function of the distance from a player's ideal point, as follows

$$u_i(t_i) = -\sqrt{(t_i - t_i^*)^2 + t_j^2} \tag{8.7}$$

The tariff issue space is illustrated in Figure 8.1. State 1's tariff is on the horizontal axis, and state 2's is on the vertical axis. State 1's ideal point is when it imposes a tariff of t_1^* and State 2 imposes a tariff of 0, illustrated on the horizontal axis. State 2 has a corresponding ideal point on the vertical axis. Each side has circular indifference curves indicating a progressive loss of utility as they move away from their ideal point. The straight line joining the ideal points is the Pareto optimal set; on the line it is not possible to move and make both parties better off (see the discussion of the Edgeworth Box in Chapter 2).

---

[9] The additional conditions that assure that a player in bad standing will wish to apologize are left to an exercise.

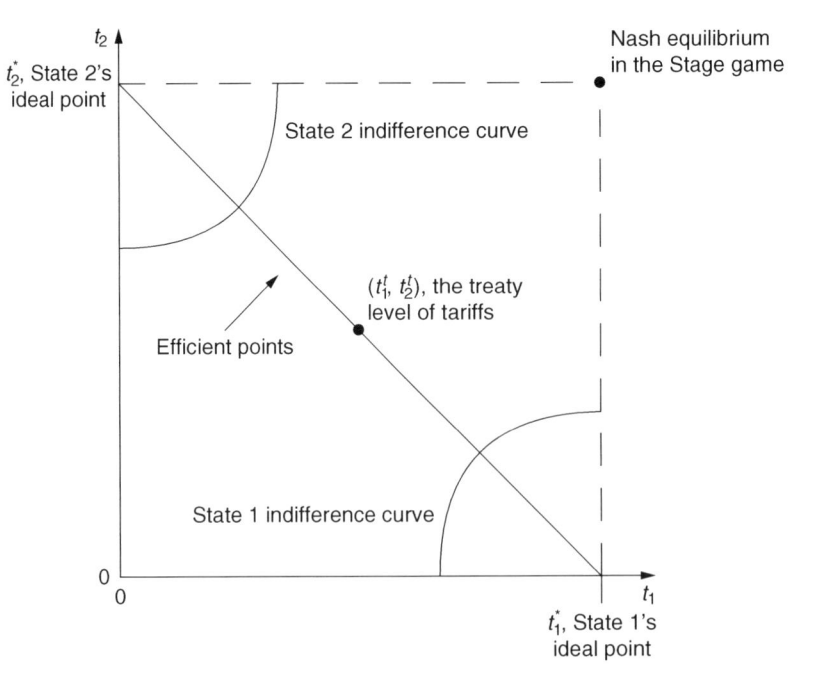

Figure 8.1 The Tariff game issue space

What is the Nash equilibrium of the Stage game? Looking at Equation (8.7), we can easily see that it is maximized when $t_i = t_i^*$, regardless of the tariff level of the other side. So the Nash equilibrium in the Stage game is simply the ideal tariffs for each side, (t_1^*, t_2^*), which is illustrated at the intersection of the dotted lines drawn from the ideal points. This Stage game equilibrium is clearly not Pareto optimal; it is well away from the contract curve of points linking the two ideal points. Moving down to this line through joint reductions in tariff levels would be Pareto improving, just as in the Prisoner's Dilemma.

Let us assume, therefore, without modeling it explicitly, that the two states agree on a treaty for reducing their tariffs to the agreed upon level (t_1^t, t_2^t), as illustrated in the middle of the contract curve in Figure 8.1. It is clear that this would be unenforceable in a single shot game; each side would immediately defect to their optimal tariff level, t_i^*. Could it be enforced in the repeated setting using the CTFT strategy? First, let's tailor the definition for this setting.

Definition 8.6 *The strategy* CTFT *in the Repeated Tariff Barrier game*

- *Good and bad standing are defined as follows:*
  - *both players begin the game in good standing;*
  - *a player enters bad standing if its tariff exceeds the treaty level, $t_i > t_i^t$, when the other player is in good standing;*

- a player leaves bad standing if its tariff is at or below the treaty specified level, $t_i \leq t_i^t$.
- If only the other side is in bad standing, choose the optimal tariff level $t_i = t_i^*$.
- Otherwise, choose the treaty tariff level $t_i = t_i^t$.

When is CTFT a Nash equilibrium with itself? The equilibrium payoff in the Stage game is $u_i(t_i^t, t_j^t)$, which corresponds to R in the discrete RPD game. Therefore, the payoff over time in the repeated game is

$$\frac{u_i(t_i^t, t_j^t)}{1 - \delta}$$

What deviations should we consider? Defecting in the first round to the ideal tariff level would maximize the short-term payoff, leading to a payoff of $u_i(t_i^*, t_j^t)$ in that round, corresponding to T in the discrete RPD. In the next round, it would be punished by the other side, leading to a payoff of $u_i(t_i^t, t_j^*)$, corresponding to S. The long-term payoff for such a one-round deviation is the following

$$u_i(t_i^*, t_j^t) + \delta u_i(t_i^t, t_j^*) + \frac{\delta^2}{1 - \delta} u_i(t_i^t, t_j^t)$$

The equilibrium beats the defection if

$$(1 + \delta) u_i(t_i^t, t_j^t) \geq u_i(t_i^*, t_j^t) + \delta u_i(t_i^t, t_j^*)$$

which can be solved for a constraint on the discount factor

$$\delta \geq \frac{u_i(t_i^*, t_j^t) - u_i(t_i^t, t_j^t)}{u_i(t_i^t, t_j^t) - u_i(t_i^t, t_j^*)} \tag{8.8}$$

This condition is the same as that found in Equation (8.5). This shows that even with a continuous strategy space, there is a natural equilibrium involving an arbitrarily specified treaty that looks much like the dichotomous RPD models. If states can agree upon a treaty, they will be able to enforce it with similar strategies. Of course, we have abstracted away from the negotiation phase which produces the treaty, as well as any noise that might complicate the task of identifying whether the other side has defected or not. More advanced models address these complications (Fearon 1998a, Downs and Rocke 1990, Bednar 2006, Schultz 2010).

8.8 The folk theorem and multiple equilibria

If the players value future payoffs sufficiently, we have seen that both Grim Trigger and CTFT are subgame perfect equilibria in a RPD. Both of them produce the same result along the equilibrium path: mutual cooperation forever. As it turns out, there are other equilibria as well, many of which yield different payoffs than simply the present value of perpetual mutual cooperation. The "Folk Theorem," so named because it first circulated as a widely known but unpublished result, proves that any payoff pair that is at least as good as the player's min–max payoffs can be sustained by suitable strategies in equilibrium (McCarty and Meirowitz 2006, 258–263). This result is certainly interesting theoretically; however, applied work typically focuses on simple equilibria that yield payoffs on the Pareto frontier and involve simple symmetrical behavior, such as mutual cooperation. States may bargain over the ultimate equilibrium, which may produce a game with a more focused prediction.

8.9 Empirical investigations

There is a large empirical literature on cooperation in repeated Prisoner's Dilemma settings, Tit for Tat, and the general subject of reciprocity. On the security side, Goldstein and Freeman (1990) investigate the US–Soviet–Chinese relationship by looking at events data coded from journalistic sources and scaled on a conflict to cooperation scale. They look for evidence of reciprocity using vector autoregression. They find evidence of reciprocity in each dyad. Goldstein and colleagues also find reciprocity in some relationships in the Middle East (Goldstein *et al.* 2001). Goldstein and Pevehouse (1997) analyze cooperation among participants in the Bosnian conflict in the early 1990s and find that Serbs cooperated towards Bosnians after being punished by NATO, what they call inverse triangular reciprocity. What this seems to highlight, however, is that the repeated Prisoner's Dilemma model is probably not the correct one for what is essentially a long-term bargaining process, as Fearon (1998a) pointed out. NATO was engaged in coercive bargaining by punishing the Serbs in an effort to get them to cease their attacks in Bosnia. As I discussed earlier, the repeated PD is a poor model of bargaining, and we must be careful to distinguish conceptually and empirically between bargaining failure and defection in a PD setting.[10]

On the political economy side there is a debate about the importance of reciprocity in enforcing international agreements. The "managerial school" argues that most states wish to abide by their international agreements and so do not need, or often use, punishment strategies such as Tit for Tat (Chayes and Chayes 1993). Downs *et al.* (1996) argue that states do mostly comply with their commitments, but that this is because they negotiate such minimal agreements that there is really very little real cooperation, in the sense of states doing something that they would not have otherwise done. Issue linkage has also been investigated in the RPD framework (McGinnis 1986, Lohmann 1997).

---

[10] For other analyses along these lines see Rajmaira (1997).

8.10 Conclusion

Cooperation is possible in the Repeated Prisoner's Dilemma if the shadow of the future is long enough and if players play appropriate strategies that punish defections but do not produce cycles of retaliation. This insight is extremely pervasive in international relations and has led to a large body of literature examining cooperation from many angles and in many issue areas. Of course, caring about the future does not always promote cooperation. Fearon pointed out that the more actors care about the future the harder they bargain – and prolonged bargaining can be extremely costly (Fearon 1998a). Concern for the future could even motivate preventive war. In Chapter 5, I did not explicitly discount the payoffs of the second round. If we do this, we can easily show that preventive war becomes more attractive the more future payoffs are valued. War in the present is a temporary cost paid to secure a better future than would otherwise be the case. The more we care about the future, the more we are willing to pay the cost in the present. Thus, if we think of war as an investment that pays dividends in the future, a long shadow of the future would promote war. The shadow of the future can cut both ways. Careful attention to the context is necessary to determine whether temporary costs are followed by future benefits, or temporary benefits are followed by future costs. For situations in the latter category, the RPD model shows how concern for the future should promote cooperation.

EXERCISES

8.1 Consider a RPD game as illustrated in Table 8.6. Consider a potential equilibrium in which both players play Contrite Tit for Tat.

Table 8.6 The Prisoner's Dilemma

		Player 2 Cooperate	Player 2 Defect
Player 1	Cooperate	R, R	S, T
	Defect	T, S	P, P

1. Show under what conditions a deviation consisting of defecting twice in a row (and then returning to CTFT) is not profitable. (Do not bother solving the quadratic equation, just express it in terms of something needs to be bigger than $T - R$.)
2. Show under what conditions a deviation consisting of defecting n times in a row (and then returning to CTFT) is not profitable.
3. How do these conditions compare with those that ensure that a one-round defection and deviating to All Defect are not profitable?

8.2 Consider a RPD game as illustrated in Table 8.6. Consider a "slow time" version of the game in which it takes two rounds to discover what the other side has done, and every choice to cooperate or defect lasts for two rounds. Posit a potential equilibrium in which both players play Contrite Tit for Tat. Describe the conditions under which a player in bad standing has an incentive to play CTFT rather than defect for one more round, when the other player is expected to play CTFT and is currently:

1. in good standing.
2. in bad standing.

9 Diplomacy and signaling

COMMUNICATION is an important aspect of international relations. While diplomacy goes back to antiquity, the institution of diplomacy as we know it was developed during the Italian Renaissance to facilitate communication between states (Nicolson 1954). We have already seen how private information can lead to conflict, and we, therefore, have a convincing rationale for how communication could prevent conflict. This chapter will introduce the topic of communication in international relations. First, I will discuss a class of models in which the communication is costless, so it is designed to represent ordinary verbal communication such as diplomacy in which the parties may lie if it suits their interests with no direct penalty, other than what the strategic situation they are in provides. These models are denoted "cheap talk" models in economics. We will see that there are limits to the effectiveness of cheap talk in dealing with situations in which the players have conflicting interests. In some cases, therefore, states resort to "costly signals," in which the means of communication have direct costs attached. Examples include threats that invoke a state or leader's reputation or domestic job security and mobilization of military power and engaging in actions that generate a risk of war.

9.1 Communication in international relations

The study of communication and signaling in international relations has a long history. An eighteenth-century French diplomat, François de Callières, wrote a treatise on diplomacy that continues to be read today (de Callières 1994). International relations as a discipline grew out of the study of diplomatic history and international law (Nicolson, 1939). Influential works in the field focused heavily on diplomatic maneuverings and included case studies of important diplomatic conferences such as the Congress of Vienna that followed the Napoleonic wars (Taylor 1954, Kissinger 1954).

Schelling pioneered the analysis of communication in the context of international bargaining with a particular focus on how to make threats and commitments credible to adversaries when they might have reason to doubt that a state would fulfill them (Schelling 1960, 1966). In particular, with the advent of nuclear weapons, if not before, war between the superpowers had become extremely costly, such as to greatly outweigh the stakes of almost any conflict that might arise between them. In such a context, there is good reason to suspect that a state would prefer to surrender a stake rather than fight a nuclear war over it. However, since this can be said of both sides, a Chicken-like dynamic arises in which each side attempts to leave the other the last chance to avoid war. Schelling pioneered insights such as the potential utility of being thought mad, or at least mad enough to risk nuclear war, and the use of trip wires, or token deployments that will not be militarily useful, but would make it impossible not to fight back if they were overrun. Jervis (1970) pioneered the distinction between what he called "signals" that could be manipulated and hence may not be credible, and "indices" that are either not manipulable or too costly to manipulate, and hence carry inherent credibility.

The game theoretic literature in international relations began to turn its attention to communication when it began considering incomplete information games in the late 1980s. The distinction between cheap talk and costly signals had developed in economics at this point and was imported into political science (Farrell and Rabin 1996). Iida (1993a) and Morrow (1994) developed cheap talk models in which states attempted to communicate about matters of shared uncertainty so as to better coordinate their activities, but their ability to do so was weakened as their preferences diverged, or were thought likely to diverge. In crisis bargaining models, where states are assumed to have sharply divergent preferences, states "escalate" or fail to concede the good in dispute, and that serves as a costly signal because it generates delay in reaching an agreement and possibly an increased risk of war (Powell 1990). Fearon (1994) introduced the concept of *audience costs* in a similar model in which escalation increased the penalty a state would pay if it ultimately backed down. Fearon argued that domestic audiences would punish the leader for escalating and then backing down, and this concept led to a number of attempts to clarify why and when they would do so (Smith 1998, Schultz 1998, 2001a, Tarar and Leventoglu 2009). A variety of challenges have arisen in attempting to establish the existence of audience costs (Snyder and Borghard 2011), although they appear to exist in experimental settings (Schultz 2001b, Tomz 2007, Trager and Vavreck 2011, Levendusky and Horowitz 2012). International audiences may also punish lying (Sartori 2002).

The claim that cheap talk cannot be useful in bargaining contexts where states have strongly opposed preferences has led to a growing literature pushing back and noting that in fact states do use cheap talk in such contexts and it seems to matter. Trager (2010) presents a model showing that if the state receiving the signal can take hostile steps that injure the sending state, then threatening cheap talk may be credible because it may cause the receiving state to harm the first and, therefore, be indirectly costly.[1]

Fearon (1997) also introduced the distinction between *sunk cost* signals and *tying hands* signals. Sunk cost signals are immediately costly to make, regardless of what else happens in the interaction. The simplest form of sunk cost signal is analogous to burning money, destroying value in a way that achieves no other purpose (Austen-Smith and Banks 2000). Tying hands signals are costly only if the other state challenges and the state sending the signal then backs down. In reality, as he acknowledges, most examples of costly signals involve both sinking costs and tying hands at least to some extent. For instance, military mobilization or arms buildups can be used to signal strength and resolve, while at the same time actually producing strength and resolve (Jervis 1976, Slantchev 2005, 2011). This has the effect of conveying a willingness to fight and improving the payoff if it comes to war.

In what follows, I will first briefly discuss the theory of how beliefs are updated in response to new information. Then I present a model of cheap talk in the context of states deliberating over whether to ratify a treaty. Then I will shift to a crisis bargaining context and examine a model where states can invoke audience costs by making a public threat. In each case, we will see what makes communication possible in equilibrium and how it can help states coordinate their interests.

9.2 Updating beliefs and Bayes' Rule

In order to study how communication can affect beliefs, we must first understand how new information in general should affect beliefs. Probability theory, in particular Bayes' Rule, provides the key.

The basic intuition can be seen in a simple example. A "king cake" is a cake with a small figurine baked in with the idea that someone will find it in their piece. If there are eight equal sized pieces and the figurine is randomly distributed, then each of the eight pieces has a $\frac{1}{8}$ chance of having the figurine. Let's say the group of eight sit down to eat, but decide to have each person eat their cake in turn to see who has the figurine. After the first person has eaten their cake and found nothing, what is the chance it is in one of the remaining pieces? Intuition suggests, and the laws of probability confirm, that it is just $\frac{1}{7}$ since there are seven remaining pieces and each is equally likely. Another way of arriving at this is to divide the prior belief, $\frac{1}{8}$, by the total remaining prior probability of each of the pieces, as follows

---

[1] See Kurizaki (2007) for a model arguing that secret communication can be more efficient than public communication.

$$\frac{\frac{1}{8}}{\frac{1}{8}+\frac{1}{8}+\frac{1}{8}+\frac{1}{8}+\frac{1}{8}+\frac{1}{8}+\frac{1}{8}} = \frac{\frac{1}{8}}{\frac{7}{8}} = \frac{1}{7}$$

The idea is to renormalize the likelihoods based on the smaller set of remaining possibilities.

A more general formula applies when the pieces of cake are of unequal sizes, and hence unequal likelihoods of having the figurine. Let $L = l_1, l_2, l_3, \ldots, l_n$ represent the likelihoods that the king is in each of n pieces, such that $l_i \in [0, 1], \forall i$ and $\sum_i l_i = 1$. Let's say we have learned that it is not in piece j. What is the new likelihood that it is in piece i? The following formula gives the answer

$$\frac{l_i}{\sum_{-j} l_i} \tag{9.1}$$

The numerator is just the prior likelihood that it was in piece i. The denominator is the sum of the remaining likelihoods, not counting l_j, which has been eliminated.

This formula can be extended to the case of continuous probability distributions as well. For instance, consider a probability density over the positive reals, $f(x)$, as illustrated in Figure 9.1. There will be an associated cumulative density, $F(x) = \int_0^x f(y) dy$, interpreted as the area under the curve from 0 up to x, and since we know that all probability distributions must sum to 1, we know that as x increases, $F(x)$ converges to 1. Furthermore, the area to the left of any point, say T_1, is $F(T_1)$, and the area to the right is $1 - F(T_1)$.

Now let's say that we are interested in the probability that x exceeds the second threshold, T_2, which we can write as $P(x \geq T_2)$. Through some means, we have been informed that x is certainly above the first threshold, T_1. The likelihood that $x > T_2$ given that $x > T_1$, can be written as $P(x > T_2 | x > T_1)$ in the conditional probability notation. The prior probability that $x > T_2$ is $1 - F(T_2)$, and the prior probability that $x > T_1$ is just $1 - F(T_1)$. Using the same logic as in the discrete probability case, we know the updated likelihood that $x > T_2$ is the following

$$P(x > T_2 | x > T_1) = \frac{1 - F(T_2)}{1 - F(T_1)} \tag{9.2}$$

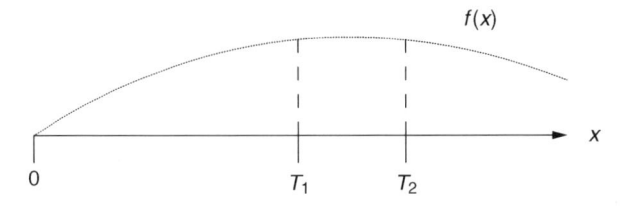

Figure 9.1 Bayes' Rule with continuous probability

9.2 UPDATING BELIEFS AND BAYES' RULE

Graphically, this is the area under the curve to the right of T_2 divided by the area to the right of T_1. This result is useful in games with continuous types where there are thresholds separating types that pursue different strategies, as in the Costly Signaling game considered below.

Another way of looking at the problem is to think about how likely the new information would be depending on whether the question we are interested in is answered one way or another. For instance, let's say one state is attempting to determine the "type" of another state, where the type could be "good" or "bad." Good types make up one half of the population, bad types the other half. They are playing a game in which they may cooperate or defect. Good types defect only when forced to by domestic factors, which happens with probability $\frac{1}{4}$. Bad types defect every time. Let's say the state has observed a defection. What should it believe about the likelihood that it faces a good type?

Let A stand for the other player being good. "Not A," or $\neg A$ stands for the other player being bad. We know that the prior probability of being good is one half, so $P(A) = \frac{1}{2}$ and $P(\neg A) = \frac{1}{2}$. Let B stand for seeing a defection. The likelihood of seeing a defection if the other side is good is $\frac{1}{4}$, so in conditional probability notation, $P(B|A) = \frac{1}{4}$. The likelihood of seeing a defection if the other side is bad is $P(B|\neg A) = 1$. With these ingredients, Bayes' Rule tells us that the posterior, or updated, belief that the other side is good, having observed a defection, is given by the following formula

$$P(A|B) = \frac{P(B|A)p(A)}{P(B|A)p(A) + P(B|\neg A)P(\neg A)} \tag{9.3}$$

In the numerator, we have the likelihood that B would be observed if A was the case times the prior likelihood that A is the case, and in the denominator we have this quantity again plus the likelihood that B would be observed if A was not the case times the prior probability that A is not the case. Plugging in the numbers from the example just discussed, we get the following

$$P(A|B) = \frac{\frac{1}{4} \times \frac{1}{2}}{\frac{1}{4} \times \frac{1}{2} + 1 \times \frac{1}{2}} = \frac{\frac{1}{8}}{\frac{5}{8}} = \frac{1}{5} = 0.2$$

This tells us that the probability that the other side is the good type is now only 20%, down from 50%. The defection makes us more suspicious of the other side because bad types are more likely to defect than good types.

What if we observed cooperation instead? Intuition suggests that since only good types cooperate, we should become certain that the other side is good. If we reinterpret B to mean observing cooperation, we can plug in the numbers as follows

$$P(A|B) = \frac{\frac{3}{4} \times \frac{1}{2}}{\frac{3}{4} \times \frac{1}{2} + 0 \times \frac{1}{2}} = \frac{\frac{3}{8}}{\frac{3}{8}} = 1$$

Bayes' Rule provides the answer our intuition had already arrived at.

The denominator in Equation (9.3) is equivalent to the total likelihood of observing B, so the formula can be expressed in an alternative format as follows

$$P(A|B) = P(B|A)\frac{P(A)}{P(B)} \qquad (9.4)$$

Note, this is a generalization of the formulas given above in Equations (9.1) and (9.2) for the discrete and continuous probability cases, in which we add an additional term, $P(B|A)$. In the examples above, $P(B|A) = 1$, but it may not always be.

9.3 Cheap talk and diplomacy

The point of communication is to convey information from someone who has it to someone who does not. The first person tells the second something. Should the second person believe it? Should the second person act on it? This is the kind of situation that cheap talk models were developed to study. The knowledgeable party is often called the *sender*, while the uninformed party is the *receiver*. The simplest, most general cheap talk model has the sender observing the value of a random variable and then sending a message to the receiver. The receiver then takes an action that affects both his own and the sender's payoffs. We will complicate this simple picture slightly to increase the applicability to a common international relations event: securing agreement on a treaty or other arrangement to act jointly on some issue.

9.3.1 The Treaty game

Let's consider a group of countries contemplating the problem of climate change (Kydd 2010). A treaty has been proposed that would impose costs c_i on member states by constraining carbon emissions, and would have some positive benefit b by reducing the global warming problem. The basic normal form game is illustrated in Table 9.1. I assume for simplicity that the treaty only goes into effect if both sides support it; if one or both sides oppose it, then the status quo remains in place, with payoffs of $0, 0$.

With complete information, the equilibria in the game are quite simple. Both sides opposing is always an equilibrium, since if only one side supports the treaty it does not pass, and the status quo obtains. Both sides supporting the treaty can be an equilibrium if

$$b \geq \max_i(c_i) \qquad (9.5)$$

9.3 CHEAP TALK AND DIPLOMACY

Table 9.1 The Treaty game

		State 2 Oppose	State 2 Support
State 1	Oppose	0, 0	0, 0
	Support	0, 0	$b - c_1, b - c_2$

One side supporting while the other side opposes can be an equilibrium, so long as the opposing side finds the costs outweigh the benefits, $b < c_i$. But if both sides find the benefits outweigh the costs, then a shift to the treaty is possible in equilibrium, and this equilibrium Pareto dominates the alternative, in which neither side supports the treaty, so the game is similar to an Assurance game from Chapter 3.

Now consider how uncertainty might influence the possible equilibria in the game. Imagine that a debate has erupted concerning the science, and in particular as to whether climate change is a serious problem that justifies the proposed treaty or not. Formally, let there be a set of possible *states of the world*, Ω, with two members, $\Omega = \{\omega_1, \omega_2\}$. If ω_1 is true, then climate change is a less serious problem, and if ω_2 is true, then climate change is more serious. So if we rank $\omega_1 < \omega_2$, then ω is an indicator of the seriousness of climate change. Let the benefit of cooperation through the climate treaty be a function of the state of the world, $b(\omega)$. Since higher ω corresponds to the worse climate change, assume that the benefit of taking action increases with ω

$$0 < b(\omega_1) < b(\omega_2) \tag{9.6}$$

I assume that the treaty is better than 0, even if climate change is not a big problem, to reflect the idea that environmentalists might like the treaty for other reasons; for instance it may lower pollution or reduce other environmental externalities. Let's further assume that state 2 would want to implement the climate change treaty if it were certain that climate change was real and not if it were not.

$$0 < b(\omega_1) < c_2 < b(\omega_2) \tag{9.7}$$

This implies that state 2's actions will be contingent on its beliefs. State 2 is persuadable – it will at least in theory respond to new information. The question then becomes: Under what conditions will this work? For state 1, we will assume only that the costs are non-negative, $c_1 \geq 0$. This leads to three possibilities. First, it could be that $c_1 < b(\omega_1)$, so state 1 would prefer to implement the treaty even if global warming were not a serious problem. I call these types the environmentalists. Second, it could be that $c_1 \in [b(\omega_1), b(\omega_2)]$, in which case state 1's preference for the treaty will hinge

```
Environmentalists          Oil lobby
       |                       |
       |   Open-minded types   |
       |   ┌───────────────┐   |
       ▼   │               │   ▼
   ┌───┬───┴───┬───────┬───┴───┬──────▶ c₁
   0  b(ω₁)   c₂     b(ω₂)
```

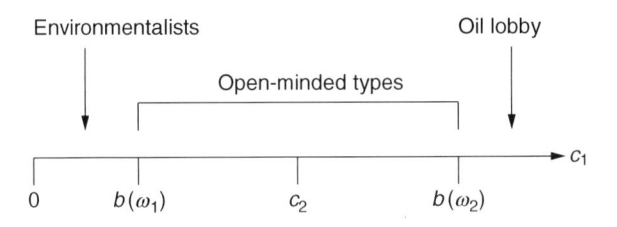

Figure 9.2 Types in the Treaty game

on whether global warming is serious or not. I call these types the open-minded types, because if they had adequate information, they would act on it. Finally, it could be that $c_1 > b(\omega_2)$, in which case state 1 finds the cost of the treaty so great it would not support it even if global warming were serious. I call these types the oil lobby.

These types are illustrated in Figure 9.2. The axis c_1 is state 1's costs for implementing the treaty. Environmentalists have low costs, open-minded types have middling costs, and the oil lobby has high costs. State 2's costs, c_2, are in the open-minded range.

To represent the states' uncertainty about the state of the world, let the prior probability that climate change is serious be denoted $P(\omega_2)$, so the corresponding likelihood that climate change is less serious is $P(\omega_1) = 1 - P(\omega_2)$. Note, so far this is a shared uncertainty.

When will the states be willing to cooperate in the game with uncertainty over global warming? The expected utility of the treaty is $P(\omega_1)b(\omega_1) + P(\omega_2)b(\omega_2) - c_i$, which is positive for both states when

$$P(\omega_1)b(\omega_1) + P(\omega_2)b(\omega_2) \geq \max_i(c_i) \tag{9.8}$$

When this holds, then both sides will find the treaty worthwhile, even though there is a risk that global warming is not serious, so there will be an equilibrium in which both sides support the treaty. Another way to express this result is to think in terms of how likely global warming is to be a problem, $P(\omega_2)$. Each state will have a critical threshold for this belief, over which it will be willing to support the treaty, defined as follows

$$P_i^*(\omega_2) \equiv \frac{c_i - b(\omega_1)}{b(\omega_2) - b(\omega_1)} \tag{9.9}$$

Note, given the assumption about state 2's preferences embodied in Equation (9.7), state 2's critical belief will be between 0 and 1, $P_2^*(\omega_2) \in (0, 1)$, so that if state 2 were certain, one way or the other it would act accordingly. As far as state 1 is concerned, for the environmentalists this will be negative, so they will always support the treaty, and for the oil lobby it will be greater than 1, so they will always oppose the treaty. Only the open-minded types with a middling cost for the treaty will have a critical belief between 0 and 1, and so will be willing to shift their behavior depending on their beliefs.

Table 9.2 The truthful communication equilibrium with scientific certainty

State 1	If ρ_1, say μ_1; if ρ_2, say μ_2
	If ρ_1, oppose; if ρ_2, support
State 2	If μ_1, oppose; if μ_2, support
Conditions	$b(\omega_1) \leq c_1 \leq b(\omega_2)$

9.3.2 Diplomacy with scientific certainty

So far, however, we have modeled uncertainty but not communication. To bring communication into the picture, let's assume that state 1 has a climate science team that is studying the problem. They come up with a report that says either that climate change is serious, or that it is not. We model this by assuming that state 1 receives a report from nature about the true state of the world. The report is either ρ_1, meaning that the true state is ω_1, or ρ_2 corresponding to ω_2. For now, we assume that these reports are perfectly accurate, so the scientists are able to discover with certainty what the true state of the world is. State 1's posterior beliefs after receiving the ρ_1 report are, therefore, that global warming is not happening, $P_1(\omega_2|\rho_1) = 0$, whereas if state 1 gets the ρ_2 report, its belief is that global warming is happening for sure, $P_1(\omega_2|\rho_2) = 1$, where the subscripts indicate the state that has those beliefs.

Next, we posit a communication opportunity for state 1 before the states have to support or oppose the treaty. Let state 1 have a move in which it can say μ_1 or μ_2, corresponding to ω_1 and ω_2. We assume that state 2 receives the message from state 1 but does not have access to the underlying report. Honest communication would have state 1 send the μ_1 message when in receipt of the ρ_1 report, and the μ_2 message upon receipt of the ρ_2 report. In this case, state 2's posterior beliefs would be the same as state 1's, so that $P_2(\omega_2|\mu_1) = P_1(\omega_2|\rho_1) = 0$, and $P_2(\omega_2|\mu_2) = P_1(\omega_2|\rho_2) = 1$.

When is honest communication possible in an equilibrium of the modified game? Consider the equilibrium as described in Table 9.2. In this equilibrium, state 1 reports μ_1 if the report says ρ_1 and μ_2 after receiving the ρ_2 report, thereby honestly revealing what report it received. State 2, therefore, updates its beliefs to reflect this honest communication, and its beliefs become the same as state 1. State 1 then supports the treaty if the report is ρ_2, and opposes it otherwise. State 2 supports the treaty if it receives the μ_2 message, and opposes it otherwise. Note, off the equilibrium path if the report is ρ_1 but state 1 says μ_2, or if the report is ρ_2 but state 1 says μ_1, one state will oppose the treaty, resulting in the status quo payoffs (of 0) for both states.

Under what conditions is this equilibrium possible? We have assumed that state 2 is open minded. Since $c_2 \in (b(\omega_1), b(\omega_2))$, under honest communication, state 2 will be willing to support the treaty after hearing the μ_2 message and oppose it after hearing the μ_1 message. Another way of looking at this is to note that state 2's critical belief is $P_i^*(\omega_2) \in [0, 1]$, so certainty either way will change its behavior. Therefore, state 2 will be willing to act on an honest message from state 1 as the equilibrium specifies.

Now consider whether state 1 has an incentive to follow its strategy. First, consider the case where $c_1 < b(\omega_1)$, so state 1 is an environmentalist who supports the treaty even if global warming is not a big problem. If state 1 gets the ρ_2 report, saying that global warming is a problem, does it have an incentive to honestly communicate this and then support the treaty? Saying μ_2 causes state 2 to support the treaty, in which case if state 1 supports the treaty, it will go into effect for a payoff of $b(\omega_2) - c_1$, which is positive for the environmentalist type. So this checks out. However, what if state 1 gets the ρ_1 report saying that global warming is not so serious? In this case, sending the μ_1 message causes state 2 to not support the treaty for a payoff of 0, whereas lying would cause state 2 to support the treaty. State 1 could then deviate again and support the treaty, giving a payoff of $b(\omega_1) - c_1$, which, for environmentalists, is also greater than 0. Therefore, state 1 has an incentive to claim that the report says global warming is a problem even if it says the opposite, thereby getting state 2 to support the treaty, and then support it itself. Thus environmentalist state 1 has no incentive to send the μ_1 signal and oppose the treaty. Note, this unwillingness to send the μ_1 signal also implies that the μ_2 signal cannot be trusted. Since state 1 will send the μ_2 signal with certainty, regardless of its information, state 2 will rationally not update its beliefs. Its posterior belief after receiving the μ_2 message is the same as the prior belief

$$P_2(\omega_2|\mu_2) = \frac{1 \times P(\omega_2)}{1 \times P(\omega_2) + 1 \times (1 - P(\omega_2))} = P(\omega_2)$$

Next, consider the oil lobby type. If an oil industry type gets the ρ_1 report, conveying this to state 2 gets state 2 to not support the treaty, for a payoff of 0, which beats any deviation. However, if the report is ρ_2, the equilibrium requires state 1 to be honest, which would convince state 2 to support the treaty, and then to support the treaty itself. However, for the oil lobby type, the treaty's value is negative even when global warming is a serious problem, so state 1 will have an incentive to deviate in this case, either by lying or by not supporting the treaty after telling the truth.

Finally, consider the open-minded type of state 1, for whom $c_1 \in (b(\omega_1), b(\omega_2))$. For this type, if the report says ρ_1, then conveying this honestly and not supporting the treaty results in a payoff of 0, which beats $b(\omega_1) - c_1$ from the treaty. If the report says ρ_2, then conveying this honestly and supporting the treaty results in a payoff of $b(\omega_2) - c_1$, which beats 0, which would be the payoff for lying or not supporting the treaty. Therefore, if state 1 is open minded, it will have an incentive to honestly communicate with state 2 about the severity of global warming and to support a treaty to deal with the problem if global warming is serious.[2]

9.3.3 Diplomacy with scientific uncertainty

It would be ideal if scientific reports could reach the truth with certainty, but this is rarely the case. More practically, science can serve to refine our beliefs, if not perfect them. To model this, we can posit that the report is more likely to be right than wrong, but has an $\epsilon \in (0, 0.5)$ chance of being in error. After receiving the report, state 1 will update its beliefs about the likelihood that climate change is serious, but the beliefs will no longer move to certainty. From Bayes' Rule, the posterior probability that climate change is serious after the ρ_1 report is

$$P_1(w_2|\rho_1) = \frac{\epsilon P(w_2)}{\epsilon P(w_2) + (1-\epsilon)(1-P(w_2))} \tag{9.10}$$

and after receiving the ρ_2 report it is

$$P_1(w_2|\rho_2) = \frac{(1-\epsilon)P(w_2)}{(1-\epsilon)P(w_2) + \epsilon(1-P(w_2))} \tag{9.11}$$

We can see that state 1 will become less convinced that global warming is real after a negative report and more convinced after a positive one, that is

$$P_1(w_2|\rho_1) < P(w_2) < P_1(w_2|\rho_2) \tag{9.12}$$

Note, that as the likelihood that the report is in error converges to 0, these beliefs converge to 0 and 1, respectively. That is, as the report becomes more certain, state 1 will be more certain after receiving it, either that global warming is real or that it is not worth bothering about.

How does scientific uncertainty change the game? First, not all of the previously open-minded types in the middle will actually be open minded, in the sense of being willing to condition their behavior on the report. Since the report has become less certain, types close to the edges of either environmentalism or the oil lobby will start to disregard it. This is illustrated in Figure 9.3. I relabel the open-minded types "potentially open minded" to reflect the fact that they would be open minded if the report were sufficiently accurate (ϵ sufficiently low). However, there are two new cut-off points, c_1^l and c_1^h, that bound the "actually open-minded" types who will be willing

---

[2] An alternative type of equilibrium, possible regardless of the parameter values, is the so-called *babbling equilibrium*. As the name suggests, the sending state does not condition its communication on its information, and the receiving state does not condition its behavior on the sender's communication. In this case, the equilibrium payoff for any babbling equilibrium is 0 if the prior belief falls below the critical threshold required for cooperation for both states. But cooperation is possible if the prior exceeds the threshold for state 2, and state 1 is open minded and receives the μ_2 signal.

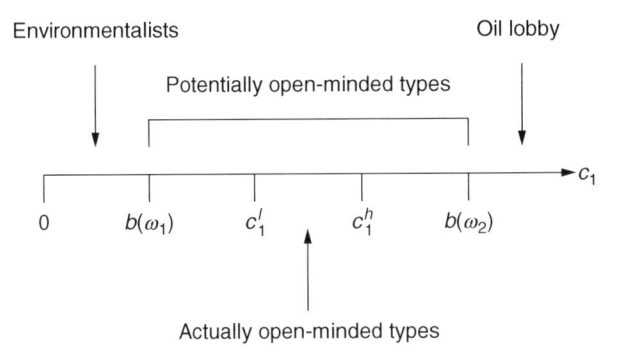

Figure 9.3 Cost cutoff points with scientific uncertainty

to condition their behavior on the report, given how accurate it actually is. Players with costs below c_1^l prefer the treaty no matter what the report says, types with costs above c_1^h prefer inaction to the treaty regardless of the report, and types in the middle will be willing to condition their behavior on the report. The distance between c_1^l and c_1^h is increasing in the accuracy of the report. As ϵ shrinks, c_1^l falls and c_1^h rises because of the effects on the posterior beliefs, until in the limit as ϵ goes to 0 these become equal to $b(\omega_1)$ and $b(\omega_2)$, respectively.

How do we solve for these these new cutoff points? The lower threshold, c_1^l, is the level of costs that makes state 1 indifferent between the treaty and the status quo after receiving the ρ_1 signal that global warming is not a problem. Any lower, and the state would support the treaty no matter what. Thus, it is the level of c_1 such that $P_1^*(\omega_2) = P_1(\omega_2|\rho_1)$ which can be solved as follows

$$P_1^*(\omega_2) = P_1(\omega_2|\rho_1)$$

$$\frac{c_1 - b(\omega_1)}{b(\omega_2) - b(\omega_1)} = P_1(\omega_2|\rho_1)$$

$$c_1^l = (b(\omega_2) - b(\omega_1))P_1(\omega_2|\rho_1) + b(\omega_1)$$

$$c_1^l = P_1(\omega_2|\rho_1)b(\omega_2) + (1 - P_1(\omega_2|\rho_1))b(\omega_1)$$

The upper cutoff point is the level of costs that makes state 1 indifferent between the treaty and the status quo having received the ρ_2 signal that global warming is serious. Any higher and the state would oppose the treaty no matter what. Therefore, c_1^h is the level of c_1 such that $P_1^*(\omega_2) = P_1(\omega_2|\rho_2)$. Solving for c_1^h, we get the following,

$$P_1^*(\omega_2) = P_1(\omega_2|\rho_2)$$

$$\frac{c_1 - b(\omega_1)}{b(\omega_2) - b(\omega_1)} = P_1(\omega_2|\rho_2)$$

$$c_1^h = (b(\omega_2) - b(\omega_1))P_1(\omega_2|\rho_1) + b(\omega_1)$$

$$c_1^h = P_1(\omega_2|\rho_2)b(\omega_2) + (1 - P_1(\omega_2|\rho_2))b(\omega_1)$$

9.3 CHEAP TALK AND DIPLOMACY

Table 9.3 The truthful communication equilibrium with scientific uncertainty

State 1	If ρ_1, say μ_1; if ρ_2, say μ_2
	If ρ_1, oppose; if ρ_2, support
State 2	If μ_1, oppose; if μ_2, support
Conditions	$P(\omega_2\|\rho_1) < P_i^*(\omega_2) < P(\omega_2\|\rho_2)$
	$c_i^l < c_i < c_i^h.$

Note that, as anticipated, $b(\omega_1) < c_1^l < c_1^h < b(\omega_2)$, because the ρ_2 signal increases the likelihood of the higher level of benefits.

Now we can address the key question: Can a truth-telling equilibrium such as the one we found with scientific certainty be supported in an environment of scientific uncertainty? The answer is yes, but only for the actually open-minded types, given the level of accuracy of the report. The equilibrium is shown in Table 9.3.

With honest communication, state 2's beliefs will once again be the same as state 1's, $P_1(\omega_2|\rho_1) = P_2(\omega_2|\mu_1)$ and $P_1(\omega_2|\rho_2) = P_2(\omega_2|\mu_2)$. State 2 must condition its behavior on the signal from state 1. This means that the μ_2 signal must convince state 2 that it is worthwhile supporting the treaty and μ_1 must convince it that it is not worth it. In terms of the critical threshold, this means the following must be true

$$P_2(\omega_2|\mu_1) < P_2^*(\omega_2) < P_2(\omega_2|\mu_2) \tag{9.13}$$

Now consider state 1. First, consider the case in which state 1's science team reports that global warming is serious, ρ_2. State 1 must then report μ_2, which will convince state 2 to support the treaty. State 1 will also support the treaty, so the treaty will be implemented. Deviating by opposing the treaty or sending the wrong message will result in a payoff of 0. For this strategy to be worthwhile, it must be the case that the posterior belief after receiving the report exceeds the critical threshold for state 1, $P_1^*(\omega_2) < P_1(\omega_2|\rho_2)$, so state 1 prefers the treaty to the status quo when global warming is believed to be serious.

Next, consider the case where the scientists say global warming is not serious, ρ_1. In this case, state 1 must report μ_1 and not support the treaty, leading to a payoff of 0. Deviating to saying μ_1 and supporting the treaty or saying μ_2 and opposing it will produce the same payoff of 0. Deviating to saying μ_2 and supporting the treaty will be not worthwhile, so long as the posterior belief after getting the ρ_1 report is below the critical threshold, $P_1(\omega_2|\rho_1) < P_1^*(\omega_2)$. Putting these two conditions together we have the following

$$P_1(\omega_2|\rho_1) < P_1^*(\omega_2) < P_1(\omega_2|\rho_2) \tag{9.14}$$

This means that the truth-telling equilibrium is possible in this game so long as for both states the critical threshold of belief required to support action on global warming is between the two levels of belief that result from the scientific study of the problem. The reason telling the truth works is that once again the preferences of the sender and receiver are aligned. The sender and receiver both want to support the treaty if global warming is serious and oppose it if it is not. Therefore, they can agree to condition their actions on the science as uncovered by state 1, even though the science is not perfect.

Translating back into the cost terms, the equilibrium is supported but only in the $[c_1^l, c_1^h]$ interval, which is smaller than under scientific certainty. In the limit, if the science was worthless, $\epsilon = 0.5$, then the equilibrium would be unsupportable, and cooperation could only occur if it were supported by the prior beliefs.

9.3.4 Diplomacy with uncertainty about the sending side

Scientific uncertainty reduces the range of types for which honest communication is possible. Another impediment to communication is uncertainty about the motivations of the speaker. So far, we have assumed that the preferences of state 1 are known to state 2. What happens if we relax this assumption? What happens if state 1 may or may not have the proper incentive to be honest?

Consider a slight variation on the game just described. Let there be some uncertainty about state 1's costs for adopting the treaty. In particular, let c_1 be distributed according to the cumulative distribution, $F(c_1)$, over the positive real numbers, $\mathbb{R}^+$. This means that all the types of state 1 will be possible. Types with costs below c_1^l prefer the treaty even if they know global warming is not serious. Types with costs between c_1^l and c_1^h will support the treaty only if the data suggest it is necessary. Types above c_1^h will oppose the treaty no matter what the report says about the true state of the world. We can attach probabilities to each range of types as well. The likelihood that state 1 prefers to adopt the treaty regardless of the science is $F(c_1^l)$. The likelihood that state 1 would be willing to go with the science is $F(c_1^h) - F(c_1^l)$. Finally, the likelihood that state 1 is committed to the status quo is $1 - F(c_1^h)$.

Is honest communication possible with uncertainty over the sender's motivations? Consider the equilibrium shown in Table 9.4. State 2 once again conditions its behavior on the signal, supporting the treaty if state 1 says global warming is serious and opposing it otherwise. State 1's strategy depends on its type. Low cost types who prefer the treaty even if the report says it is not worth it will send the μ_2 message and support the treaty. High cost types who would not prefer the treaty even if they get the ρ_2 report will send the μ_1 message and oppose the treaty. Types who are willing to condition their behavior on the report play as in the last equilibrium, saying global warming is

9.3 CHEAP TALK AND DIPLOMACY

Table 9.4 The truthful communication equilibrium with uncertainty over sender's motivations

State 1	If $P_1^*(w_2) < P_1(w_2\|\rho_1)$, say μ_2 and support.
	If $P_1^*(w_2) \in [P_1(w_2\|\rho_1), P_1(w_2\|\rho_2)]$, then
	If ρ_1, say μ_1; if ρ_2, say μ_2
	If ρ_1, oppose; if ρ_2, support
	If $P_1(w_2\|\rho_2) < P_1^*(w_2)$, say μ_1 and oppose
State 2	If μ_1, oppose; if μ_2, support
Conditions	$P(w_2\|\mu_1) < P_2^*(w_2) < P(w_2\|\mu_2)$

serious and supporting the treaty if they get the ρ_2 report saying it is not worth it and opposing the treaty if they get the ρ_1 report.

When is this equilibrium possible? State 1's strategy checks out straightforwardly given the discussion of the previous equilibrium. Each type is playing a strategy that will bring about their favored outcome: low cost types will get state 2 to support the treaty, high cost types will get state 2 to oppose it and middling cost types will get state 2 to follow the signal just as they are.

The only remaining question is when state 2 will be willing to follow its strategy. The condition specified in Table 9.4 is correct, but general, state 2's critical value for belief must lie between its posterior beliefs after receiving an honest message, so that it is willing to act on the message. We need to know what are these posterior beliefs in this case, given that the signal has been degraded by uncertainty about the sender's motivations?

So let us examine state 2's posterior beliefs after receiving state 1's message. If w_2 is the case, state 1 will send the μ_1 message if it has high costs, probability $1 - F(c_1^h)$, or if it has medium costs and got the ρ_1 report, which would be an error and hence have probability ϵ. The total likelihood is, therefore, $1 - F(c_1^h) + (F(c_1^h) - F(c_1^l))\epsilon$. Conversely, if w_1 is the case, state 1 will send the μ_1 message when it has high costs, or if it has middling costs and got the correct report, likelihood $1 - \epsilon$, for a total likelihood of $1 - F(c_1^h) + (F(c_1^h) - F(c_1^l))(1 - \epsilon)$. Bayes' Rule says the posterior likelihood that global warming is serious after the μ_1 message is

$$P_2(w_2|\mu_1) = $$

$$\frac{(1 - F(c_1^h) + (F(c_1^h) - F(c_1^l))\epsilon)P(w_2)}{(1 - F(c_1^h) + (F(c_1^h) - F(c_1^l))\epsilon)P(w_2) + (1 - F(c_1^h) + (F(c_1^h) - F(c_1^l))(1 - \epsilon))P(w_1)}$$

Note, the more likely the state is to be the high cost type who sends the μ_1 message regardless of the report, the more the posterior belief converges to $\frac{P(w_2)}{P(w_2)+P(w_1)}$, which is equivalent to the prior belief, $P(w_2)$. This means that the signal is conveying less information, because state 1 is believed to be so heavily biased in favor of sending that signal. Conversely, if there are no high cost types, $F(c_1^h) = 1$, then this posterior belief is the same as the previous one when state 1 had middling costs for sure. As $F(c_1^h)$ decreases, the belief increases until in the limit it is equal to the prior belief.

Now consider the case where state 2 receives the μ_2 signal. It is the low cost type that is biased in favor of sending this signal. The posterior belief after the communication is

$$P_2(\omega_2|\mu_2) = \frac{(F(c_1^l) + (F(c_1^h) - F(c_1^l))(1 - \epsilon))P(\omega_2)}{(F(c_1^l) + (F(c_1^h) - F(c_1^l))(1 - \epsilon))P(\omega_2) + (F(c_1^l) + (F(c_1^h) - F(c_1^l))\epsilon)P(\omega_1)}$$

Here, if there are no low cost types, $F(c_1^l) = 0$, then this belief is equal to the one in the previous model without uncertainty over the sender's type. The bigger c_1^l, the closer this posterior belief gets to the prior belief.

The upshot is that this equilibrium is much like the one in the previous case, but the uncertainty about state 1's preferences degrades the information content of state 1's message to some extent. The bigger $F(c_1^l)$ is and the smaller $F(c_1^h)$ is, the less likely the message is to actually convey information. This further shrinks the range of types of state 2 who would be persuadable by the message. A certain amount of uncertainty about state 1's preferences is not fatal to the equilibrium, however. Honest communication can tolerate a certain amount of both scientific uncertainty about whether the information is correct or not, as well as suspicion about the motives of the communicator.

Result 9.1 *States can share information about the state of the world provided that their preferences on what to do based on the information are aligned. States that would prefer to do the same thing regardless of the state of the world cannot convey information credibly. The greater the uncertainty about the preferences of the communicating state, the less credible their information.*

9.4 Costly signals and crisis bargaining

We have seen how diplomatic communication can be undermined by uncertainty about the state of the world, diverging preferences, and uncertainty over preferences. This has led to exploration of mechanisms designed to reinforce the credibility of verbal communication. Two main mechanisms are posited as to why such threats should be credible. The first is domestic audience costs, the concept that domestic audiences will

9.4 COSTLY SIGNALS AND CRISIS BARGAINING

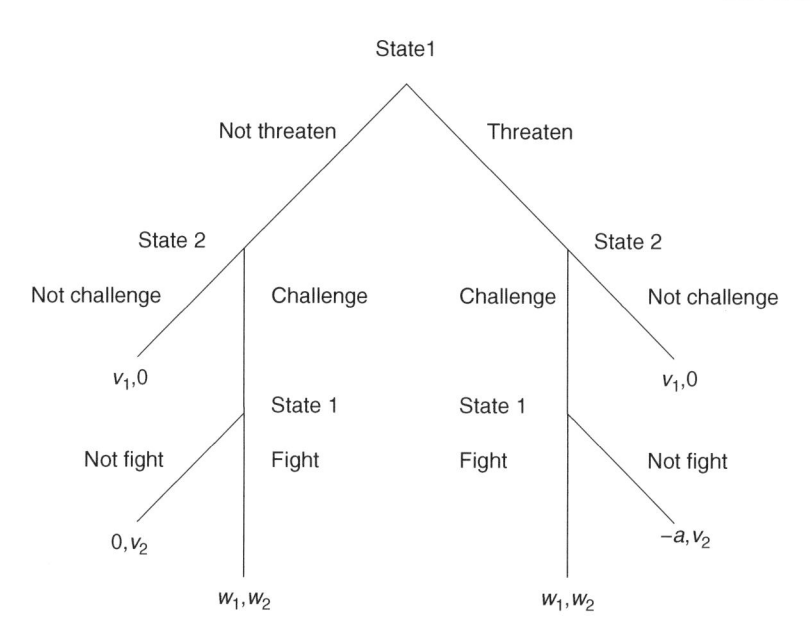

Figure 9.4 The Costly Signaling game

[Game tree: State 1 chooses Not threaten or Threaten.

Not threaten branch: State 2 chooses Not challenge ($v_1, 0$) or Challenge. If Challenge, State 1 chooses Not fight ($0, v_2$) or Fight (w_1, w_2).

Threaten branch: State 2 chooses Challenge or Not challenge ($v_1, 0$). If Challenge, State 1 chooses Fight (w_1, w_2) or Not fight ($-a, v_2$).]

punish leaders for retreating from commitments once made. This concept has been explored in an extensive literature (Fearon 1994, Smith 1998, Schultz 1998, 2001b, Tarar and Leventoglu 2009). The domestic audience cost concept faces some difficulties however. For one thing, it is unclear why domestic audiences should punish their leader for bluffing, when bluffing may be the policy that does best for the state as a whole. For another, empirically it is unclear that publics punish leaders for acting contrary to their statements, rather than contrary to the preferences of the public. That is, it is not clear that a dovish public would punish a leader for backing down after a threat, or that a hawkish public would punish a leader for fighting although previously saying he would not. A related mechanism is that of international reputation. Leaders may be honest because they value their reputation with other states for honesty abroad. If a leader were to be caught out in a bluff, this leader could be discounted in the future, so it might be worthwhile to maintain a reputation for honesty at the cost of occasionally sacrificing short-term gains that could be had by bluffing (Sartori 2002, Guisinger and Smith 2002).

Both of these forms of audience costs make communication more credible by attaching costs that are paid if a state acts contrary to its statement. Fearon (1997) calls these "tying hands" signals, to distinguish them from "sunk cost" signals in which the cost of the signal is paid up front. Because of the widespread interest in them, I will discuss a tying hands costly signaling model here.

Consider the game tree illustrated in Figure 9.4. State 1 first moves, either sending a signal of resolve or not. State 2 then has an opportunity to challenge state 1 or not.

If state 2 challenges, then state 1 has an opportunity to fight back or not. If state 2 does not challenge, then the status quo is assumed to remain in place, with payoffs v_1 for state 1 and 0 for state 2, reflecting that state 1 starts off in possession of a good in dispute worth v_i to each state. If state 2 challenges and state 1 fights back, then war is assumed to take place, with payoffs of w_1, w_2. I assume that war is a simple lottery, so $w_i = p_i v_i - c_i$. If state 2 challenges and state 1 does not resist, then state 2 gains v_2 and state 1 loses v_1. For instance, when North Korea invaded South Korea in 1950, if the US had not resisted, it would have lost the value of South Korea and the Soviet Union would have made a corresponding gain. Finally, if state 1 makes a threat, state 2 challenges, and state 1 does not fight, then state 1 suffers an audience cost from backing down on the threat, a.

9.4.1 Equilibria with complete information

We can solve the game under complete information using the subgame perfect equilibrium concept. State 1 will fight having not made a threat if $p_1 v_1 - c_1 > 0$, and having made a threat if $p_1 v_1 - c_1 > -a$. We can, therefore, distinguish three categories of state 1 differentiated by how much they value the good. Those for whom $v_1 < \frac{c_1 - a}{p_1}$ care so little for the good that they would not be willing to fight for it even if they have made a threat. Those for whom $\frac{c_1 - a}{p_1} < v_1 < \frac{c_1}{p_1}$ value the good enough to fight for it only if they have made a threat. Finally, those for whom $\frac{c_1}{p_1} < v_1$ will be willing to fight for it even if they have made no threat. Similarly, the different types of state 2 can be distinguished between those unwilling to fight rather than accept the status quo if $p_2 v_2 - c_2 < 0$, or $v_2 \leq \frac{c_2}{p_2}$, and those willing to fight rather than accept nothing, $v_2 > \frac{c_2}{p_2}$.

With these cut points in mind, we can identify seven pure strategy equilibria in the model, illustrated in Figure 9.5. The horizontal axis is state 1's valuation for the good, v_1, and the vertical axis is state 2's valuation for the good, v_2. In the description of the equilibria, S1 and S2 stand for state 1 and state 2, respectively, T stands for threaten, NT for not threaten, C for challenge, NC for not challenge, F for fight, and NF for not fight. For state 2's strategy and state 1's second move, the first entry is what is done after no threat and the second is after a threat, so C, NC means that player 2 challenges after no threat but does not challenge after a threat. In equilibrium 1, state 1 cares so little for the good that it would not fight for it even if it made a threat. If state 1 will not fight even having made the threat, then state 2 will challenge whether or not state 1 makes the threat, because it will anticipate that state 1 will not fight and so it will receive v_2, which beats the payoff for not challenging, which is 0. Given that state 2 challenges no matter what state 1 does, state 1 will prefer to not make the threat, and get 0 after backing down, rather than $-a$.

9.4 COSTLY SIGNALS AND CRISIS BARGAINING

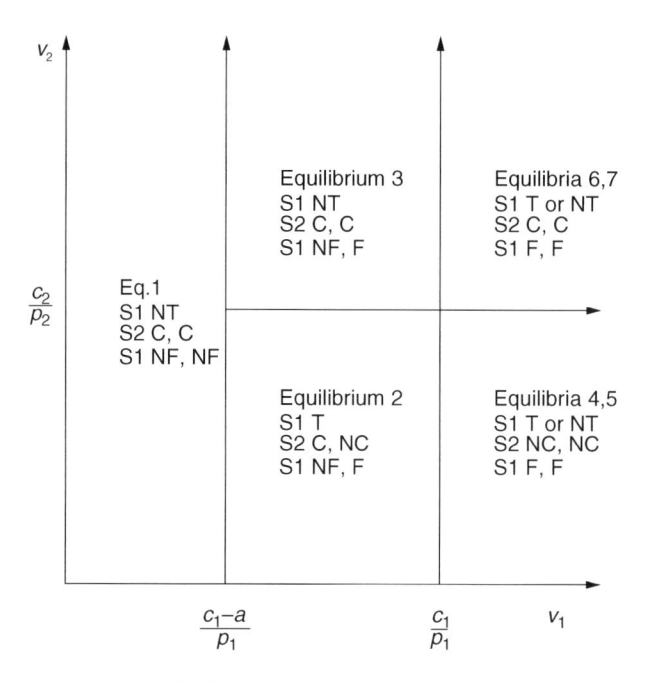

```
V₂ ↑
         │         │
         │ Equilibrium 3    │ Equilibria 6,7
         │ S1 NT            │ S1 T or NT
         │ S2 C, C          │ S2 C, C
         │ S1 NF, F         │ S1 F, F
c₂/p₂ ───┤                  │
   Eq.1  │                  │
   S1 NT │                  │
   S2 C, C│                 │
   S1 NF, NF                │
         │                  │
         │ Equilibrium 2    │ Equilibria 4,5
         │ S1 T             │ S1 T or NT
         │ S2 C, NC         │ S2 NC, NC
         │ S1 NF, F         │ S1 F, F
         │                  │
         └──────────────────┴──────────────→
                (c₁-a)/p₁      c₁/p₁       v₁
```

Figure 9.5 Costly Signaling game: complete information equilibria

If state 1 cares enough about the issue to fight but only having made the threat, then there are two cases to consider. In equilibrium 2, state 2 does not care enough about the issue to fight for it, and so will not challenge if state 1 makes a threat, but will challenge if state 1 does not make a threat. If state 2 will not challenge after a threat, then state 1 will make the threat since that will give v_1 rather than 0. In equilibrium 3, state 2 does care enough about the issue to fight for it, so it will challenge after a threat. State 1, therefore, will not make the threat because it would only serve to commit itself to fight over an issue that it would prefer not to fight over.

If state 1 will fight whether or not it made the threat, there are again two cases to consider. In equilibria 4 and 5, state 2 does not value the issue enough to fight over and, therefore, does not challenge no matter whether state 1 threatens or not. In equilibria 6 and 7, state 2 prefers to fight, so it challenges whether or not state 1 has threatened. In either case, state 1 is indifferent between threatening and not threatening because it will never incur the audience cost, since it will fight in both cases. Hence, the two versions of the equilibria here.

Note, threats are made when they can serve to commit state 1 to fighting, and when that will deter a challenge from state 2. They may also be made when they are irrelevant, that is, when state 1 would fight even without a threat. There is no possibility of bluffing here: state 1 will never make a threat and subsequently back down. There is also no communication of information, given that there is complete information to start with.

```
                        Challenge            Challenge
State 2                 Not challenge        Challenge
           ├────────────────┼──────────────────┼──────────────▶
           0                v₂*                                 v₂
```

```
                  Not threaten   Not threaten   Threaten     Threaten
                  Not fight      Not fight      Not fight    Fight
                  Not fight      Fight          Fight        Fight
State 1
(No bluff
equilibrium) ├────────┼──────────────┼──────────────┼──────────▶
             0     (c₁−a)/p₁        v₁*           c₁/p₁        v₁
```

```
                  Not threaten   Threaten      Threaten     Threaten
                  Not fight      Not fight     Not fight    Fight
                  Not fight      Not fight     Fight        Fight
State 1
(Bluffing
equilibrium) ├─────────┼──────────────┼──────────────┼──────────▶
             0        v₁*         (c₁−a)/p₁        c₁/p₁       v₁
```

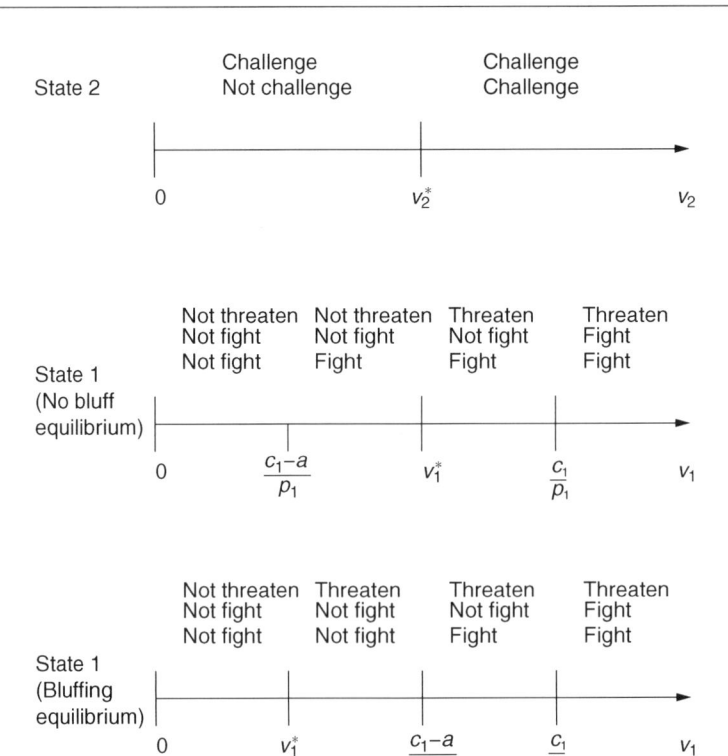

Figure 9.6 Costly Signaling game: strategies for each state/type

9.4.2 Incomplete information

Now assume that each side's value for the good in question is distributed over the positive real numbers $\mathbb{R}^+$, according to continuous and strictly positive densities $v_i \sim f_i$, and associated distributions F_i. We can now solve for perfect Bayesian equilibria. In particular, since we are interested in the possibility of communication in high conflict situations, I will consider separating equilibria, in which some types of state 1 threaten and other types do not, so the threat is informative about the type of state 1. Even more specifically, I am interested in equilibria in which types with high values of v_1 are more likely to threaten than types with low values, so the threat serves as a signal that state 1 is likely to fight over the issue if challenged. The challenge, therefore, is to find equilibria in which types that are willing to fight threaten and types not willing to fight do not.

The strategies for two such equilibria are illustrated in Figure 9.6. For state 2, there will be a cutoff point between those who do not challenge and those with higher values for the good that do, conditional on whether there has been a threat or not. As we will see, state 1 never fights after not making a threat in equilibrium, so all types of state 2 will wish to challenge after seeing no threat. However, after a threat, some types may

9.4 COSTLY SIGNALS AND CRISIS BARGAINING

wish to not challenge, and some will prefer to challenge anyway. Call the cutoff point between these two ranges v_2^*.

State 1's choice over fighting after a challenge is the same as it was before, types with $v_1 < \frac{c_1-a}{p_1}$ will not fight whether or not they have made a threat, types between $\frac{c_1-a}{p_1}$ and $\frac{c_1}{p_1}$ will fight only if they have made a threat, and types above $\frac{c_1}{p_1}$ will fight in either case. There will also be a threshold separating those who threaten and those who do not threaten, which I will call v_1^*. This threshold could be either below $\frac{c_1-a}{p_1}$ or above it. (It can be shown that it will not be above $\frac{c_1}{p_1}$ in equilibrium.) If it is above, illustrated in the middle line in Figure 9.6, then types below $\frac{c_1-a}{p_1}$ will not threaten and not fight whether or not they have threatened. Types between $\frac{c_1-a}{p_1}$ and v_1^* will not threaten, and will fight only if they have threatened. Types above v_1^* but below $\frac{c_1}{p_1}$ will threaten and fight only if they make a threat, and types above $\frac{c_1}{p_1}$ will threaten and fight whether or not they have made a threat. Note, in this case there is no bluffing. The only types that threaten are sufficiently committed by their threat to carry it out, so they fight if they threaten.

In the second case, illustrated in the bottom row of Figure 9.6, v_1^* is below $\frac{c_1-a}{p_1}$. In this case, types below v_1^* will not threaten or fight under any circumstances, types between v_1^* and $\frac{c_1-a}{p_1}$ will threaten but not fight even if they threatened (hence their threat is a bluff), types above $\frac{c_1-a}{p_1}$ and below $\frac{c_1}{p_1}$ will threaten and fight only if they have threatened, while types above $\frac{c_1}{p-1}$ will threaten and fight whether or not they threaten. We will consider these two equilibria in turn.

The no bluffing equilibrium

In the no bluffing case, we know that a threat from state 1 implies that state 1 will fight with certainty. The threat is perfectly informative and removes all doubt. Therefore, the only types of state 2 who wish to challenge after a threat are those who prefer war to the status quo, so we know that the cutoff point for state 2 after a threat is the following

$$v_2^* = \frac{c_2}{p_2} \tag{9.15}$$

Note that state 2's threshold depends solely on its own war-related parameters: its cost for fighting and its likelihood of winning. In particular, it does not depend on state 1's cutoff level.

Turning to state 1, we can now find v_1^* by equating the payoff for not threatening, which will lead this type of state 1 to not fight after a challenge for a payoff of 0, and threatening, which will lead it to fight after a challenge for a payoff of $F_2(v_2^*)v_1 + (1 - F_2(v_2^*))(p_1 v_1 - c_1)$. The threshold value is, therefore, $v_1^* = \frac{(1-F_2(v_2^*))c_1}{F_2(v_2^*)+(1-F_2(v_2^*))p_1}$ or, rearranged slightly

$$v_1^* = \frac{c_1}{\frac{1}{\frac{1}{F_2(v_2^*)}-1} + p_1} \tag{9.16}$$

With these two cutoff points, we have a well-defined equilibrium. The threat serves as a perfectly informative signal that state 1 intends to fight. Therefore, only those types of state 2 who prefer war to the status quo challenge.

Note, v_1^* is decreasing in $F_2(v_2^*)$. The more likely state 2 is to not challenge after a threat, the lower v_1^* is, that is, the more types of state 1 will wish to issue a threat. Conversely, if almost everyone challenges after a threat, so $F_2(v_2^*) \approx 0$, then v_1^* is almost equal to $\frac{c_1}{p_1}$. This means that almost all the types who are threatening would fight even without a threat. As $F_2(v_2^*)$ increases, v_1^* declines and more and more types will threaten until the threshold $\frac{c_1 - a}{p_1}$ is eventually crossed, and we transition to the equilibrium in which some types are bluffing. Therefore, there is an upper limit on how likely state 2 is to acquiesce after a threat. $F_2(v_2^*)$ cannot get too great or the lower value types of state 1 will be tempted to threaten as well, thereby introducing bluffing.

We can analyze other comparative statics in the equilibrium as well. Increasing state 2's cost for war, c_2, increases v_2^*, so more types will not challenge after a threat. This will in turn increase $F_2(v_2^*)$ and decrease v_1^*, leading more types of state 1 to threaten. Increasing c_1 increases v_1^*, causing fewer types to threaten. If state 1 becomes stronger, p_1 increases. This will cause p_2 to decrease and v_2^* to increase, and state 2 becomes less likely to challenge after a threat. As for v_1^*, increasing p_1 has a direct effect through its appearance in the denominator and an indirect one through its effect on v_2^*, but both point in the same direction and reduce v_1^*, making state 1 more likely to threaten.

The probability of war in this equilibrium is the product of the likelihoods that state 1 threatens and that state 2 is willing to fight, or

$$P(W) = (1 - F_1(v_1^*))(1 - F_2(v_2^*)) \tag{9.17}$$

The bluffing equilibrium

Now we turn to the bluffing equilibrium. This time let's start with state 1, and derive the v_1^* cutoff point, the type that is indifferent between threatening and not threatening, given that they will not fight after a threat, so that their threat is a bluff. The payoff for not threatening for types who will not fight is 0, and the payoff for threatening and not fighting is $F_2(v_2^*)v_1 + (1 - F_2(v_2^*))(-a)$. The type of state 1 who is indifferent between these options is

$$v_1^* = \left(\frac{1}{F_2(v_2^*)} - 1\right) a \tag{9.18}$$

Just as before, the higher $F_2(v_2^*)$ is, that is, the more types of state 2 that do not challenge in response to a threat, the lower v_1^* is, the more types of state 1 that are willing to bluff by threatening even if they are not willing to fight.

Now consider the type of state 2 who is indifferent between challenging and not after state 1 threatens. The payoff for not challenging is just 0 as before. The payoff for challenging after a threat will depend on how likely state 1 is to fight after having made a threat – call this $P(F|T)$. Then state 2's payoff for challenging after a threat is $(1 - P(F|T))v_2 + P(F|T)(p_2 v_2 - c_2)$. The type who finds this equivalent to 0 is $\frac{P(F|T)c_2}{1-P(F|T)+P(F|T)p_2}$, so

$$v_2^* = \frac{c_2}{\frac{1}{P(F|T)} - 1 + p_2} \quad (9.19)$$

We can see that the higher $P(F|T)$ is, that is, the fewer types of state 1 are bluffing, the higher v_2^* is, or the fewer types of state 2 that will challenge in response to a threat. Comparing this cutoff point with that in the no bluffing equilibrium, we can see that it is smaller (because $\frac{1}{P(F|T)} > 1$). This means that more types are challenging after a threat in the bluffing equilibrium, which stands to reason since there is now a chance that the threat is not genuine.

Finally, we need to know the posterior belief that state 1 will fight, given that it has threatened, $P(F|T)$. Types from v_1^* upwards will threaten, but only types above $\frac{c_1-a}{p_1}$ will fight after a threat. Therefore, from Bayes' Rule, the posterior likelihood that state 1 fights, having threatened, is the following

$$P(F|T) = \frac{1 - F_1(\frac{c_1-a}{p_1})}{1 - F_1(v_1^*)} \quad (9.20)$$

The crucial insight here is that the higher v_1^*, the higher $P(F|T)$, so the more likely state 1 is to be willing to fight having made the threat. Note, this posterior belief, having truncated the types below v_1^*, places higher probability on types higher than that and hence raises the expected likelihood that state 1 will fight. However, unlike in the previous case, it does not raise it to 1, because of the possibility of bluffing.

We now have expressions for v_1^* and v_2^* in the bluffing equilibrium case. They depend on the exogenous parameters, such as relative power p_i, costs of war, c_i, and the audience cost of the statement, a. However, they also depend on each other, and so must be solved simultaneously. This stands to reason since they should obviously depend on each other. The fewer types of state 1 are bluffing, the fewer types of state 2 will challenge after a threat. The fewer types of state 2 that challenge after a threat, the more incentive there is to bluff, and so forth. We can solve them analytically by substituting the expression for one into the other, but it will be more intuitive to proceed graphically.

The equations for v_1^* and v_2^* are shown in Figure 9.7. State 1's cutoff point as a function of state 2's is denoted $v_1^*(v_2^*)$, and is the downward sloping line. Therefore, as state 2 gets less likely to challenge after a threat, state 1 becomes more likely to bluff. State 2's cutoff point as a function of state 1's, $v_2^*(v_1^*)$, is the upward sloping line, so as state 1 becomes less likely to bluff, state 2 becomes less likely to challenge after a threat. There

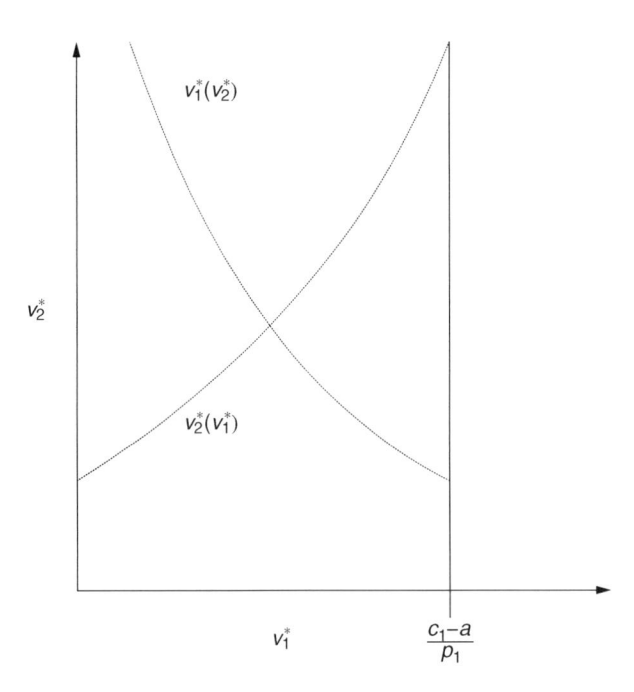

Figure 9.7 Bluffing equilibrium in the Costly Signaling game

is an upper bound for v_1^* for this equilibrium at $\frac{c_1-a}{p_1}$, because if v_1 were to exceed this amount then all types of state 1 would fight if they threaten, so $P(F|T)$ would be maximized at 1 and we would be back in the no bluffing equilibrium. The intersection of the two curves gives the equilibrium in the cutoff points. In this equilibrium, there will be a certain amount of bluffing, so the signal will not be a perfectly credible indication of resolve to fight.

We can now consider comparative statics in the bluffing equilibrium, considering the variables discussed previously, p_1, c_1, and c_2, and also a which did not appear in the previous equilibrium because audience costs were never paid there. Let's start with the variables that only appear in the equation for v_2^*, namely, the balance of power, p_1, and war costs, c_1 and c_2. Increasing c_2 increases v_2^*, so it shifts the v_2^* curve upwards, as illustrated in Figure 9.8. The original equilibrium is at the point labeled A and increasing c_2 shifts the curve up, leading to a new equilibrium at point B. This has the effect of shifting the equilibrium cutoffs downwards for state 1 and upward for state 2. This implies that more types of state 1 will bluff and fewer types of state 2 will resist after a threat. Next, consider c_1, state 1's cost of war. Increasing c_1 decreases $P(F|T)$, the likelihood that state 1 fights after a threat, and so it reduces v_2^*, lowering the curve, leading to a new equilibrium at point C. Lowering the v_2^* curve shifts the equilibrium down and to the right, so fewer types of state 1 bluff and more types of state 2 challenge, despite a threat.

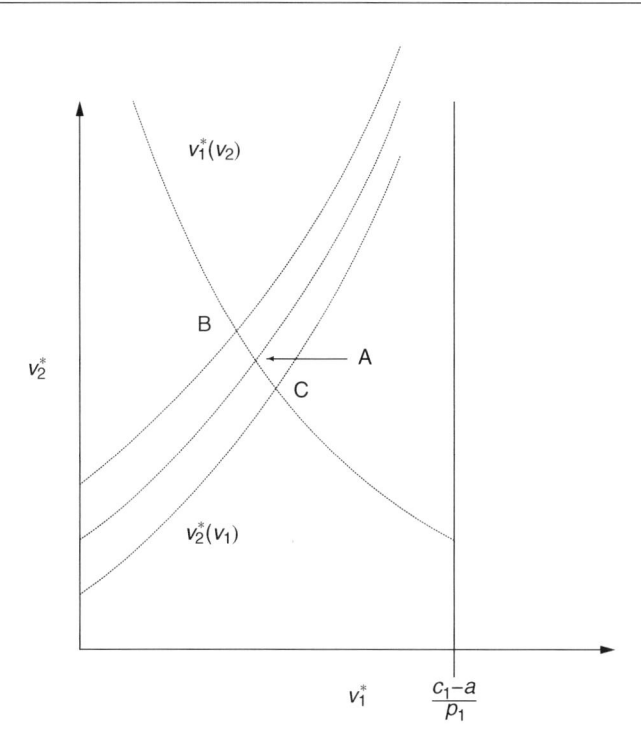

Figure 9.8 Comparative statics in the bluffing equilibrium

Increasing p_1 will increase $P(F|T)$, making state 1 more likely to fight after a threat, which increases v_2^*, making state 2 less likely to challenge after a threat. In addition, increasing p_1 decreases p_2, which has a direct effect, increasing v_2^*. These two effects reinforce each other, so the effect will be to raise v_2^* and lower v_1^*, so state 1 will be more likely to bluff but state 2 will be less likely to challenge after a threat.

Lastly, consider a. This parameter appears in the equations for both v_1^* and v_2^*. Increasing a increases v_1^*, shifting the curve to the right. By itself this would increase both v_1^* and v_2^*, so state 1 would be less likely to bluff and state 2 would be less likely to challenge after a threat. Increasing a also has the effect of increasing $P(F|T)$, the likelihood of fighting after a threat, which increases v_2^*, shifting the curve upward. This reinforces the increase in v_2^*, so we know that state 2 will be less likely to challenge after a threat. However, it counteracts the effect on v_1, so it is unclear which effect will dominate as far as whether state 1 is more likely to bluff or not.

Finally, we can derive the expression for the likelihood of war in the bluffing equilibrium. In the bluffing equilibrium, war occurs when state 1 threatens, state 2 challenges anyway, and state 1 decides to fight. The ex ante likelihood of this occurring is the joint likelihood that state 1 has a value for the good above the threshold for fighting, $1 - F_1(\frac{c_1-a}{p_1})$, and the likelihood that state 2 fights after a signal, or $1 - F_2(v_2^*)$

$$P(W) = \left(1 - F_1\left(\frac{c_1 - a}{p_1}\right)\right)(1 - F_2(v_2^*)) \tag{9.21}$$

Anything that makes state 2 more likely to challenge after a threat increases the chance of war.

No bluffing vs. bluffing equilibria

The existence of an equilibrium with bluffing in this model differs from the result in Fearon (1997). In that model, Fearon assumes that state 1 is able to generate any level of audience cost it wishes, rather than the fixed amount modeled here by the exogenous constant a. As a result, no bluffing occurs. The logic is as follows. Given that some types of state 2 will challenge even if they expect state 1 to fight for certain, there will always be a risk of war. Types of state 1 who will never pay audience costs because they will never back down can easily choose a very high level of audience costs. Types of state 1 who value the good less will, therefore, be confronted with a choice between getting 0 by not making a threat and backing down, or making a threat and either paying a large audience cost for backing down or fighting a war over a good they do not care about, the payoff for either one would be less than 0. Since the high value types never pay the audience costs, it is in their interest to drive them up to the point that maximizes their signaling value, where no bluffers would remain.

In the context of the simpler game with fixed audience costs, we can consider when bluffing occurs and when it does not. The key constraint is that the likelihood of not challenging after a threat cannot be too high to tempt bluffers, $\frac{c_1 - a}{p_1} < v_1^*$, or

$$\frac{c_1 - a}{p_1} < \frac{c_1}{\frac{1}{F_2\left(\frac{c_2}{p_2}\right)} - 1} + p_1 \tag{9.22}$$

If this condition holds, the no bluffing equilibrium will be possible; if it is violated, the bluffing equilibrium takes over. Note, if a can be expanded at will, then this condition can always be satisfied. Since the types who will never pay audience costs are not affected by the magnitude of a directly, and the no bluffing equilibrium is better for them because it minimizes the likelihood of a challenge from state 2 (maximizes v_2^*), they have an incentive to increase a if they can.

It is an interesting question empirically how much bluffing is apparent in the historical record, and what accounts for it. It could be that it is not easy for states to run up audience costs sufficiently to eliminate the incentive for less interested states to bluff. Democracies and some authoritarian states with powerful domestic audiences are thought to be able to generate higher audience costs, and so may be able to enact no bluffing equilibria, while personalistic dictatorships may be doomed to bluffing equilibria (Weeks 2008).

Result 9.2 *In a crisis bargaining situation, states that would suffer audience costs from backing down can send credible verbal signals that will deter some types from challenging. If states cannot generate unlimited audience costs, however, there may be bluffing, so that the signal is not perfectly credible and hence does not deter all potentially deterrable types of adversary.*

Cheap talk vs. costly signals

A final question to consider is: What would happen if the threat carried no costs, and so was an example of cheap talk rather than costly signals? This would be the case if $a = 0$. If this were the case, first of all we would be in the bluffing equilibrium because the condition just discussed making the no bluffing equilibrium possible cannot hold for $a = 0$. In the bluffing equilibrium, if $a = 0$, $v_1^* = 0$ as well; that is, all types will send the signal. In this case, the posterior belief that state 1 is going to fight after a threat would be equal to the prior belief, $P(F|T) = 1 - F_1\left(\frac{c_1}{p_1}\right)$. Since the signal would be uninformative, state 2's likelihood of challenging will be based on its prior beliefs. The costliness of the signal is, therefore, crucial to underpinning meaningful communication in this context.

9.5 Conclusion

Because uncertainty is so common in international relations, and its consequences can be so negative, communication is very important. We have seen that in conditions where states have shared uncertainty and shared preferences, communication is relatively easy with ordinary diplomacy, or cheap talk. Even in the face of scientific or other uncertainty about how the world works, states can communicate their knowledge and overcome uncertainty, thereby reaping the rewards of cooperation if it is indicated. Uncertainty about the preferences of the states can erode the ability to communicate using ordinary diplomacy, but a little need not be fatal. If the interests of the states are known to be opposed, however, cheap talk by itself will not help alleviate uncertainty. In that case, costly signals are required. In a model of crisis bargaining, states can send informative signals about how much they value the object at stake so long as they were to pay at least some cost if they were to be caught in a lie. In particular, states can threaten to fight if challenged, and if they were to be punished in some way for failing to back up that threat, it can serve as an informative signal of their true value for the object in contention and their intention to fight. As a result, diplomacy, both in ordinary times and in times of crisis, is a vital component of international relations.

EXERCISES

9.1 Consider the Treaty game model, only now assume that the severity of global warming can range across the positive real numbers, instead of being restricted to just two values, so $\omega \in \mathbb{R}^+$. Let the density be f and the cumulative distribution be F. As before, let $b(\omega)$ be a (strictly) increasing function, so the treaty produces more benefit the worse the problem of global warming is.

1. Under what conditions would a player with costs c_i prefer the treaty to inaction?
2. Imagine the scientific report takes the form of putting a floor on how bad global warming will be. In probability terms, it truncates the distribution from below. There are two potential values for the report, A and B, where $0 < A < B$. If the report is A, then the new distribution is truncated from below at A, similarly for B. Under what conditions will a truth-telling equilibrium exist in which state 1 honestly conveys which report it received, and if the report is A, the two states oppose the treaty, and if the report is B, the two states support the treaty?

9.2 Consider an alternative Costly Signaling game in which the signal cost is paid up front, like a sunk cost signal, but also has the effect of reducing the cost paid in fighting if war occurs. Let the cost be k, so the payoff for not being challenged after a threat is $v_1 - k$, the payoff for being challenged and backing down after a threat is $-k$, and the war payoff after a threat is $w_1 + k$. Describe the complete information equilibria in the game as a function of v_1 and v_2.

1. Under what conditions will player 1 not fight whether or not it has made a threat?
2. Under what conditions will player 1 fight only if it has made a threat?
3. Under what conditions will player 1 fight whether or not it has made a threat?
4. If player 2 expects that challenging will lead to war, under what conditions will it prefer to challenge?
5. If player 2 is expected to not challenge in response to a threat, and player 1 will fight only if it makes a threat, when will it prefer to make a threat?
6. If player 2 is expected to challenge in response to a threat, and player 1 will fight only if it makes a threat, when will it prefer to make a threat?
7. Use all of these conditions to create a figure analogous to Figure 9.5.

10 Multilateral cooperation

So far, we have considered interactions between pairs of states, using two player games. This is perfectly acceptable for a wide range of contexts. The Cold War was the heyday of bipolarity, in which the main security interactions were between the United States and the Soviet Union. Most wars (Levy 1983) and over 80% of militarized international disputes (Ghosn et al. 2004) are bilateral. The vast majority of international treaties are bilateral (Koremenos 2013). However, many international interactions involve more than two states. The major wars of the past 200 years, the Napoleonic Wars and the First and Second World Wars, each involved many states. The World Trade Organization has over 150 members, the International Monetary Fund over 180, and over 160 states have signed the United Nations Convention on the Law of the Sea. Thus, how states interact in groups of more than two is an important subject of study.

While multilateral bargaining has received some attention in international relations (Sebenius 1984, Gilligan 2004), most of the interest has been in the subject of multilateral cooperation. The main theoretical lens through which this problem has been examined is the theory of public goods (Samuelson 1954). The foundational work on this question in political science is Olson (1965).[1] Olson was the first to ask how groups form to pursue their collective interests, given that individuals have an incentive to "free ride" off the efforts of others, what he dubbed the *collective action problem*. His main theoretical claim is that cooperation is harder to achieve the more actors are involved. Small groups find it easier to organize and overcome the collective action problem, and so can often prevail politically against larger but less well-organized groups. Applied to states, many have argued that small numbers of states find it easier to cooperate than large numbers (Oye 1986). Taken to its logical extreme, this argument has been used to support the claim that a *hegemon* or predominant state is needed to provide international public goods. Kindleberger (1974) famously attributed the relative international openness and harmony of the nineteenth

---

[1] See also Hardin (1982).

century and the post Second World War era to British and US hegemony, respectively, and the interwar chaos to the fact that Britain could no longer, and the US chose not to, provide the needed stabilizing force. Hegemonic stability theory (HST) developed this thesis and applied it to economic and security affairs (Lake 1993), while Keohane (1984) argued that cooperative institutions, once set up by hegemons, could continue to foster cooperation "after hegemony."

States do often choose to cooperate multilaterally, and often create large international institutions and multilateral treaties that eventually achieve substantial, and in some cases near universal, membership. This has been a particular hallmark of the post Second World War period, with notable treaties and organizations such as the United Nations (UN), the North Atlantic Treaty Organization (NATO), the International Monetary Fund (IMF), the World Bank, the General Agreement on Tariffs and Trade (GATT) which became the World Trade Organization (WTO), and the Nuclear Non-Proliferation Treaty (NPT). The concept of international regimes was developed in an attempt to explain these and less formal examples of widespread cooperation (Krasner 1983), and the particular causes, advantages, and disadvantages of multilateralism as an alternative to bilateral cooperation were also investigated (Ruggie 1993). Koremenos *et al.* (2001) developed conjectures on how institutions should be designed to cope with different strategic problems, information environments, and numbers of actors. Some of the interesting debates include whether efforts at cooperation should start small and grow over time or be inclusive from the beginning (Downs *et al.* 1998, Gilligan 2004), and whether agreements should incorporate flexibility, opt out clauses or renegotiation provisions (Rosendorff and Milner 2001, Koremenos 2001, 2005).[2]

In what follows, I will introduce two broad classes of models: public goods games and tipping models. Public goods models are often used to analyze the role of small groups and hegemons in providing international cooperation. Tipping models are often invoked when widespread international cooperation is observed, particularly in large multilateral treaties. Both classes of models can be applied in a variety of issue areas, including security, political economy, and the environment.

10.1 Public goods

Many goods can be differentiated along two dimensions. First, is excludability. If the good is produced and some people enjoy it, can other people be prevented from enjoying it too? If they can, they can easily be charged money for the privilege of enjoying it; if not, they will enjoy it for free. Second, is rivalness. Does one person's use of the good

---

[2] Gilligan and Johns (2012) provide a review of the institutions literature.

Table 10.1 Different types of goods

	Excludable	Not excludable
Not rival	Club goods (Alliance defense)	Public goods (National defense)
Rival	Private goods (Territory)	Commons goods (Fish stocks)

diminish the amount left over for another to enjoy? If so, then more will need to be produced for each user; if not, then the same amount will suffice for many users. These two dimensions generate a two-by-two table with four entries, as shown in Table 10.1.

Private goods are excludable and rival, so you can prevent people from enjoying them unless they pay for the good, and more needs to be produced for each consumer. An example in the international relations context is land; the territory of states is privately enjoyed, and states jealously guard their rights to it. Economists tend to think that private goods are provided efficiently by the market. This does not stop them from becoming the object of political contention, of course – there is a lot of bargaining and conflict over who gets to enjoy what private goods. However, from the perspective of thinking about how groups form and how benefits can be provided, private goods are thought to be unproblematic. So it is the other three categories that are interesting from the point of view of this chapter.

Public goods are not rival and not excludable. The problem with goods that are not excludable is that it is hard to get someone to pay for them (Samuelson 1954). For instance, consider the case of radio broadcasts. People buy radios, which are private goods. But they do not pay for radio broadcasts, and there is no way to make them. Public radio asks for donations but typically does not make enough from listener contributions to stay in business. Ordinary stations make money by selling advertisement space, which is excludable for the companies that want airtime. An international relations example is national defense, considered from the perspective of the individuals within a state. If the state is defended, everyone in the state enjoys that defense. The state cannot refuse to defend an individual within its borders just because that person did not pay their taxes. Therefore, the state needs to use coercion to extract revenues to provide national defense, otherwise it would be undersupplied.

A related concept is *externalities* or "public bads." Pollution is the classic example. Each country produces a certain amount of greenhouse gasses from its factories and vehicles. Taken together, the greenhouse gasses warm the planet and impose costs on all. However, every state would prefer that other states control their externalities for the public benefit, while being free to produce and drive its own cars in the normal way. Coase (1960) famously argued that the market will take care of externalities efficiently if property rights are clearly allocated and transaction costs are absent. Countries that dislike pollution can pay others not to pollute. If they don't find it worthwhile to compensate others for not polluting, then it is not economically efficient to reduce production for the sake of alleviating pollution. Following on from this concept, a common solution to this problem today is the market for pollution, or the "cap and trade" system. Firms are allocated rights to pollute, and they can then trade these rights. If they develop a process to cheaply reduce their pollution, they can sell their right to pollute to a company that wishes to expand production.

Club goods are a hybrid form which are not rival but excludable. A club can form to provide the good for its members, and charge admission to the club. Once inside the club, use of the good does not detract from anyone else, but each member must pay to get into the club. Alliance defense is a plausible international relations example. A group of states gets together and pledges to defend each other but does not pledge to defend anyone outside the group, so the good is excludable. If countries can credibly be threatened with expulsion for not contributing to the alliance's defense, then the club can extract contributions from the members. In some cases, however, the threat of expulsion may not be credible, so the alliance becomes more nearly a public good, as we will explore below. Two other significant examples are the European Union and the WTO. For both of these institutions, states must go through long accession negotiations and make many policy adjustments in order to achieve membership. Once in the club, they receive many benefits in terms of improved access to export markets, capital, etc.

The final category is commons goods. Commons goods are especially problematic because they are not excludable but are rival. A famous paper by Garrett Hardin (1968) called the "Tragedy of the Commons" lays out the logic. Let's say you have a village with a commons used for grazing animals. Each villager has a certain number of sheep and anyone can graze as many as they want. In this context, each villager will be tempted to add an additional sheep to their flock. This will increase their profits and the harm on the resource will be slight. But if everyone does this, the commons will be overgrazed, and eventually no one will be able to use it. Elinor Ostrom won the Nobel prize for studying these sorts of issues (Ostrom 1998). A classic example in the international relations context is fisheries. Fisheries worldwide are over fished; too many boats are competing for too few fish. This is the subject of many international negotiations over border fisheries, such as the Grand Banks shared by US and Canada. Within each country also, government officials are trying to put limits on catches in order to preserve fish stocks. One solution is to "privatize" the commons, or sell them off to individuals. Individuals will supposedly not have an incentive to overgraze because they would just destroy their own livelihood. However, cooperative management of commons goods is feasible under certain circumstances.

Because they are the most widely applied models of collective action problem, let us examine a few examples of public goods in more detail.

10.1.1 Binary choice public goods games, small numbers, and hegemony

One of the simplest public goods models is the n person Prisoner's Dilemma. Consider a world of n states. Each one can choose to have low tariffs, L, or high tariffs, H, on foreign goods. Each state bears a cost, c, from having an open economy that lets in imports which compete with domestic producers and put inefficient companies out of business. Each country derives a benefit, b, from each other country that has low tariff barriers, because that gives them an additional export market. Let p_i be a binary variable with value 1 if player i has low tariffs, and 0 if player i has high tariffs. Player i's payoff for having high tariffs can then be expressed as

$$U_i(H) = \sum_{-i} p_j b$$

while the payoff for having low tariffs is

$$U_i(L) = \sum_{-i} p_j b - c$$

This game can be illustrated as shown in Figure 10.1. On the horizontal axis is the number of states with low tariffs, the vertical axis is utility. In the figure, $c = 5$ and $b = 1$. The payoff for having high tariffs is the upper line starting at 0, the line for having low tariffs is the lower line starting at −5. Because the payoff for having high tariffs is always above that for having low tariffs, no matter how many other states have low tariffs, there is a unique Nash equilibrium in this model – states have dominant strategies to have high tariffs. Switching to low tariffs incurs a cost for you, while conferring benefits on the other actors. Hence, if this is your model of the international political economy, you would predict high tariffs all around. This game, therefore, closely resembles the binary Prisoner's Dilemma. Each player has a dominant strategy to defect, or have high tariffs, but this leaves them worse off than they might have been if they had all cooperated by having low tariffs. The payoff if everyone defects is 0, while the payoff if all ten states (in Figure 10.1) were to lower their tariffs would be 5.

Although the game has a unique Nash equilibrium involving no cooperation, scholars often speculate on when cooperation would be "easier" to achieve in such games.[3]

---

[3] Technically speaking, this involves going beyond the model as specified, involving implicit hunches about what might happen in a repeated version of the game, or with some other modification. Nonetheless, it raises some interesting aspects of the model, which can be more rigorously examined with more advanced tools.

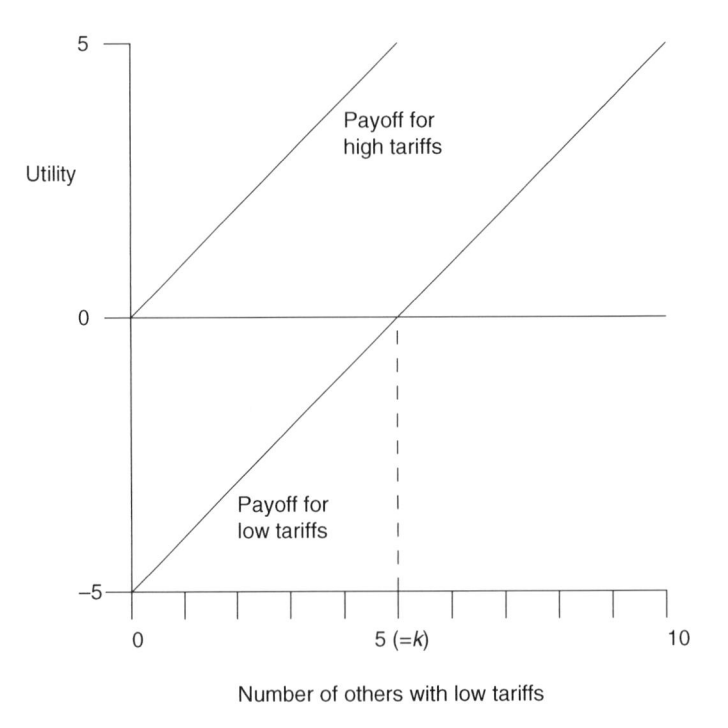

Figure 10.1 The N person Prisoner's Dilemma

One index of how easy it would be to cooperate in the public goods game is the minimum number of cooperators it would be necessary to assemble for them to do better than they would have done by defecting. That is, if it takes a lot of cooperators to break even, then cooperation seems unlikely, but if it takes only a few working together, then it seems like this might be easier to achieve. For instance, in the game illustrated in Figure 10.1, the payoff for each state if no one cooperates (has low tariffs) is 0. If five states get together and have low tariffs, they will just break even, receiving a payoff of 0. Six states would show a strict profit by agreeing to cooperate; their payoff would be 1. This break-even point is often denoted k and the minimum number of players needed to break even is known as the *k-group* (Snidal 1985b). Solving for k explicitly, we set the payoff if no one cooperates, 0, equal to the payoff for cooperating if k actors cooperate

$$0 = kb - c$$

$$k = \frac{c}{b}$$

With $c = 5$ and $b = 1$, $k = 5$, illustrated as the point where the low tariff payoff intersects the 0 line for no cooperation in Figure 10.1.

Note that if the costs of cooperation go down, k goes down. This means that fewer players need to get together and cooperate to break even, which may make cooperation easier.[4] The central Olsonian argument is that small groups are easier to form than large ones because of the ease in monitoring contributions (Olson 1965). Hence, small interests may prevail over larger ones. If the k group is small, then the group is more likely to form, which will make it more likely to achieve its ends.

A common modification of the n person Prisoner's Dilemma in the context of international political economy is to consider states of different sizes in a slightly different strategic environment. This model can be used to think about the effects of hegemony, or the presence of a strong actor. Consider the Hegemonic Stability game (Snidal 1985b). Assume that you have a world of n states, each with size s_i. They face a public goods problem that is slightly different from the previous one, in that each state benefits somewhat from its own provision of the public good, depending on its size. Each state faces a cost of contribution to the public good, which is c and is the same regardless of the size of the state. Each derives a benefit from the amount of public good provided, which depends on its size and how many others are contributing. As before, let p_i be a binary variable with value 1 if player i contributes, and 0 if player i does not contribute. Player i's payoff for not contributing can then be expressed as

$$U_i(N) = \sum_{-i} p_j s_j b$$

while the payoff from contributing is

$$U_i(C) = \sum_{-i} p_j s_j b + s_i b - c$$

A state should contribute if

$$\sum_{-i} p_j s_j b + s_i b - c \geq \sum_{-i} p_j s_j b$$

which simplifies to

$$s_i b - c \geq 0$$

or

$$s_i \geq \frac{c}{b} = k \qquad (10.1)$$

This gives us a lower bound on the size a state must have to contribute. The size must exceed the k threshold. Using the previous numbers, a state with size 5 would just break even by contributing. Any state with size greater than 5 has a dominant strategy to contribute. Thus, larger states have a greater incentive to contribute, even if they know others will not. This result continues to hold in more sophisticated public goods

---

[4] Once again, this is not equilibrium analysis; the only Nash equilibrium in the game is universal non-cooperation.

models as well. The idea that large states contribute disproportionately to international public goods has become a mainstay of international relations theory. It provides the theoretical rationale for hegemonic stability theory (Lake 1993), which helps it retain theoretical interest despite empirical challenges.

A problem with hegemonic stability theory when formulated along these lines is that it implies that only one or two large actors will provide international public goods, and the rest of the world will free ride. This has been called the "benign" view of hegemony and may seem unrealistic. In addition, we often see what appears to be widespread cooperation in institutions such as the WTO, IMF, etc. Are the small cooperating, and, if so, what accounts for it? Two common answers in the political economy literature are coercive hegemony and reciprocity. Basically, non-cooperation is punished, either by the hegemon or by other states more generally. To analyze this requires a more sophisticated model of hegemony or a repeated game framework (Alt et al. 1988, Lichbach 1992, Pahre 1994, Stone et al. 2008).

10.1.2 Military spending among allies

Models with continuous levels of public goods provision are widely applied, including to military spending among allies.[5] Consider the alliance modeling tradition beginning with Olson et al. (1966), and reviewed by Sandler (1993). Each country has an income level, I^i, which can be spent on a private good, y^i, and a public good (defense spending), q^i. The other countries in the alliance spend Q_{-i}, for a total alliance level of spending of $Q = q^i + Q_{-i}$, and the alliance faces a threat T. The utility function for country i is

$$U^i = U^i(y^i, Q, T)$$

which is increasing at declining rates in y^i and the total defense spending of the alliance, Q, and declining in the threat, T. Thus, each country wants more of the private good and more alliance defense spending which produces deterrence.

Each country also faces a budget constraint in which the price of the private good is 1, and the price of the public good is p

$$I^i = y^i + pq^i$$

---

[5] In some cases, alliance defense is more of a club good than a fully public one, since allies do not have to defend non-cooperative partners. For some countries behind the front line, however, the alliance may be effectively public. For instance, if NATO stopped Soviet tanks on the inter-German border, countries behind that border, such as France, could free ride to some extent, as the US and Germany could not credibly threaten not to defend France. For other alliances, however, states can credibly threaten not to come to the aid of their ally if the ally acts provocatively (Snyder 1984).

Each country should maximize its utility subject to the budget constraint. If we take the derivative of the utility function with respect to q^i, and set it equal to 0 we can find the optimum.

$$\frac{\partial U^i}{\partial y^i}\frac{\partial y^i}{\partial q^i} + \frac{\partial U^i}{\partial Q}\frac{\partial Q}{\partial q^i} = 0$$

The quantity of the private good produced is $y^i = I^i - pq^i$. The derivative of this with respect to q^i is just $-p$. The derivative of Q with respect to q^i is just 1. So we have

$$\frac{\partial U^i}{\partial y^i}(-p) + \frac{\partial U^i}{\partial q_i} = 0$$

or

$$\frac{\frac{\partial U^i}{\partial q_i}}{\frac{\partial U^i}{\partial y^i}} = p \qquad (10.2)$$

The numerator is the marginal utility of an additional unit of military defense; the denominator is the marginal utility of an additional unit of the private good. This ratio must equal the price of the military good. So if the price of the defense good is 2, you buy enough so that you would get twice as much utility from an additional unit of defense as you would from an additional unit of the private good.

As an example, consider the model of arms competition from Chapter 3. This time, let there be three actors, players 1, 2, and 3. Players 1 and 2 are allied, and so on the same side. I assume they care about the overall power of the alliance and their own individual cost of military spending, $\gamma_i m_i$. Player 3 is the adversary. Player 1's utility function is

$$u_1(m_1, m_2, m_3) = \frac{m_1 + m_2}{m_1 + m_2 + m_3} - \gamma_1 m_1 \qquad (10.3)$$

player 2 has a similar utility function and player 3's is

$$u_3(m_1, m_2, m_3) = \frac{m_3}{m_1 + m_2 + m_3} - \gamma_3 m_3 \qquad (10.4)$$

Player 1 maximizes utility by setting the derivative equal to 0

$$\frac{(m_1 + m_2 + m_3) - (m_1 + m_2)}{(m_1 + m_2 + m_3)^2} - \gamma_1 = 0$$

$$\frac{m_3}{(m_1 + m_2 + m_3)^2} = \gamma_1$$

$$(m_1 + m_2 + m_3)^2 = \frac{m_3}{\gamma_1}$$

$$m_1^*(m_2, m_3) = \sqrt{\frac{m_3}{\gamma_1}} - (m_2 + m_3)$$

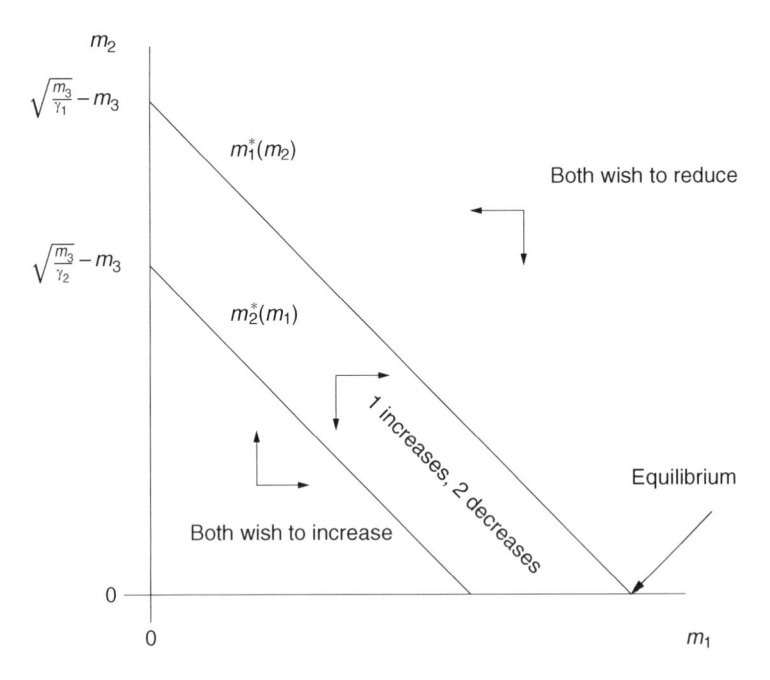

Figure 10.2 Military spending among allies

Since player 3 is the only one on player 3's side, its reaction function is similar to before

$$m_3^*(m_1, m_2) = \sqrt{\frac{m_1 + m_2}{\gamma_3}} - (m_1 + m_2) \qquad (10.5)$$

Note, the more player 2 spends, the greater m_2, the less player 1 spends. Player 2's reaction function is symmetrical, so the more player 1 spends, the less player 2 spends. Each ally's spending is just as good as its own, so there is a one-to-one substitution rate between them – every dollar spent by one ally leads to a dollar less spent by the other. This implies that for any fixed amount spent by the adversary, the two players' reaction functions will be lines of slope −1, with the one for the low cost player further out than the one for the high cost player, as illustrated in Figure 10.2. Here we assume that player 1 has lower cost for arming, perhaps because its economy is larger, so $\gamma_1 < \gamma_2$. In the region above and to the right of $m_1^*(m_2)$, both allies will wish to reduce their spending. In the region below and to the left of $m_2^*(m_1)$, both allies wish to increase their spending. In between $m_1^*(m_2)$ and $m_2^*(m_1)$, player 1 wishes to increase its spending and player 2 wishes to decrease its spending. Therefore, the equilibrium is for the low cost player 1 to spend the entire amount that it wants and the high cost player 2 to free ride completely. The alliance burden will, therefore, be carried entirely by its lowest cost member. Note, we could add additional higher cost members and get the same result: player 1 will always bear the entire burden of the alliance. The Multilateral Alliance game, therefore, reduces to a Bilateral Arms game between the leader of the alliance and the opposing state, between player 1 and player 3, and the equilibrium is derived in the same way as before.

A classic stylized fact about the NATO alliance is that the small exploit the large, in the sense that smaller countries spend less on the common defense than larger ones as a fraction of GDP. In the military spending game we just studied, this can be interpreted as the large state having lower costs (per capita) for weapons. In the more general framework discussed previously, this is explained by arguing that at Nash levels, each country is equating its marginal rate of substitution to the price. If we think of a large country, such as the US, this could imply billions of dollars of spending, and still be a reasonable fraction of GDP, like the late Cold War average of 6%. For a small country like Belgium, if you are already getting billions of dollars in defense courtesy of the US, the marginal utility of an additional small amount that you might spend is negligible, so you will spend little or nothing. This idea led to a cottage industry on "burden sharing" in the alliance literature that still has echoes today in the debates over NATO enlargement.

Result 10.1 *In multilateral cooperation over public goods like situations, the degree of cooperation will tend to be sub-optimal, in the sense that all players could be made better off by increasing their degree of cooperation. The burden of cooperation is also disproportionately borne by the largest actors in the group, with the smaller actors tending to free ride.*

10.2 The Tipping game

Public goods games typically predict that only a few states cooperate and the rest free ride. However, as pointed our previously, there are a number of very large multilateral treaties and organizations, such as NATO, the EU, the WTO, the NPT, etc. It is possible that these organizations do not actually require any real cooperation from their members, so signing is essentially equivalent to free riding for them (Downs et al. 1996). However, it is certainly worth entertaining the possibility that there are large multilateral cooperative endeavors, and thinking about how they could be accounted for. The tipping model is the usual framework applied to such problems.

Let's say that a friend has decided to throw a party. Invitations are sent out to a group of mutual friends, specifying the date and time. A characteristic feature of parties is that well-attended parties are fun and people are usually glad they came, while poorly attended parties are embarrassing and everyone wants to leave. This sets up self-reinforcing dynamics. The more people are expected to go, the more people will want to go, reinforcing their decision to attend. The fewer people are expected to go, the less

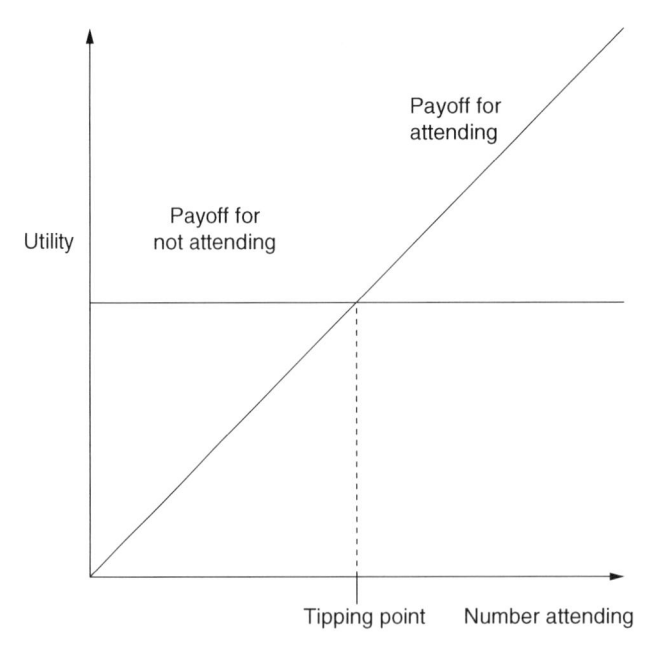

Figure 10.3 The Tipping game

enjoyable the party is expected to be, reinforcing a tendency to stay home and watch television. Two obvious equilibria in such a situation are full attendance by the invitees, and no attendance at all. If everyone thinks everyone will go, everyone will want to go, so they will in fact go, confirming expectations. If everyone thinks no one will go, no one will go, confirming that expectation too.

This type of situation, analysed by Schelling (1978) and many others,[6] can be represented with the diagram in Figure 10.3. The horizontal axis is the number of (other) people attending, while the vertical axis is a measure of utility. Starting in the lower left corner, at 0 attendance, the utility for attending the party gradually increases as the number of people attending increases. At a certain point, this line intersects the line representing the utility of not attending the party, which is horizontal in this case because it does not depend on the number of people who attend (the television show will not improve if more people go to the party). To the right of the intersection point, the utility for attending the party beats that of staying home and watching television. The intersection point is sometimes called the tipping point, because if people expect that more than that number of people will attend, everyone will want to attend, so the attendees will reach their maximum at the right-hand end of the scale. If the expected attendance is below the tipping point, the utility for going will be less than that for staying home, so no one wants to go. Thus, the tipping point is the boundary between

---

[6] See Laitin (1993, 1994) for an application to language choice and Karklins and Peterson (1993) for an application to the eastern European revolutions of 1989.

two very different zones, one which leads to full attendance, and one which leads to no attendance at all. Small changes in expectations can cause the process to tip in either direction, if the starting expectation is right around the tipping point.

While the Tipping game may seem unlike the games previously considered, it is strategically equivalent to an n-person version of the Assurance game. People's preferences have the classic Assurance game characteristic; if everyone else will attend (cooperate) each person wants to attend (cooperate), while if everyone else is going to stay home (defect), then each person wants to stay home (defect) as well. The difference, of course, is that each player must be assured, not just that one other player will cooperate, but that several others will, in order to be willing to cooperate themselves. This may pose greater difficulties for achieving cooperation than are found in the two actor case. The problem is one of coordinating everyone's expectations, getting everyone to believe that everyone will cooperate, so they will be willing to cooperate. Beliefs need to be coordinated on the better, cooperative equilibrium, rather than on the not so good non-cooperative equilibrium. The tipping point will vary from situation to situation, but the basic coordination problem is the same: convince everyone that the number of cooperators will exceed the tipping level, so everyone will then be willing to cooperate, fulfilling the expectation. This process is aided by the fact that the cooperative equilibrium is everyone's favorite equilibrium, making it a "focal point" in the game (Schelling 1960, 54).

10.2.1 The Landmines Convention game

Just as the Assurance game has found application to the context of arms races and arms control, the multilateral Assurance game, or Tipping game, has been applied to multilateral arms control treaties. An especially striking example is the treaty banning landmines. Landmines went from being a perfectly normal weapon in the arsenal of almost every country in the world to being normatively objectionable and banned by international treaty in the space of less than ten years (Price 1998, Rutherford 2000). Tipping models seem especially relevant to understanding such rapid international changes.

Consider a game among n countries about whether or not to get rid of landmines, illustrated in Figure 10.4. Each country has a choice between either giving up its landmines or keeping them. Let us assume for simplicity that retaining mines produces a certain level of military utility, $m > 0$, but in the presence of an international treaty banning them there is a cost of social opprobrium, $c > 0$, which is multiplied by the number of countries who have signed, s, producing a total cost of cs. The payoff for retaining mines is, therefore, $m - cs$. The payoff for getting rid of them is 0, the military benefit is not obtained, and the social cost is not paid.

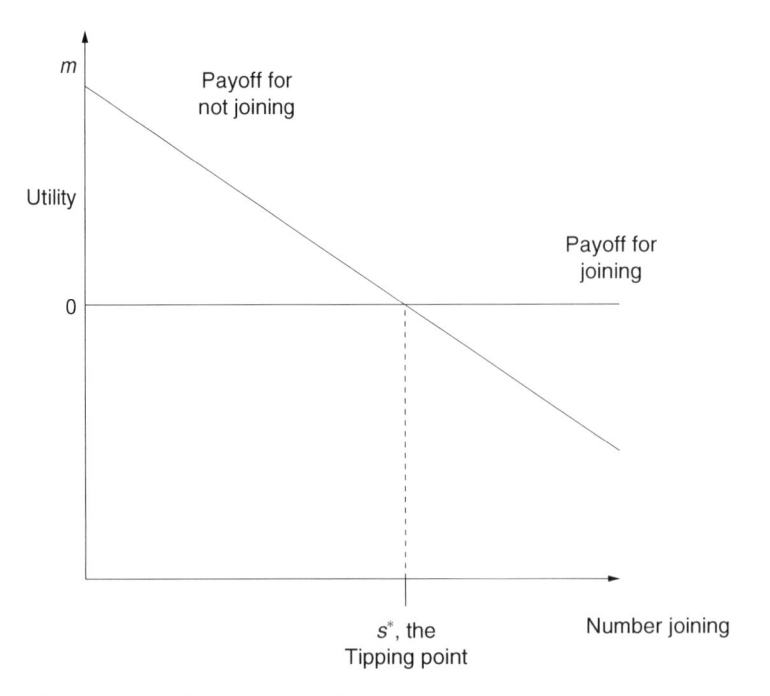

Figure 10.4 Landmines Convention game

If we assume that $m - cn < 0$, then the game has the structure of a Tipping game. Every country wishes to retain their mines if no one else will sign the treaty, but every country also wishes to give them up if assured that every other country will as well. The tipping point is obtained by setting the payoff for retaining mines equal to the payoff for getting rid of them and solving for s^*

$$m - cs = 0$$
$$s^* = \frac{m}{c} \tag{10.6}$$

So if over $\frac{m}{c}$ countries sign the accord, then everyone will want to, and the treaty will reach universal status. Thus, with these assumptions, there are two Nash equilibria in the game: universal retention of land mines and universal adherence to the treaty.

10.2.2 Tipping games with interior equilibria

Some treaties have universal or nearly universal membership. In the arms control issue area, the Nuclear Non-proliferation Treaty and the Chemical Weapons Convention are examples. However, some treaties acquire many members without becoming universal, and the Landmines Convention is an example. What accounts for the existence of tipping phenomena with holdouts, or interior equilibria?

10.2 THE TIPPING GAME

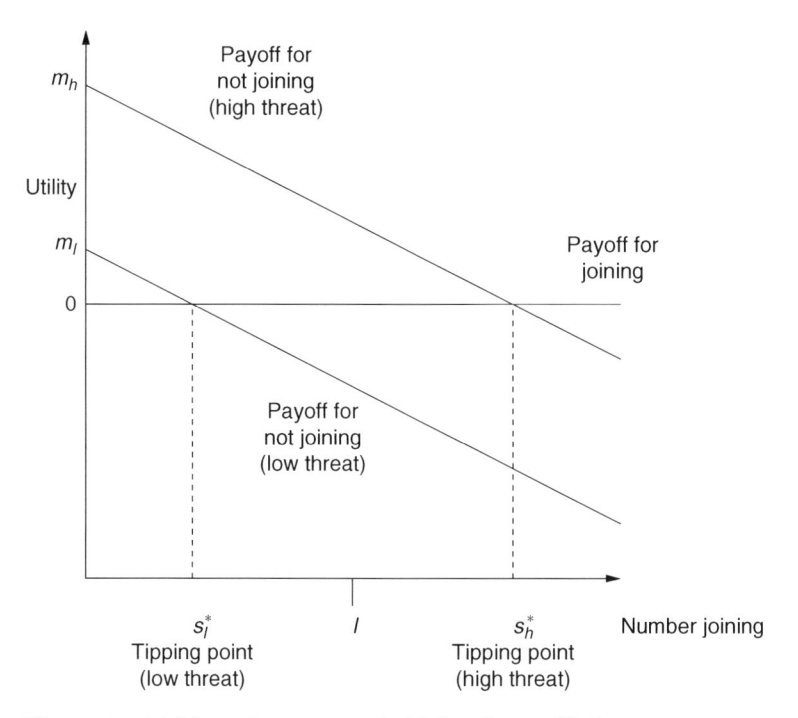

Figure 10.5 Multilateral arms control with interior equilibria

Let the military benefit of possessing landmines be particular to each state, m_i. In this case, every country will have its own tipping point

$$s_i^* = \frac{m_i}{c} \quad (10.7)$$

With particular tipping points it is easy to explain interior equilibria. Imagine two groups of countries with different levels of utility for landmines. One, the high threat countries, are engaged in military rivalries that could break out into war. Their utility for landmines is m_h. The other group are the low threat countries, who are not involved in military rivalries, and hence have less utility for landmines, m_l, where $m_h > m_l$. Let there be h high threat states and l low threat states, where $h + l = n$. The tipping point for the low threat states is $s_l^* = \frac{m_l}{c}$ and the tipping point for high threat states is $s_h^* = \frac{m_h}{c}$. We know that the tipping point for the high threat states is higher than that for the low threat states, $s_l^* < s_h^*$. This case is illustrated in Figure 10.5.

How can we get interior equilibria? If there are more low threat states than their tipping point, but not as many as the high threat states' tipping point, we have

$$s_l^* < l < s_h^*. \quad (10.8)$$

In this case, if all the low threat states get rid of their landmines, they will all be content to have done so, since $s_l^* < l$. However, the high threat states will not be content to get rid of their weapons in this case because $l < s_h^*$, so their tipping point has not been reached. Therefore, there will be three equilibria in this game: no states get rid of their weapons, only the low threat states get rid of their weapons, and all states get rid of their weapons. Note, if the high threat states value mines a great deal, so that $m_h > nc$, the last equilibrium will not exist, because the high threat states will prefer to keep their weapons, even if all other states in the world get rid of theirs.

Result 10.2 *In multilateral cooperation over issues resembling the tipping game, there can be rapid shifts from non-cooperation to cooperation, and possibly back. Interior solutions in which some players cooperate and some do not can be understood as a result of divergent preferences over the issue at stake, such that different classes of actors have different tipping points and the higher tipping points have not been reached.*

10.3 Conclusion

Cooperation can be difficult to sustain with more than two players. In public goods games and especially commons dilemmas, there is a tendency to free ride or exploit the cooperation of others that can be socially sub-optimal. However, as the Tipping game points out, with slightly different assumptions there can be rapid and beneficial social change if most actors prefer it and can coordinate their activities to achieve it. Given the ready availability of diplomacy, it would seem that coordinating on Pareto superior equilibria should be possible in international relations, although mistrust may be an obstacle (Kydd 2005, Chapter 5). Hegemony, so seemingly essential in the public goods context, may also be helpful in the Tipping game context, in helping focus expectations on the preferred equilibrium. However, the Landmines Convention shows that hegemony is not necessary; the Ottawa treaty was negotiated against US wishes, and the US has not signed. The role of non-governmental norm entrepreneurs was crucial in this case, in alliance with anti-landmine states such as Canada. Tipping models, therefore, form a potentially fruitful bridge between the rationalist and constructivist approaches to norm change in the international system (Finnemore and Sikkink 1998).

EXERCISES

10.1 A group of n states are considering an environmental treaty to reduce air pollution. Air pollution provides economic benefits in a linear fashion but the costs that it imposes are rising quadratically with the overall level of pollution. Their individual level of pollution is p_i, the sum total level of pollution is $P = \sum_i p_i$, and their utility from pollution is $p_i - \sigma P^2$, where $\sigma > 1$ is an environmental parameter measuring how sensitive to pollution the environment is. Assume all players are symmetrical.

1. What is the Nash level of pollution? Graph this as a function of the number of states.
2. What is the utility associated with this level of pollution? Graph this as a function of the number of states.
3. How many states in the system must there be for the countries to be better off not polluting at all (setting $p_i = 0$)?

10.2 Consider the following stylization of the tragedy of the commons. A group of n states face the choice to permit fishing or ban fishing. If they choose B for ban, their payoff is 0. If they choose F for permit fishing, their payoff is either 0 or $m - p$, whichever is greater, where m is a positive integer, and p is the number of other players choosing F.

1. Under what condition is there a Nash equilibrium in which anyone has a payoff greater than 0?
2. If it exists, is it unique?

10.3 Consider a more complicated version of the previous game. Each player can choose a number x_i between 0 and 1 representing her level of effort devoted to fishing. The greater effort you exert, the more costs you pay, and the more fish you catch, depending on what the others are doing. The utility function for each player is the following

$$U_i = \frac{x_i}{\sum_j x_j} b_i - x_i^2 c_i$$

where b_i is a constant representing benefits, c_i is a constant representing costs, and $\sum_j x_j$ is the sum total of the other players' efforts.

1. Find the Nash equilibrium level of effort for player i.
2. What utility does this level of effort yield?
3. How and why does this game differ from the previous version in terms of its overall implications for cooperation?

11 Domestic politics and international relations

Domestic politics has an extremely important impact on international relations.[1] To begin to address this impact, it is possible to use unitary actor models that differentiate the actors according to variables that represent features of their domestic political makeup, for instance, their costs for fighting or their level of transparency. However, for some aspects of domestic politics, it is necessary to go beyond this and leave behind the unitary state assumption that I have maintained so far. Following the overall rationalist approach and commitment to parsimony, however, I will depart from it as little as possible. The usual method is to recast the state as an individual executive or leader, and add an additional (unitary) actor to the model, representing a domestic institution such as a legislature. If the other state is left unitary, this procedure results in a three actor model that is often quite useful without being overly complex.

11.1 The impact of domestic politics

The role of domestic politics in international relations, and vice versa, has been debated for centuries. Some nineteenth-century historians, such as Leopold von Ranke, argued for the "primat der aussenpolitik" or primacy of foreign policy, holding that international relations has a profound impact on domestic politics. Otto von Hintze (1975) famously argued that Prussia was autocratic because its exposed position on the European plain necessitated a strong state, while England had the freedom to develop democracy because it was protected from foreign threat by the English Channel. Marx, of course, focused on the class structure within states as the most important variable in explaining their behavior, and his disciple Lenin (1996 (1916)) blamed the origins of the First World War on capitalist imperialism. Subsequent historians attempting to come to grips with Germany's record of aggression in the twentieth century placed

---

[1] Bueno de Mesquita and Smith (2012) survey the formal literature on domestic influences on international relations. Gehlbach (2013) provides an introduction to formal models of domestic politics.

the blame squarely on domestic factors, arguing for the "primat der innenpolitik," or primacy of domestic politics. Historians such as Kehr (1965), Fischer (1967), and Mayer (1981) all argued that aristocratic/industrial regimes in an era of mass mobilization used nationalism to fight calls for liberal democracy and socialism, with results that eventually led to war.

This debate continued in political science in a conversation between realism and its alternatives. Waltz (1954) divided the explanations for war into three categories: the first relating to psychology, the second relating to domestic politics, and the third relating to international factors. Waltz endorsed the third category, equating it with political realism, and went on to write the definitive brief for it in his *Theory of International Politics* (Waltz 1979). This led to much subsequent discussion of the "levels of analysis" question, or how the same event can be explained using variables at different levels (Singer 1961). Peter Gourevitch (1978) revived Hintze's thesis in a famous essay arguing for the "second image reversed," or the influence of international factors on domestic politics. Other scholars took up the cause of domestic factors which became particularly salient in the United States as the Vietnam era eroded the relative foreign policy consensus of the early Cold War (Rosenau 1967). Moravcsik (1997) argues for a version of liberalism that posits the internal determination of state preferences as the most important factor explaining state behavior, of far greater significance than relative power, information, or international institutions.

Domestic political actors are usually thought to influence international events by either *constraining, rewarding and punishing*, or *selecting* the state leader. First, they may be able to veto actions or agreements undertaken by the executive, and so pose a constraint on the leader's behavior, sometimes called a "ratification constraint" in the context of treaties. In the presence of such "veto players," the executive must play a "two-level game" between international and domestic actors (Putnam 1988, Tsebelis 1991, 2002). This kind of constraint is often built into the constitutional process in a democracy, where institutions like the legislature must ratify treaties or vote for war. Following Putnam's influential article, a group of scholars applied this metaphor to a variety of security and political economy contexts (Evans *et al.* 1993). Game theorists took up the concept and developed a series of closely related models investigating the effect of domestic constraints on one side, both sides, and with and without uncertainty (Iida 1993b, 1996, Mo 1994, 1995, Milner 1997, Tarar 2001, 2005). One key question was whether domestic constraints help in bargaining internationally, a conjecture attributed to Schelling (1960, 28). The conjecture was generally supported but with some exceptions.

Second, domestic audiences can reward a leader for doing something they like and punish a leader for pursuing policies they do not like, even if they cannot stop the leader from pursuing them. Models of trade protection often feature domestic interests offering a schedule of rewards and punishments to the leader to encourage them to adopt preferred economic policies (Grossman and Helpman 1994, 1996). The inducements are often conceived of as campaign contributions and the punishments as contributions to opposing candidates.

Finally, and most fundamentally, domestic actors may be able to replace the leader with someone else, which means that leaders must take into account not just their own preferences but those of actors who could potentially fire them.[2] The institutions for selecting leaders may, therefore, be very important in determining international behavior, by determining to whom, and how, the leader must pay attention in formulating international policies. The literature on the democratic peace is built on this insight. Empirical researchers have found that democracies rarely fight each other (Russett 1993). Theorists have attempted to account for this finding in a number of ways. Bueno de Mesquita *et al.* (2003) argue that democratic leaders are beholden to large groups that cannot be bought off with private goods, as the supporters of authoritarian leaders can be. This means that they must produce public goods such as successful foreign policies, which lead them to avoid wars unless the chance of victory is very high. Democracies are held to choose their conflicts more wisely, fight harder and win more often (Lake 1992, Reiter and Stam 2002). And, as discussed in Chapter 9, democratic states are thought to be able to send more credible signals because of their ability to generate a risk of being punished by domestic actors for lying. Fiona McGillivray and Alastair Smith developed the related concept of *leader-specific punishments* (McGillivray and Smith 2000, 2005, 2006, 2008). The idea is that leaders, rather than the state itself, are held responsible for the cooperation or defection of a state. This gives the population an incentive to replace leaders who defect in the international system, which can help sustain cooperation and honesty.

Related to the selection issue, leaders who are insecure in office are sometimes held to be more belligerent, in a phenomenon known as *diversionary war* (Smith 1996, Tarar 2006). Snyder (1991) generalized the earlier historical arguments about German aggression and argued that authoritarian states facing pressures for democratization were particularly war prone (Mansfield and Snyder 1995). Leaders who feel that they are likely to lose power may be willing to start a war in the hope that a triumph will extend their lease on office. Similarly, once a war is underway, some leaders will feel that they have little incentive to settle on moderate or losing terms, since they will be kicked out of office in any event, so they might as well keep fighting so long as there is any hope of gains sufficient to appease the population. This is sometimes known as *gambling for resurrection* (Downs and Rocke 1995, Goemans 2000, Chiozza and Goemans 2011).

---

[2] Of course, replacement is itself a form of punishment, so these last two forms of influence are related.

A related literature in economics focuses on "principal–agent" models (Laffont and Martimort 2001). In these models, the principal empowers an agent to act on its behalf. Typically, the principal has resources, such as money, but limited time and attention, and wishes to hire the agent to carry out its wishes in a specific context. The agent will often have divergent preferences, it may wish to slack off and not work as hard as the principal wishes, or it may even have different preferences over the outcome of the game. The agent may also have an informational advantage associated with closer study of the issue, or spending more time on it. This means that the principal must design a contract that gets the agent to follow its wishes as closely as possibal, compensating for the agent's different preferences and superior information. In international relations, the principal is sometimes thought to be "the people" or more modestly the median voter, and the leader is the agent.

This literature is too large and diverse to do justice to in a single chapter. In what follows, I will focus on the mechanism of domestic ratification or two-level games. I develop a model where the executive is constrained by a legislature and see how this affects international bargaining. Key questions include: When do domestic constraints shift the bargaining outcome, and to whose advantage? Was Schelling right, are domestic constraints an advantage to a negotiator? I will also be able to address the question of whether bargaining leads to efficient outcomes, and from whose perspective, a topic that has not been well developed yet by the extensive literature on the topic. In particular, I will show that once we add a domestic actor with preferences that differ from the leader's, there is no longer a simple answer to the question of what constitutes the set of efficient outcomes between two states, and whether bargaining will achieve an outcome in it.

11.2 Domestic constraints in bargaining

Let's consider a two-dimensional issue space designed to represent an issue area in which each side controls some policy variable that affects their own and the other side's utility.[3] To make things more concrete, let's think of them as tariffs. Each side has a tariff level, t_i. This generates a two-dimensional space of tariffs, illustrated in Figure 11.1. The horizontal axis is player 1's tariff level, t_1, and the vertical axis is player 2's, t_2. Each player has a utility function defined over the space, $u_i(t_1, t_2)$. This utility function will

---

[3] The setup follows Milner and Rosendorff (1997) (see also Martin 2000, 40). Typically, this problem is modeled as a one-dimensional bargaining space between the two states where the leaders on both sides have a status quo payoff of 0, but the legislature has a positive value for the status quo that imposes an additional floor on what the leader can accept (see the papers by Iida, Mo, and Tarar, cited above). This makes it hard to understand why the legislature does not benefit from some agreements that benefit the leader, and so leaves the legislatively imposed floor somewhat mysterious. The setup used here provides one possible explanation for this.

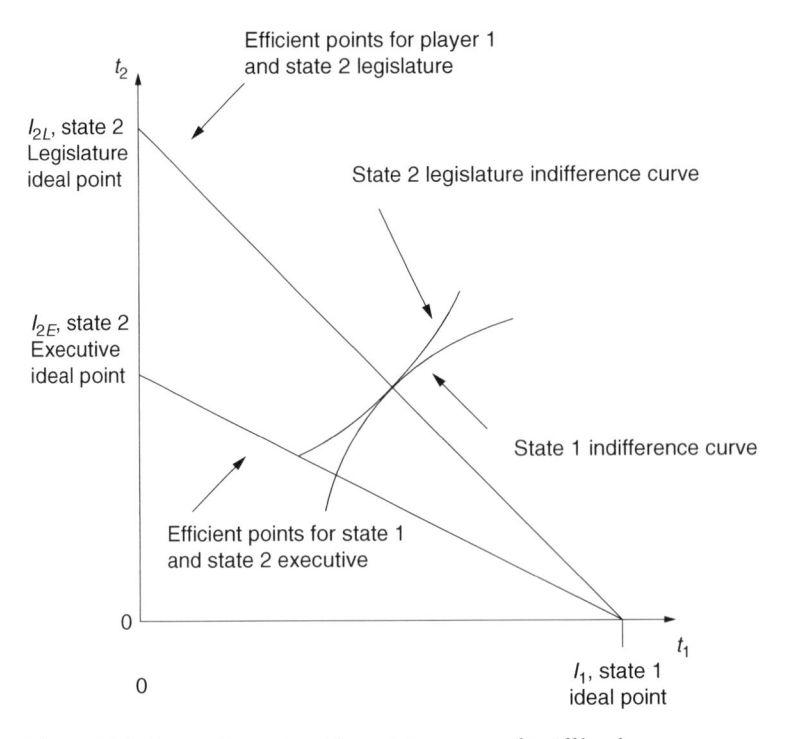

Figure 11.1 A two-dimensional bargaining space of tariff levels

have a maximum at the player's ideal point. I assume that everyone wants the other side's tariff to be 0, and has a most preferred tariff for their own side. State 1 is assumed to be unitary, and its ideal point is on the horizontal axis at $(I_1, 0)$. State 2 is assumed to be divided into an executive, with a lower ideal point at $(0, I_{2E})$, and a legislature, with a higher one at $(0, I_{2L})$, where $I_{2E} < I_{2L}$. Therefore, the executive prefers lower tariffs than the median voter of the legislature, reflecting the usual idea that the executive represents a national constituency and so is more attuned to the welfare benefits of free trade. For simplicity, let's also assume that the utility functions of the players are a simple function of the distance to the ideal point as follows

$$u_1(t_1, t_2) = -\sqrt{(t_1 - I_1)^2 + t_2^2} \tag{11.1}$$

$$u_{2E}(t_1, t_2) = -\sqrt{t_1^2 + (t_2 - I_{2E})^2} \tag{11.2}$$

$$u_{2L}(t_1, t_2) = -\sqrt{t_1^2 + (t_2 - I_{2L})^2} \tag{11.3}$$

This implies that the indifference curves or level sets of the utility functions are circles around the ideal point. A pair of indifference curves are illustrated in Figure 11.1 for state 1 and for the legislature of state 2. A point of tangency between the indifference curves of two players, such as the one illustrated, is efficient from their perspective; no one player can be made better off by moving from such a point without making the

11.2 DOMESTIC CONSTRAINTS IN BARGAINING

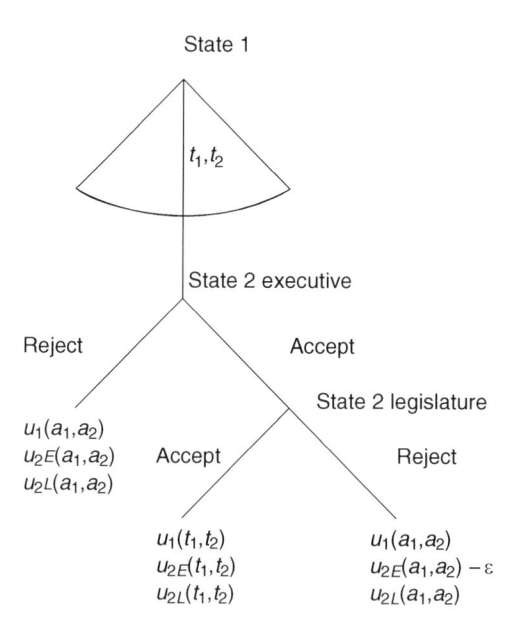

Figure 11.2 Bargaining with ratification

other one worse off. By finding all such points of tangency between state 1's indifference curves and those of the legislature of state 2, we can find the set of efficient outcomes from their perspective. We can do the same between state 1 and the executive of state 2. Because the indifference curves for each player are circles, the set of Pareto optimal or efficient points between player 1 and either version of player 2 will be a straight line between the ideal points of the two players, as illustrated in Figure 11.1.[4] The set of efficient points if we count all three actors is the triangle between the ideal points. From any point in this triangle, any move will make at least one actor worse off.

With this bargaining space in mind, let's return to the basic bargaining model of Chapter 4. Let player 1 make an offer, this time in two dimensions, (t_1, t_2), and player 2 can accept it or reject it, as illustrated in Figure 11.2. I will assume that war is effectively off the table due to its costs in comparison with the stakes at issue, so rejecting the offer simply leaves the status quo in place, denoted (a_1, a_2).[5] If the executive on state 2's side accepts the offer, it then goes before state 2's legislature for an up or down vote. If the legislature vetoes the deal, then the status quo remains in place; if the legislature approves it, then the deal is implemented. I assume that the executive on state 2's side suffers a small cost, ε, if the deal is rejected in the legislature, so they would prefer to reject it themselves if they anticipate that it will be rejected by the legislature.[6]

---

[4] See Chapter 2 for discussion of the Edgeworth Box and contract curve.
[5] See Trager (2011) for a multidimensional bargaining model in the crisis bargaining context.
[6] The model is essentially a one-round spatial choice problem with two dimensions, three players, and unanimity rule, where one player makes a proposal and any player can veto it.

Table 11.1 Equilibria in the Bargaining game with domestic constraints

State 1	Propose (t_1^*, t_2^*)
State 2E	Accept if $u_{2L}(t_1, t_2) \geq u_{2L}(a_1, a_2)$ and $u_{2E}(t_1, t_2) \geq u_{2E}(a_1, a_2)$, reject otherwise
State 2L	Accept if $u_{2L}(t_1, t_2) \geq u_{2L}(a_1, a_2)$, reject otherwise

11.2.1 Equilibrium

The game can be easily solved for subgame perfect equilibria. The legislature on state 2's side will accept a deal if it is as least as good as the status quo, $u_{2L}(t_1, t_2) \geq u_{2L}(a_1, a_2)$, and not otherwise. If the legislature will reject the deal, then the executive on state 2's side prefers to reject it. If the legislature will accept it, then the leader will accept it only if it beats the status quo, $u_{2E}(t_1, t_2) \geq u_{2E}(a_1, a_2)$. Let (t_1^*, t_2^*) be the best point for state 1 that satisfies both of those constraints. If it beats the status quo, then state 1 will offer it. The equilibrium can be summed up in Table 11.1.

The deal, therefore, must satisfy both the leader and the legislature from state 2. This much is obvious. The interesting question arises when we consider where (t_1^*, t_2^*) is in the bargaining space, how it compares with the status quo, and how it compares with what would have happened had the leader of state 2 not been constrained.

We can analyze this graphically by considering Figure 11.3. Here the status quo point, (a_1, a_2), is assumed to be above the efficient line of deals between state 1 and the legislature of state 2, so mutual gains are possible even between state 2's legislature and state 1. Indifference curves for the executive and legislature of state 2 through the status quo point are illustrated. It is clear that the curve for the legislature is more constraining, from state 1's perspective, in that any deal that lies along the indifference curve of the legislature and is closer to the efficient set of points between state 1 and the legislature of state 2 will automatically be acceptable to state 2's executive. The best such point from state 1's perspective is where one of state 1's indifference curves is tangent to the legislature's curve that passes through the status quo point, which must be on the line of efficient points, and is denoted (t_1^*, t_2^*). State 2's legislature will (weakly) be willing to accept such a proposal, as it provides the same utility as the status quo. It makes state 1 as well off as it can be and still satisfy state 2's legislature. State 2's executive prefers it to the status quo. Hence, it is the equilibrium offer of the game.

Looking at this point, we can deduce several implications for the game. First, because the legislature of state 2 has a more extreme ideal point, it will be barely satisfied with the treaty. State 1 will select a treaty that barely buys off the legislature of state 2. Second, the executive of state 2 benefits from the existence of the legislature's harder line. If the executive were unencumbered by a legislature, state 1 would offer the point on the executive's indifference curve through the status quo that is best for itself, shown

11.2 DOMESTIC CONSTRAINTS IN BARGAINING

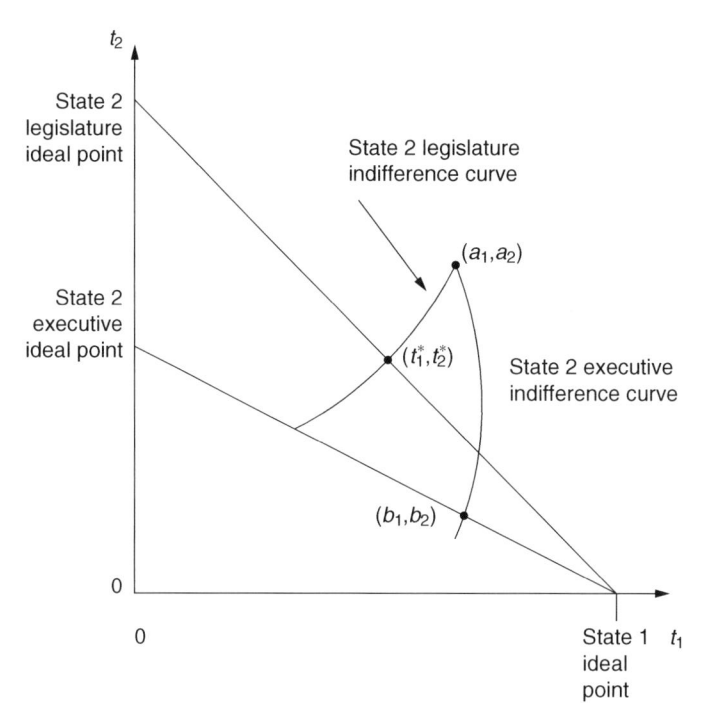

Figure 11.3 Equilibrium in the Two-Level Bargaining game

as (b_1, b_2) in Figure 11.3. In comparison with the equilibrium point, state 1 has higher tariffs and state 2 has lower ones, and state 2's executive is worse off. Thus, confirming Schelling, the existence of the harder-line legislature strengthens the hand of the executive and results in a better deal from the executive's perspective.

Next, both the executive of state 2 and that of state 1 benefit from the equilibrium in comparison with the status quo, so the equilibrium of the Bargaining game is a Pareto improvement from their point of view. In fact, while the legislature does not strictly benefit from the change, state 1 and the executive of state 2 experience strict improvements in utility, so they are definitely better off having bargained to an agreement.

Finally, although both state 1 and the executive of state 2 benefit from the agreement, the equilibrium is not efficient from their point of view. From the perspective of the leaders, there are still joint gains going unrealized, because the equilibrium is north east of the line of efficient outcomes linking their ideal points. This inefficiency may lead them to wish they could outmaneuver the legislature of state 2 and negotiate a second agreement not subject to their veto. But as long as state 2's legislature can veto an agreement, state 1 and the executive of state 2 cannot realize all the joint gains they could if left to their own devices.

These findings help us understand some of the qualitative patterns surrounding complex international negotiations. In particular, international negotiations often proceed in stages that grow progressively more difficult, prolonged, and subject to breakdown. The rounds of negotiations focusing on world trade are an example. The General Agreement on Tariffs and Trade (GATT) was negotiated in 1948 and then extended in subsequent rounds of negotiations that have covered increasingly intrusive subjects and taken increasingly long to complete. The model above suggests that after initial gains are reaped that make domestic veto players barely satisfied with the deal, further progress will be difficult without disenfranchising those veto players. Further rounds of negotiation will, therefore, run up against the fact that, while leaders see room for joint gains, domestic veto players do not. As a result, once initial gains have been realized, leaders have more interests in common with the leader on the other side than they do with their own domestic veto player.

Result 11.1 *The presence of a legislative constraint benefits the executive in international negotiations. The resulting deal is barely acceptable to the legislature and better for the executive than it would have negotiated without the constraint. However, the executives on each side will find it Pareto inferior to alternative deals involving greater cooperation.*

11.3 Two-sided constraints

We can make the game more symmetrical by adding a legislature on state 1's side which also must pass on the deal. The game tree is illustrated in Figure 11.4. The game is the same as before except for a new final move in which state 1's legislature must approve the deal. I assume that each executive suffers a cost of embarrassment if their own legislature vetoes the deal but not if the other side does.

The equilibrium is similar to the one-sided case, and is illustrated in Table 11.2. The legislatures accept the deal if it is as good as their payoff for the status quo. State 2's executive accepts the deal if it will be ratified by its legislature and if it prefers it to the status quo and rejects it otherwise. State 1's executive will choose the best deal for itself that will be approved by all three of the other players.

Once again, the key question is what the initial offer, (t_1^*, t_2^*), will look like. The new constraints are shown in Figure 11.5. Now four ideal points are illustrated, for the executive and legislature of each side. The lines connecting them are the contract curves, or efficient points between each pair of players. The efficient set for the four players taken together is the quadrilateral bounded by the contract curve linking the legislatures' ideal points, that linking the executives' ideal points, and the connecting segments of the axes. No point in this set is a Pareto improvement or any other point in the set.

11.3 TWO-SIDED CONSTRAINTS

Table 11.2 Equilibria in the Bargaining game with two-sided constraints

State 1E	Propose (t_1^*, t_2^*)
State 2E	Accept if $u_{2L}(t_1, t_2) \geq u_{2L}(a_1, a_2)$ and $u_{2E}(t_1, t_2) \geq u_{2E}(a_1, a_2)$, reject otherwise
State 2L	Accept if $u_{2L}(t_1, t_2) \geq u_{2L}(a_1, a_2)$, reject otherwise
State 1L	Accept if $u_{1L}(t_1, t_2) \geq u_{1L}(a_1, a_2)$, reject otherwise

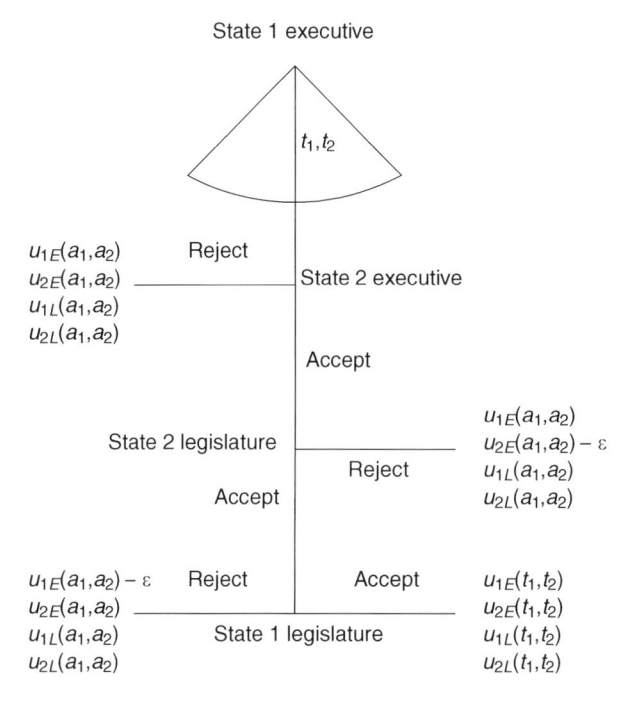

Figure 11.4 Bargaining with two-sided ratification

The status quo is illustrated as the point (a_1, a_2). Indifference curves for the legislatures through this point define a lens of outcomes that both legislatures would consider at least as good as the status quo. For clarity, I have not drawn the corresponding lens for the executives, but it is clear that the lens for the legislatures is contained in that for the executives, and there is no point that would be acceptable to the legislatures that would be unacceptable to either executive, so it is the legislatures that pose the binding constraints.

The executive of state 1, therefore, faces the task of picking the best outcome for itself in the lens of deals preferred by the legislatures. This turns out to be the lower tip of the lens, labeled (t_1^*, t_2^*). State 1's leader clearly prefers points on the lower boundary of the lens, defined by the indifference curve of state 2's legislature. The best such point would be a point of tangency, as in the previous case, where there was no legislature on state 1's side. In this case, however, state 1's legislature would veto the point of tangency, so

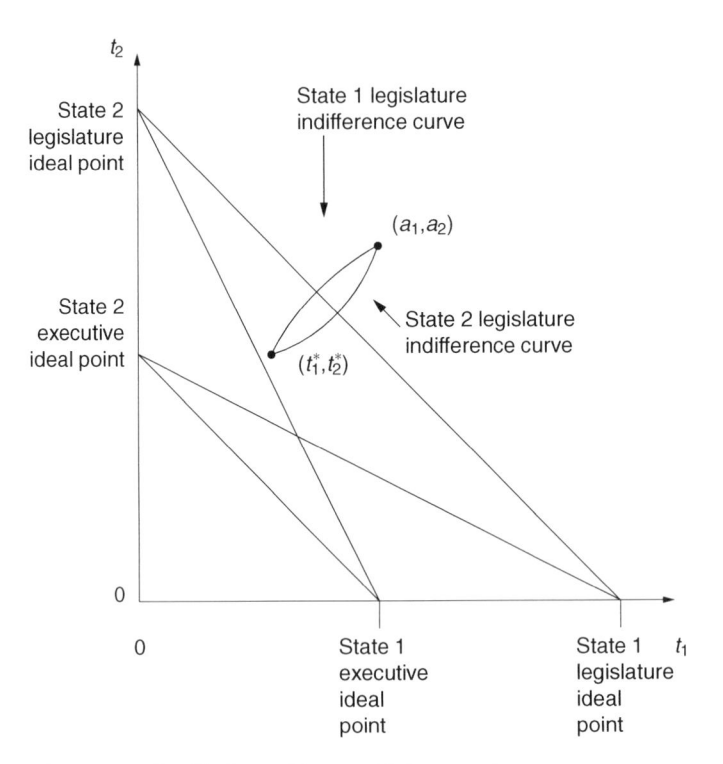

Figure 11.5 Equilibrium with two-sided constraints

state 1's executive chooses the closest point to it that is acceptable to state 1's legislature, namely the lower tip of the lens. Thus, both constraints are binding in this case, both legislatures exercise a constraining effect on their executives. Interestingly, the executive of player 2 would also pick this point, as the lower end of the lens is the best point in the lens from its perspective as well. In this case, it does not matter which executive gets to make the proposal – they would both pick the same point.

This equilibrium point is in the Pareto optimal set for the four players considered together. However, it is not on the contract curve between any two particular players, so no pair of players considers it Pareto optimal. The two legislatures could reap joint gains by mutual increases in tariffs. The two executives could reap joint gains by reducing tariffs. Each executive and the legislature of the other side would also prefer mutual reductions, although smaller ones than the two leaders would deem optimal. The outcome, therefore, although acceptable to everyone, is deemed optimal by no pair of players; all of them would like to renegotiate the agreement if only they could dispense with one of the other players, possibly their own domestic counterpart.

As far as the Schelling conjecture goes, we can easily see that state 2's executive still benefits from having a legislature. The constraint imposed by state 2's legislature pulls the equilibrium point much closer to the executive of state 2's ideal point than it would be without the legislature. Player 1, however, is not benefiting by having a legislature, in fact it is slightly harmed by it. Without state 1's legislature, state 1's leader would pick the best outcome that state 2's legislature would accept. With a legislature of its own, state 1's leader must depart from this point to some extent. However, this is an extreme case because state 1 is allocated all the bargaining power here by virtue of moving first, so any additional constraint can only harm it.

Result 11.2 *With legislative constraints on both sides, the resulting deal may be determined wholly by constraints imposed by the two legislatures. The executives on each side may agree on the best possible deal given legislative constraints. The resulting deal will be efficient from the perspective of all four actors, but will not be Pareto optimal for any pair. In particular, the executives will agree that greater cooperation would be Pareto improving.*

The equilibrium may not always be at the lower tip of the lens of the constraints imposed by the legislatures. If the status quo point, (a_1, a_2), were further out, the lower tip of the lens would be correspondingly further towards the origin. If the contract curve between the executive of state 1 and the legislature of state 2 intersected the lens, then the lower point of intersection would be the equilibrium. This case would then be just as in the previous case in which state 1 was unitary. State 1's legislature would be content with the best deal that state 1's executive could extract from state 2's legislature, so state 1's legislature (and state 2's executive) would not impose a binding constraint. This illustrates the common observation of spatial models, that is, the worse the status quo is, the more leeway the proposer has in altering it to its satisfaction. The more actors that like the status quo, the less leeway there is for change.

In all the cases so far discussed, the deal is not optimal for the executives of the two states. Left to their own devices, the leaders would prefer to renegotiate the deal. There is one version of this model, however, in which this is not true. Milner and Rosendorff (1997) look at a one-sided constraint model, but have the domestically constrained leader make the offer. That is, in terms of the first model, state 2's executive proposes a deal and then a unitary state 1 either accepts it or not, and then state 2's legislature accepts it or not. In this case, the leader of state 2 will propose the best deal on the contract curve between itself and state 1 that state 2's legislature will accept. Thus, the executives will find the deal Pareto optimal as long as the state making the proposal is the one with a domestic constraint and the other state is unitary. For instance, if the US is negotiating with an autocratic regime in a context where the US has most of the bargaining leverage, the deal may be optimal from the perspective of the leaders. If both sides have domestic constraints or if the unitary state has more leverage, however, the deal will be found wanting by the executives.

11.4 Cheap talk and negotiation with domestic constraints

We have seen that state 2's executive benefits from having a legislature that constrains what deal they will accept, confirming the Schelling conjecture. An interesting question then arises as to whether leaders can usefully communicate with each other about their domestic constraints. Anecdotally, it appears that leaders frequently do this, referring to the difficulty of getting a deal ratified in order to extract more concessions from foreign negotiators. Such communication appears to be cheap talk, in that it is private and costless. In bargaining contexts, we usually start from the premise that such talk is not credible, although there are exceptions to this rule (Trager 2014). Is talk cheap when it is about domestic constraints?

Consider the following model. As before, state 1 is unitary. State 2 has an executive and a legislature. The legislature may be moderate or extreme in its ideal point, as illustrated in Figure 11.6. Contract curves are drawn between state 1's ideal point and those of the executive and two possible legislatures for state 2. Indifference curves through the status quo point are illustrated for the two different types of legislature. The points where they intersect with their respective contract curve would be equilibria if their type was known; these points are designated (t_1^e, t_2^e) for the extreme legislature and (t_1^m, t_2^m) for the moderate legislature. By construction, I have illustrated a case in which the status quo is pretty extreme, in that state 2 has high tariffs and the extreme type of

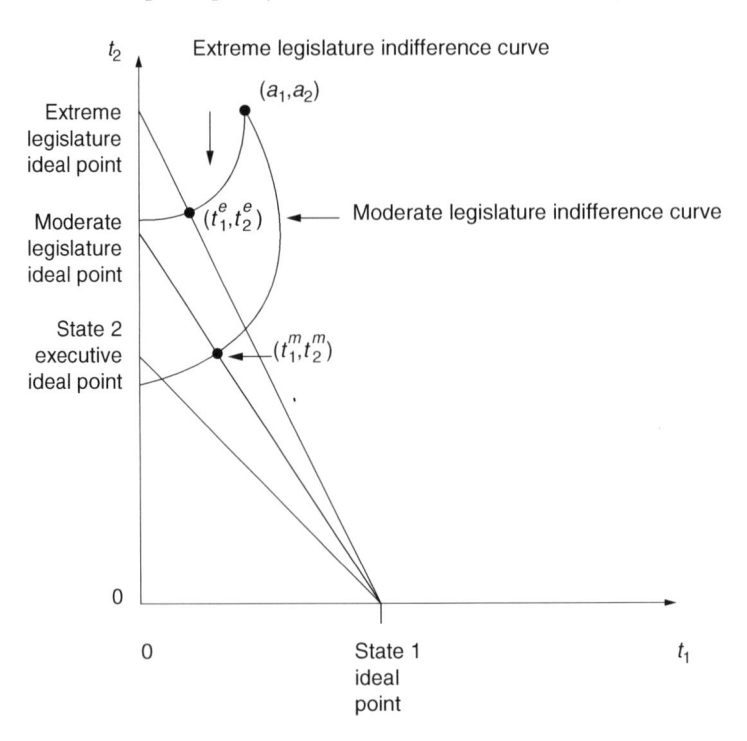

Figure 11.6 Issue space with uncertainty about state 2's legislature

11.4 CHEAP TALK AND NEGOTIATION WITH DOMESTIC CONSTRAINTS

legislature on player 2's side is quite happy with that state of affairs. Hence, the indifference curve for the extreme legislature poses a severe constraint, and the resulting equilibrium still features high tariffs for state 2. The moderate legislature would not be so happy with the status quo and the corresponding equilibrium features greatly reduced tariffs for player 2.

Crucially, again by construction, the executive of state 2 would prefer to have a moderate legislature to an extreme one. It prefers the equilibrium associated with a moderate legislature to that induced by an extreme one, $u_{2E}(t_1^m, t_2^m) > u_{2E}(t_1^e, t_2^e)$.[7] State 1 also prefers the equilibrium associated with the moderate legislature, because it results in much lower tariffs for player 2. Therefore, state 1 and the executive of state 2 have a shared preference for a moderate legislature in state 2. This common interest will make communication possible.

Let there be uncertainty about whether the legislature is moderate or extreme. The likelihood that the legislature is moderate is $P(2LM)$ and the likelihood that the legislature is extreme is $1 - P(2LM)$. Everyone on state 2's side is informed of the legislature's type, but state 1 is not. Then they play the game illustrated in Figure 11.7. The executive of state 2 can make a statement about whether their legislature is moderate or extreme. Then the game proceeds as before. State 1 makes an offer, the executive of state 2 accepts it or rejects it, and if it accepts it the deal is placed before the legislature of state 2 for final approval.[8]

The question of interest is whether there is an equilibrium with honest communication, in which the executive of state 2 honestly reveals the type of its legislature to state 1, and state 1 conditions its offer appropriately. Such an equilibrium is shown in Table 11.3. The executive of state 2 honestly communicates whether the legislature is moderate or extreme. Player 1 then conditions its offer on this information, offering the moderate point if the leader says the legislature is moderate and the extreme point if the leader says the legislature is extreme. The executive of state 2 then accepts the offer if it will be acceptable to the actual legislature and rejects if otherwise, and the legislature accepts deals they prefer to the status quo.

When is this equilibrium sustainable? The legislatures' strategies are straightforwardly optimal; they have no uncertainty. The executive's decision over accepting the offer is also straightforward, the leader knows the legislature's type and, therefore, knows what will pass muster. If the deal is acceptable to the legislature and the leader, it will be accepted. For state 1, the game is also the same as before, given the truth-telling

---

[7] Interestingly, the executive of state 2 would also prefer having the moderate legislature to none at all. In fact, we can show that there is a "best" legislative ideal point from the perspective of the executive.

[8] Note, the game tree depicted in Figure 11.7 is only a portion of the total game. The full game begins with a move by Nature to select the type of state 2's legislature. Then state 2's executive has the communication opportunity illustrated in the figure. State 1 does not observe Nature's choice.

Table 11.3 Equilibria in the Constrained Bargaining game with uncertainty

State 2E	Say "moderate" if 2LM, "extreme" if 2LE
State 1	Propose (t_1^m, t_2^m) if "moderate," (t_1^e, t_2^e) if "Extreme"
State 2E	Accept if [2LM and $u_{2LM}(t_1, t_2) \geq u_{2LM}(a_1, a_2)$ or 2LE and $u_{2LE}(t_1, t_2) \geq u_{2LE}(a_1, a_2)$] and $u_{2E}(t_1, t_2) \geq u_{2E}(a_1, a_2)$, reject otherwise
State 2LM	Accept if $u_{2LM}(t_1, t_2) \geq u_{2LM}(a_1, a_2)$, reject otherwise
State 2LE	Accept if $u_{2LE}(t_1, t_2) \geq u_{2LE}(a_1, a_2)$, reject otherwise
Conditions	$u_{2E}(t_1^m, t_2^m) \geq u_{2E}(t_1^e, t_2^e) \geq u_{2E}(a_1, a_2)$

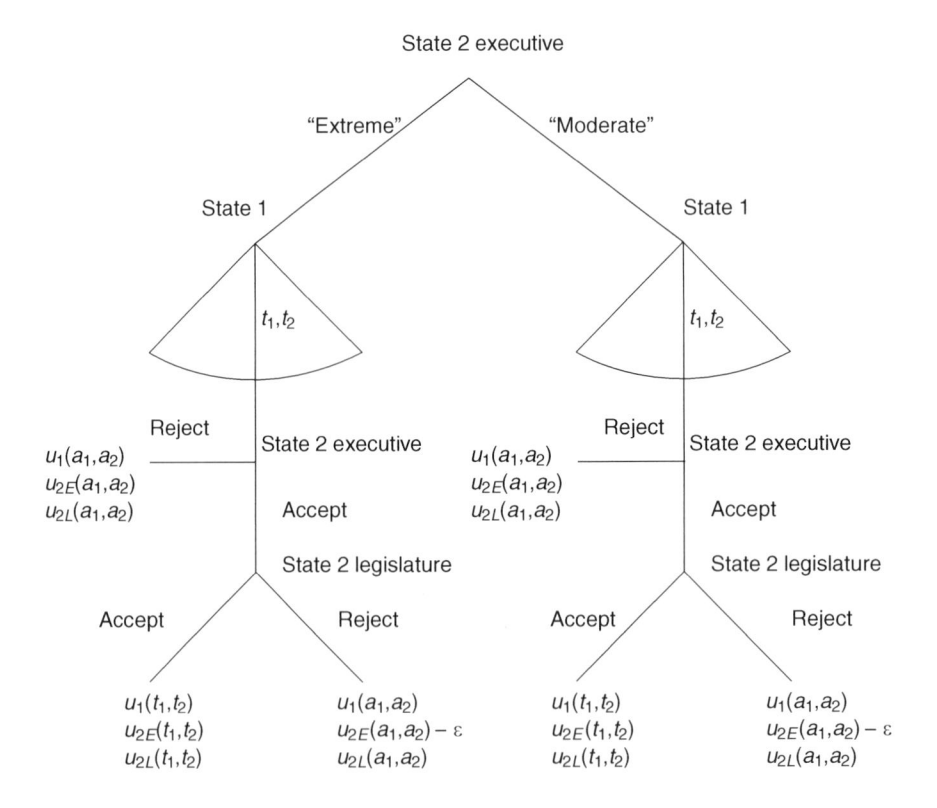

Figure 11.7 Communication and bargaining with domestic constraints

strategy of the executive of state 2. Given the executive's honesty, state 1 updates its beliefs to certainty corresponding to what the leader of state 2 says.

The key remaining question, therefore, is: Does the executive of state 2 have an incentive to be honest? Consider first if the legislature is actually extreme. If the executive is honest and says the legislature is extreme, the offer will be (t_1^e, t_2^e) for a payoff of $u_{2E}(t_1^e, t_2^e)$. Lying and saying "moderate" will result in an offer of (t_1^m, t_2^m). This offer will be rejected by the extreme legislature, so the leader will have to reject it as well, leading to the status quo for a payoff of $u_{2E}(a_1, a_2)$. So if the executive prefers the extreme legislature's equilibrium to the status quo, as it does in Figure 11.6, the executive will prefer to be honest in this case, leading to the following condition

$$u_{2E}(t_1^e, t_2^e) \geq u_{2E}(a_1, a_2) \tag{11.4}$$

Now consider if the legislature is actually moderate. Saying that the legislature is moderate will result in an offer of (t_1^m, t_2^m), which will be accepted for a payoff of $u_{2E}(t_1^m, t_2^m)$. Lying and saying that the legislature is extreme will result in an offer of (t_1^e, t_2^e). This offer will actually be acceptable to the moderate legislature as well as the leader, so it will be accepted for a payoff of $u_{2E}(t_1^e, t_2^e)$. If this payoff is not as good as the payoff associated with the moderate legislature, then honesty will be preferred. This leads to a second condition required for the equilibrium to hold

$$u_{2E}(t_1^m, t_2^m) \geq u_{2E}(t_1^e, t_2^e) \tag{11.5}$$

So if the leader of state 2 prefers the equilibrium with a moderate legislature to that with an extreme one, and the equilibrium with an extreme legislature to the status quo, then it will have the proper incentives to be honest about the ideal point of its own legislature in negotiation with state 1. If these conditions are met, the honest communication equilibrium will be possible between the executives of state 2 and state 1.

This equilibrium demonstrates that the oft-heard claim, "I would like to agree to that offer but my legislature would never ratify it" may sometimes be credible after all. It can be believable if the executives share a preference for a moderate legislature, but realize that the legislature may be extreme. In that case, the leader of the constrained state will have an incentive to honestly reveal the extent of its constraint. Given that it would not want the offer associated with an extreme constraint, it has no incentive to pretend it is severely constrained unless it truly is. Note, this would be difficult to imagine in a one-dimensional setting, where constraints can only improve the leader's bargaining outcome, unless they make agreement impossible altogether. Here the equilibrium with the extreme legislature is feasible, and preferred to the status quo, but not to the deal that would be produced by a moderate constraint, an impossibility with a one-dimensional good.

Result 11.3 *If there is uncertainty over the severity of the legislative constraint, and if the executive would prefer to have a moderate legislature rather than an extreme legislature, and an extreme legislature to none at all, the executive can be honest about the severity of its constraint, and credibly communicate information on this to the other state.*

11.5 Conclusion

The impact of domestic politics on international relations is a fertile field of research. In the corner of this literature addressed in this chapter, we have seen that domestic veto players help explain why agreements fall short of the desires of leaders, why domestic constraints may nonetheless benefit leaders, and how leaders can credibly communicate about their domestic constraints. Domestic considerations also help explain what states want from the international system, whether they are cooperative or exploitative, whether they honor their commitments or not, and when they can communicate credibly. While adding domestic actors makes modeling the domestic–international interaction more complex, scholars are increasingly coming to the conclusion that international relations cannot be adequately understood without taking domestic features into account.

EXERCISES

11.1 Consider a crisis Bargaining game with the following structure. The voters of state 2 elect a leader of state 2. Then the states play the Bargaining Game of Chapter 4 in which state 1 makes an offer, and the leader of state 2 either accepts it, rejects it, or fights. There are two candidates for leader of state 2, differentiated by their cost of fighting, a low cost type, c_{2l}, and a high cost type, c_{2h}. The voters of state 2 have a cost for fighting of c_{2v}. Assume that player 1's power, p, is less than the status quo, so $p < s$. Assume that all actors have linear utility functions.

1. Is there an equilibrium in which the voters of state 2 strictly prefer to elect the low cost type? If so, list the conditions required for it.
2. Is there an equilibrium in which the voters of state 2 strictly prefer to elect the high cost type? If not why not?

11.2 Now assume that the types of leader for player 2 are differentiated not by their cost but by their utility functions. Let the utility functions for the potential leaders of state 2 be $u(x) = (1 - x)^\rho$. Assume that the voters have linear preferences, $\rho_v = 1$, and of the two candidates for leader, one is risk acceptant, ρ_h, and one is risk averse, ρ_l, where $\rho_h > 1 > \rho_2$.

1. Is there an equilibrium in which the voters strictly prefer to elect the risk-acceptant leader? Under what conditions?
2. Is there an equilibrium in which the voters strictly prefer to elect the risk-averse leader? Under what conditions?

References

Abreu, Dilip. 1988. "On the Theory of Infinitely Repeated Games with Discounting." *Econometrica* 56(2): 383–396.

Acemoglu, Daron, Georgy Egorov, and Konstantine Sonin. 2008. "Coalition Formation in Non-Democracies." *Review of Economic Studies* 75(4): 987–1009.

Achen, Christopher H. 1988. "A State with Bureaucratic Politics is Representable as a Unitary Rational Actor." Paper presented at the annual Meeting of the American Political Science Association, Washington, DC.

Alesina, Alberto and Enrico Spolaore. 2003. *The Size of Nations*. Cambridge, MA: MIT Press.

Alt, James E., Randall L. Calvert, and Brian D. Humes. 1988. "Reputation and Hegemonic Stability: A Game-Theoretic Analysis." *American Political Science Review* 82(2): 445–466.

Arrow, Kenneth J. 1970. *Social Choice and Individual Values*. New Haven, CT: Yale University Press.

Ashley, Richard K. 1984. "The Poverty of Neo-Realism." *International Organization* 38(2): 225–286.

Austen-Smith, David and Jeffrey S. Banks. 2000. "Cheap Talk and Burned Money." *Journal of Economic Theory* 91(1): 1–16.

Axelrod, Robert. 1984. *The Evolution of Cooperation*. New York: Basic Books.

Axelrod, Robert. 1997. *The Complexity of Cooperation: Agent Based Models of Competition and Collaboration*. Princeton, NJ: Princeton University Press.

Bailey, Kathleen C. 1995. *The UN Inspections in Iraq: Lessons for On-Site Verification*. Boulder, CO: Westview Press.

Baldwin, David A., ed. 1993. *Neorealism and Neoliberalism: The Contemporary Debate*. New York: Columbia Unversity Press.

Barnett, Michael and Raymond Duvall. 2005. "Power in International Politics." *International Organization* 59(1): 39–75.

Bas, Muhammet A. and Andrew J. Coe. 2012. "Arms Diffusion and War." *Journal of Conflict Resolution* 56(4): 651–674.

Bednar, Jenna. 2006. "Is Full Compliance Possible? Conditions for Shirking with Imperfect Monitoring and Continuous Action Spaces." *Journal of Theoretical Politics* 18(3): 347–375.

Beissinger, Mark R. 2002. *Nationalist Mobilization and the Collapse of the Soviet State*. Cambridge: Cambridge University Press.

Bendor, Jonathan. 1993. "Uncertainty and the Evolution of Cooperation." *Journal of Conflict Resolution* 37(4): 709–734.

Bendor, Jonathan and Piotr Swistak. 1997. "The Evolutionary Stability of Cooperation." *American Political Science Review* 91(2): 290–307.

Bendor, Jonathan, Roderick M. Kramer, and Suzanne Stout. 1991. "When in Doubt . . . Cooperation in a Noisy Prisoner's Dilemma." *Journal of Conflict Resolution* 35(4): 691–719.

Biddle, Stephen. 2006. *Military Power: Explaining Victory and Defeat in Modern Battle*. Princeton, NJ: Princeton University Press.

Black, Duncan. 1948. "On the Rationale of Group Decisionmaking." *Journal of Political Economy* 56(1): 23–34.

Blainey, Geoffrey. 1988. *The Causes of War*. 3rd edn. New York: The Free Press.

Booth, Ken and Nicholas J. Wheeler. 2008. *The Security Dilemma: Fear, Cooperation and Trust in World Politics*. New York: Palgrave Macmillan.

Boulding, Kenneth E. 1962. *Conflict and Defense: A General Theory*. New York: Harper & Brothers.

Brams, Steven J. and Alan D. Taylor. 1996. *Fair Division: From Cake Cutting to Dispute Resolution*. Cambridge: Cambridge University Press.

Braumoeller, Bear F. 2012. *The Great Powers and the International System*. Cambridge: Cambridge University Press.

Brito, Dagobert L. and Michael D. Intrilligator. 1985. "Conflict, War and Redistribution." *American Political Science Review* 79(4): 943–957.

Brooks, Stephen G. 1997. "Dueling Realisms." *International Organization* 51(3): 445–477.

Brown, Anthony Cave. 1975. *Bodyguard of Lies*. New York: Harper & Row.

Brown, Michael E., Owen R. Cote Jr., Sean M. Lynn-Jones, and Steven E. Miller, eds. 2000a. *The Rise of China*. Cambridge, MA: MIT Press.

Brown, Michael E., Owen R. Cote Jr., Steven E. Miller, and Sean M. Lynn-Jones, eds. 2000b. *Rational Choice and Security Studies*. Cambridge, MA: MIT Press.

Bueno de Mesquita, Bruce. 1981. *The War Trap*. New Haven, CT: Yale University Press.

Bueno de Mesquita, Bruce and David Lalman. 1992. *War and Reason*. New Haven, CT: Yale University Press.

Bueno de Mesquita, Bruce and Alastair Smith. 2012. "Domestic Explanations of International Relations." *Annual Review of Political Science* 15: 161–181.

Bueno de Mesquita, Bruce, James D. Morrow, and Ethan R. Zorick. 1997. "Capabilities, Perception, and Escalation." *American Political Science Review* 91(1): 15–27.

Bueno de Mesquita, Bruce, Alastair Smith, Randolph M. Siverson, and James D. Morrow. 2003. *The Logic of Political Survival*. Cambridge MA: MIT Press.

Buthe, Tim and Walter Mattli. 2011. *The New Global Rulers: The Privatization of Regulation in the World Economy*. Princeton, NJ: Princeton University Press.

Butterfield, Herbert. 1951. *History and Human Relations*. London: Collins.

Camerer, Colin F. 2003. *Behavioral Game Theory*. The Roundtable Series in Behavioral Economics. Princeton, NJ: Princeton University Press.

Camerer, Colin F. and Ernst Fehr. 2006. "When Does 'Economic Man' Dominate Social Behavior?" *Science* 311: 47–52.

Carlsnaes, Walter, Thomas Risse, and Beth A. Simmons, eds. 2002. *Handbook of International Relations*. Sage Publications.

Carr, Edward Hallett. 1946. *The Twenty Years' Crisis, 1919–1939*. 2nd edn. New York: Harper & Row.

Carter, David. 2010. "The Strategy of Territorial Conflict." *American Journal of Political Science* 54(4): 969–987.

Carter, David B. and H. E. Goemans. 2011. "The Making of the Territorial Order: New Borders and the Emergence of Interstate Conflict." *International Organization* 65(2): 275–309.

Cederman, Lars-Erik. 1997. *Emergent Actors in World Politics*. Princeton, NJ: Princeton University Press.

Chadefaux, Thomas. 2011. "Bargaining over Power: When do Shifts in Power Lead to War?" *International Theory* 3(2): 228–253.

Chayes, Abram and Antonia Handler Chayes. 1993. "On Compliance." *International Organization* 47(2): 175–205.

Chiozza, Giacomo and H. E. Goemans. 2011. *Leaders and International Conflict*. Cambridge: Cambridge University Press.

Coase, Ronald. 1960. "The Problem of Social Cost." *Journal of Law and Economics* 3(1): 1–44.

Coe, Andrew J. 2011. "Costly Peace: A New Rationalist Explanation for War." Working paper.

Conybeare, John A. C. 1984. "Public Goods, Prisoners' Dilemmas and the International Political Economy." *International Studies Quarterly* 28(1): 5–22.

Cooper, Andrew F., Jorge Heine, and Ramesh Thakur, eds. 2013. *The Oxford Handbook of Modern Diplomacy*. Oxford: Oxford University Press.

Copeland, Dale C. 2000. *The Origins of Major War*. Ithaca, NY: Cornell University Press.

de Callières, François. 1994. *The Art of Diplomacy*. Lanham, MD: University Press of America.

Debs, Alexandre and Nuno P. Monteiro. 2014. "Known Unknowns: Power Shifts, Uncertainty and War." *International Organization* 68(1): 1–31.

DeNardo, James. 1995. *The Amateur Strategist: Intuitive Deterrence Theories and the Politics of the Nuclear Arms Race*. Cambridge: Cambridge University Press.

DiCicco, Jonathan and Jack S. Levy. 1999. "Power Shifts and Problem Shifts: The Evolution of the Power Transition Research Program." *Journal of Conflict Resolution* 43(6): 675–704.

Downs, George W. 1991. "Arms Races and War." In *Behavior, Society and Nuclear War*, ed. Philip Tetlock *et al.* New York: Oxford University Press, pp. 73–109.

Downs, George W. and David M. Rocke. 1990. *Tacit Bargaining, Arms Races, and Arms Control*. Ann Arbor, MI: University of Michigan Press.

Downs, George W. and David M. Rocke. 1995. *Optimal Imperfection: Domestic Uncertainty and Institutions in International Relations*. Princeton, NJ: Princeton University Press.

Downs, George W., David M. Rocke, and Peter N. Barsoom. 1996. "Is the Good News about Compliance Good News about Cooperation?" *International Organization* 50(3): 376–406.

Downs, George W., David M. Rocke, and Peter N. Barsoom. 1998. "Managing the Evolution of Multilateralism." *International Organization* 52(2): 397–419.

Downs, George W., David M. Rocke, and Randolph M. Siverson. 1985. "Arms Races and Cooperation." *World Politics* 38(1): 118–146.

Dunne, Tim, Milja Kurki, and Steve Smith, eds. 2013. *International Relations Theories: Discipline and Diversity*. Oxford: Oxford University Press.

Evans, Peter B., Harold K. Jacobson, and Robert D. Putnam. 1993. *Double Edged Diplomacy: International Bargaining and Domestic Politics*. Berkeley, CA: University of California Press.

Farnham, Barbara, ed. 1995. *Avoiding Losses/Taking Risks: Prospect Theory and International Conflict*. Ann Arbor, MI: University of Michigan Press.

Farrell, Joseph and Matthew Rabin. 1996. "Cheap Talk." *Journal of Economic Perspectives* 10(3): 103–118.

Fearon, James D. 1994. "Domestic Political Audiences and the Escalation of International Disputes." *American Political Science Review* 88(3): 577–592.

Fearon, James D. 1995. "Rationalist Explanations for War." *International Organization* 49(3): 379–414.

Fearon, James D. 1996. "Bargaining over Objects that Influence Future Bargaining Power." Paper presented at the Annual Meetings of the American Political Science Association, Washington, DC.

Fearon, James D. 1997. "Signaling Foreign Policy Interests: Tying Hands vs. Sunk Costs." *The Journal of Conflict Resolution* 41(1): 68–90.

Fearon, James D. 1998a. "Bargaining, Enforcement and International Cooperation." *International Organization* 52(2): 269–305.

Fearon, James D. 1998b. "Commitment Problems and the Spread of Ethnic Conflict." In *The International Spread of Ethnic Conflict*, ed. David A. Lake and Donald Rothchild. Princeton, NJ: Princeton University Press, pp. 107–126.

Fearon, James D. 2004. "Why Do Some Civil Wars Last So Much Longer Than Others?" *Journal of Peace Research* 41(3): 275–301.

Fearon, James D. and Alexander Wendt. 2002. "Rationalism v. Constructivism: A Skeptical View." In *Handbook of International Relations*, ed. Walter Carlsnaes, Thomas Risse, and Beth A. Simmons. London: Sage.

Fey, Mark and Kristopher W. Ramsay. 2007. "Mutual Optimism and War." *American Journal of Political Science* 51(4): 738–754.

Fey, Mark and Kristopher W. Ramsay. 2011. "Uncertainty and Incentives in Crisis Bargaining: Game Free Analyais of International Conflict." *American Journal of Political Science* 55(1): 149–169.

Finnemore, Martha and Katheryn Sikkink. 1998. "International Norm Dynamics and Political Change." *International Organization* 52(4): 887–917.

Fischer, Fritz. 1967. *Germany's Aims in the First World War*. New York: W. W. Norton & Co.

Fischer, Fritz. 1975. *War of Illusions*. New York: W. W. Norton & Co.

Fortna, Virginia Page. 2008. *Does Peacekeeping Work? Shaping Belligerent' Choices after Civil War*. Princeton, NJ: Princeton University Press.

Frederick, Shane, George Loewenstein, and Ted O'Donoghue. 2002. "Time Discounting and Time Preference: A Critical Review." *The Journal of Economic Literature* 40(2): 351–401.

Gaertner, Wulf. 2009. *A Primer in Social Choice Theory*. Oxford: Oxford University Press.

Garfinkel, MIchelle R. 1990. "Arming as a Strategic Investment in a Cooperative Equilibrium." *American Economic Review* 80(1): 50–68.

Gehlbach, Scott. 2013. *Formal Models of Domestic Politics*. Cambridge: Cambridge University Press.

Ghosn, Faten, Glenn Palmer, and Stuart Bremer. 2004. "The MID3 Data Set, 1993–2001: Proceedures, Coding Rules and Description." *Conflict Management and Peace Science* 21: 133–154.

Gill, Jeff. 2006. *Essential Mathematics for Political and Social Research*. Cambridge: Cambridge University Press.

Gilligan, Michael J. 2004. "Is There a Broader-Deeper Trade-off in International Multilateral Agreements?" *International Organization* 58(3): 459–484.

Gilligan, Michael J. and Leslie Johns. 2012. "Formal Models of International Institutions." *Annual Review of Political Science* 15: 221–243.

Gilpin, Robert. 1981. *War and Change in World Politics*. Cambridge: Cambridge University Press.

Glaser, Charles L. 1995. "Realists as Optimists: Cooperation as Self Help." *International Security* 19(3): 50–90.

Glaser, Charles. 2010. *Rational Theory of International Politics*. Princeton, NJ: Princeton University Press.

Goddard, Stacie E. 2006. "Uncommon Ground: Territorial Conflict and the Politics of Legitimacy." *International Organization* 60(1): 35–68.

Goemans, Henk Erich. 2000. *War and Punishment: the Causes of War Termination and the First World War*. Princeton, NJ: Princeton University Press.

Goldstein, Joshua S. and John R. Freeman. 1990. *Three-Way Street: Strategic Reciprocity in World Politics*. Chicago: University of Chicago Press.

Goldstein, Joshua S. and Jon C. Pevehouse. 1997. "Reciprocity, Bullying, and International Cooperation: Time Series Analysis of the Bosnia Conflict." *American Political Science Review* 91(3): 515–529.

Goldstein, Joshua S., Jon C. Pevehouse, Deborah J. Gerner, and Shibley Telhami. 2001. "Reciprocity, Triangularity, and Cooperation in the Middle East, 1979–1997." *Journal of Conflict Resolution* 45(5): 594–620.

Gourevitch, Peter. 1978. "The Second Image Reversed: The International Sources of Domestic Politics." *International Organization* 32(4): 891–912.

Green, Donald P. and Ian Shapiro. 1994. *Pathologies of Rational Choice Theory: A Critique of Applications in Political Science*. New Haven: Yale University Press.

Grieco, Joseph. 1988. "Anarchy and the Limits of Cooperation: A Realist Critique of the Newest Liberal Institutionalism." *International Organization* 42(3): 485–507.

Grossman, Gene M. and Elhanan Helpman. 1994. "Protection for Sale." *American Economic Review* 84(4): 833–850.

Grossman, Gene M. and Elhanan Helpman. 1996. "Electoral Competition and Special Interest Politics." *Review of Economic Studies* 63(2): 265–286.

Guisinger, Alexandra and Alastair Smith. 2002. "Honest Threats: The Interaction of Reputation and Political Insitutions in International Crises." *Journal of Conflict Resolution* 46(2): 175–200.

Hardin, Garrett. 1968. "The Tragedy of the Commons." *Science* 162: 1243–1248.

Hardin, Russell. 1982. *Collective Action*. Baltimore, MD: Johns Hopkins University Press.

Harsanyi, John C. 1967. "Games with Incomplete Information played by Bayesian Players, I–III, Part I: The Basic Model." *Management Science* 14(3): 159–182.

Harsanyi, John C. 1973. "Games with Randomly Disturbed Payoffs: A New Rationale for Mixed Strategy Equilibrium Points." *International Journal of Game Theory* 2(1): 1–23.

Hassner, Ron. 2003. "To Halve and to Hold: Conflicts over Sacred Space and the Problem of Indivisibility." *Security Studies* 12(4): 1–33.

Herz, John H. 1950. "Idealist Internationalism and the Security Dilemma." *World Politics* 2(2): 157–180.

Hirshleifer, Jack. 1989. "Conflict and Rent-Seeking Success Functions: Ratio vs. Difference Models of Relative Success." *Public Choice* 63(2): 101–112.

Hirshleifer, Jack. 1995. "Anarchy and Its Breakdown." *Journal of Political Economy* 103(1): 26–52.

Hobbes, Thomas. 1968 (1651). *Leviathan*. New York: Penguin.

Hollis, Martin. 1998. *Trust within Reason*. Cambridge: Cambridge University Press.

Hopf, Ted. 2013. *Reconstructing the Cold War: The Early Years, 1945–1958*. Oxford: Oxford University Press.

Horowitz, Michael C. 2010. *The Diffusion of Military Power: Causes and Consequences for International Politics*. Princeton, NJ: Princeton University Press.

Hug, Simon. 1999. "Nonunitary Actors in Spatial Models: How Far is Far in Foreign Policy?" *Journal of Conflict Resolution* 43(4): 479–500.

Huth, Paul K. 1998. *Standing Your Ground: Territorial Disputes and International Conflict*. Ann Arbor, MI: University of Michigan Press.

Iida, Keisuke. 1993a. "Analytic Uncertainty and International Cooperation: Theory and Application to International Economic Policy Coordination." *International Studies Quarterly* 37(4): 431–457.

Iida, Keisuke. 1993b. "When and How do Domestic Constraints Matter? Uncertainty in International Relations." *Journal of Conflict Resolution* 37(3): 403–426.

Iida, Keisuke. 1996. "Involuntary Defection in Two-Level Games." *Public Choice* 89(3/4): 283–303.

Intrilligator, Michael D. and Dagobert L. Brito. 1984. "Can Arms Races Lead to the Outbreak of War?" *Journal of Conflict Resolution* 28(1): 63–84.

Jackson, Matthew O. and Massimo Morelli. 2009. "Strategic Militarization, Deterrence and Wars." *Quarterly Journal of Political Science* 4(4): 279–313.

Jervis, Robert. 1970. *The Logic of Images in International Relations*. Princeton, NJ: Princeton University Press.

Jervis, Robert. 1976. *Perception and Misperception in International Politics*. Princeton, NJ: Princeton University Press.

Jervis, Robert. 1978. "Cooperation under the Security Dilemma." *World Politics* 30(2): 167–214.

Kadercan, Burak. 2013. "Making Sense of Survival: Refining the Treatment of State Preferences in Neorealist Theory." *Review of International Studies* 39(4): 1014–1037.

Kahler, Miles. 1998. "Rationality in International Relations." *International Organization* 52(4): 919–941.

Kahn, Herman. 1960. *On Thermonuclear War*. Princeton, NJ: Princeton University Press.

Kahneman, D., P. Slovic, and A. Tversky, eds. 1982. *Judgment under Uncertainty: Heuristics and Biases*. Cambridge: Cambridge Universty Press.

Karklins, Rasma and Roger Peterson. 1993. "Decision Calculus of Protesters and Regimes: Eastern Europe 1989." *Journal of Politics* 55(3): 588–614.

Kehr, Eckart. 1965. *Economic Interest, Militarism and Foreign Policy: Essays on German History*. Berkeley, CA: University of California Press.

Kennedy, Paul. 1980. *The Rise of the Anglo-German Antagonism 1860–1914*. London: George Allen & Unwin.

Kennedy, Paul. 1984. "Arms Races and the Causes of War: 1850–1945." In *Strategy and Diplomacy*, ed. Paul Kennedy. London: Fontana Press, pp. 165–177.

Kennedy, Paul. 1987. *The Rise and Fall of the Great Powers: Economic Change and Military Conflict from 1500 to 2000*. New York: Random House.

Keohane, Robert O. 1984. *After Hegemony*. Princeton, NJ: Princeton University Press.

Keohane, Robert O. 1986. "Reciprocity in International Relations." *International Organization* 40(1): 1–27.

Keynes, John Maynard. 1936. *The General Theory of Employment, Interest and Money*. New York: Harcourt Brace.

Kilgour, D. M. and N. M. Fraser. 1988. "A Taxonomy of All Ordinal 2 X 2 Games." *Theory and Decision* 24(2): 99–117.

Kindleberger, Charles. 1974. *The World in Depression, 1929–1939*. Berkeley, CA: University of California Press.

Kissinger, Henry A. 1954. *A World Restored: Metternich, Castlereagh and the Problems of Peace 1812–1822*. Boston, MA: Houghton Mifflin.

Kivimaki, Timo. 1993. "Strength of Weakness: American–Indonesian Hegemonic Bargaining." *Journal of Peace Research* 30(4): 391–408.

Koremenos, Barbara. 2001. "Loosening the Ties that Bind: A Learning Model of Agreement Flexibility." *International Organization* 55(2): 289–325.

Koremenos, Barbara. 2005. "Contracting around International Uncertainty." *American Political Science Review* 99(4): 549–565.

Koremenos, Barbara. 2013. "The Continent of International Law." *Journal of Conflict Resolution* 57(4): 653–681.

Koremenos, Barbara, Charles Lipson, and Duncan Snidal. 2001. "The Rational Design of International Institutions." *International Organization* 55(4): 761–800.

Krasner, Stephen D., ed. 1983. *International Regimes*. Ithaca, NY: Cornell University Press.

Kugler, Jacek and Douglas Lemke, eds. 1996. *Parity and War: Evaluations and Extensions of the War Ledger*. Ann Arbor, MI: University of Michigan Press.

Kuhn, Harold W., ed. 1997. *Classics in Game Theory*. Princeton, NJ: Princeton University Press.

Kurizaki, Shuhei. 2007. "Efficient Secrecy: Public versus Private Threats in Crisis Diplomacy." *American Political Science Review* 101(3): 543–558.

Kurizaki, Shuhei. 2014. "Threats and Assurances in Coercive Diplomacy." Working paper.

Kydd, Andrew. 1997a. "Game Theory and the Spiral Model." *World Politics* 49(3): 371–400.

Kydd, Andrew. 1997b. "Sheep in Sheep's Clothing: Why Security Seekers Do Not Fight Each Other." *Security Studies* 7(1): 114–155.

Kydd, Andrew. 2000. "Trust, Reassurance and Cooperation." *International Organization* 54(2): 325–357.

Kydd, Andrew H. 2005. *Trust and Mistrust in International Relations*. Princeton, NJ: Princeton University Press.

Kydd, Andrew H. 2008. "Methodological Individualism and Rational Choice." In *Oxford Handbook of International Relations*, ed. Christian Reuss-Smit and Duncan Snidal. Oxford: Oxford University Press, chapter 25, pp. 425–443.

Kydd, Andrew H. 2010. "Learning Together, Growing Apart: Global Warming, Energy Policy and International Trust." *Energy Policy* 38(6): 2675–2680.

Kydd, Andrew H. 2011. "Terrorism and Profiling." *Terrorism and Political Violence* 23(3): 458–473.

Kydd, Andrew and Roseanne McManus. 2014. "Threats, Assurances and Bargaining." Working paper.

Lacey, Edward J. 1996. "The UNSCOM Experience: Implications for US Arms Control Policy." *Arms Control Today* 26(6): 914.

Laffont, Jean-Jacques and David Martimort. 2001. *The Theory of Incentives: The Principal-Agent Model*. Princeton, NJ: Princeton University Press.

Laitin, David D. 1993. "The Game Theory of Language Regimes." *International Political Science Review* 14(3): 227–239.

Laitin, David D. 1994. "The Tower of Babel as a Coordination Game: Political Linguistics in Ghana." *American Political Science Review* 88(3): 622–634.

Lake, David A. 1992. "Powerful Pacifists: Democratic States and War." *American Political Science Review* 86: 24–37.

Lake, David A. 1993. "Leadership, Hegemony and the International Economy: Naked Emperor or Tatterd Monarch with Potential?" *International Studies Quarterly* 37(4): 459–489.

Lake, David A. 2011. "Why 'isms' are Evil: Theory, Epistemology, and Academic Sects as Impediments to Understanding and Progress." *International Studies Quarterly* 55(2): 465–480.

Lebow, Richard Ned and Thomas Risse-Kappen, eds. 1995. *International Relations Theory and the End of the Cold War*. New York: Columbia University Press.

Lenin, Vladimir Il'ich. 1996 (1916). *Imperialism: The Highest Stage of Capitalism*. London: Pluto Press.

Levendusky, Matthew S. and Michael C. Horowitz. 2012. "When Backing Down is the Right Decision: Partisanship, New Information and Audience Costs." *Journal of Politics* 74(2): 323–338.

Leventoğlu, Bahar and Ahmer Tarar. 2008. "Does Private Information Lead to Delay or War in Crisis Bargaining?" *International Studies Quarterly* 52(3): 533–553.

Levy, Jack S. 1983. *War in the Modern Great Power System 1495–1975*. Lexington, KY: University of Kentucky Press.

Levy, Jack S. 1988. "Declining Power and the Preventive Motivation for War." *World Politics* 40(1): 82–107.

Levy, Jack S. 1997. "Prospect Theory, Rational Choice and International Relations." *International Studies Quarterly* 41(1): 87–112.

Lichbach, Mark Irving. 1989. "Stability in Richardson's Arms Races and Cooperation in Prisoner's Dilemma Arms Rivalries." *American Journal of Political Science* 33(4): 1016–1047.

Lichbach, Mark Irving. 1990. "When is an Arms Rivalry a Prisoner's Dilemma?: Richardson's Models and 2X2 Games." *Journal of Conflict Resolution* 34(1): 29–56.

Lichbach, Mark Irving. 1992. "The Repeated Public Goods Game: A Solution Using Tit for Tat and the Lindahl Point." *Theory and Decision* 32: 133–146.

Lieber, Keir A. 2007. "The New History of World War I and What it Means for International Relations Theory." *International Security* 32(2): 155–191.

Lindley, Dan. 2007. *Promoting Peace with Information*. Princeton, NJ: Princeton University Press.

Lohmann, Susanne. 1997. "Linkage Politics." *Journal of Conflict Resolution* 41(1): 38–67.

MacDonald, Paul K. 2003. "Useful Fiction or Miracle Maker: The Competing Epistemological Foundations of Rational Choice Theory." *American Political Science Review* 97(4): 551–565.

Machiavelli, Niccolò. 2003. *The Prince*. Penguin Classics.

Maliniak, Daniel, Amy Oakes, Susan Peterson, and Michael J. Tierney. 2011. "International Relations in the US Academy." *International Studies Quarterly* 55(2): 437–464.

Mansfield, Edward D. and Jack Snyder. 1995. "Democratization and the Danger of War." *International Security* 20(1): 5–38.

March, James G. and Johan P. Olsen. 1998. "The Institutional Dynamics of International Political Orders." *International Organization* 52(4): 943–969.

Martin, Lisa L. 1992. "Interests, Power and Multilateralism." *International Organization* 46(4): 765–792.

Martin, Lisa L. 2000. *Democratic Commitments: Legislatures and International Cooperation*. Princeton, NJ: Princeton University Press.

Mas-Colell, Andreu, Michael D. Whinston, and Jerry R. Green. 1995. *Microeconomic Theory*. Oxford: Oxford University Press.

Mayer, Arno J. 1981. *The Persistence of the Old Regime: Europe to the Great War*. New York: Pantheon Books.

McCarty, Nolan and Adam Meirowitz. 2006. *Political Game Theory: An Introduction*. Cambridge: Cambridge University Press.

McDermott, Rose. 1998. *Risk Taking in International Politics: Prospect Theory in American Foreign Policy*. Ann Arbor, MI: University of Michigan Press.

McGillivray, Fiona and Alastair Smith. 2000. "Trust and Cooperation through Agent-specific Punishments." *International Organization* 54(4): 809–824.

McGillivray, Fiona and Alastair Smith. 2005. "The Impact of Leadership Turnover and Domestic Institutions on International Cooperation." *Journal of Conflict Resolution* 49(5): 639–660.

McGillivray, Fiona and Alastair Smith. 2006. "Credibility in Compliance and Punishment: Leader Specific Punishments and Credibility." *Journal of Politics* 68(2): 248–258.

McGillivray, Fiona and Alastair Smith. 2008. *Punishing the Prince: A Theory of Interstate Relations, Political Institutions and Leader Change*. Princeton, NJ: Princeton University Press.

McGinnis, Michael D. 1986. "Issue Linkage and the Evolution of International Cooperation." *Journal of Conflict Resolution* 30(1): 141–170.

McLean, Iain and Arnold Urken, eds. 1995. *Classics of Social Choice*. Ann Arbor, MI: University of Michigan Press.

Mearsheimer, John J. 1994/5. "The False Promise of International Institutions." *International Security* 19(3): 5–49.

Mearsheimer, John J. 2001. *The Tragedy of Great Power Politics*. New York: Norton.

Mearsheimer, John J. and Stephen M. Walt. 2013. "Leaving Theory Behind: Why Hypothesis Testing Has Become Bad for IR." *European Journal of International Relations* 19(3): 427–457.

Meirowitz, Adam and Anne E. Sartori. 2008. "Strategic Uncertainty as a Cause of War." *Quarterly Journal of Political Science* 3(4): 327–352.

Miller, Steven E., Sean M. Lynn-Jones, and Stephen Van Evera, eds. 1991. *Military Strategy and the Origins of the First World War*. International Security Readers, Princeton, NJ: Princeton University Press.

Milner, Helen V. 1997. *Interests, Institutions, and Information: Domestic Politics and International Relations*. Princeton, NJ: Princton University Press.

Milner, Helen V. and B. Peter Rosendorff. 1997. "Democratic Politics and International Trade Negotiations: Elections and Divided Government as Constraints on Trade Liberalization." *Journal of Conflict Resolution* 41(1): 117–146.

Mitzen, Jennifer. 2006. "Ontological Security in World Politics: State Identity and the Security Dilemma." *European Journal of International Relations* 12(3): 341–370.

Mo, Jongryn. 1994. "The Logic of Two-Level Games with Endogenous Domestic Coalitions." *Journal of Conflict Resolution* 38(3): 402–422.

Mo, Jongryn. 1995. "Domestic Institutions and International Bargaining: The Role of Agent Veto in Two-Level Games." *American Political Science Review* 89(4): 914–924.

Molinari, M. Christina. 2000. "Military Capabilities and Escalation: A Correction to Bueno de Mesquita, Morrow and Zorick." *American Political Science Review* 94(2): 425–427.

Moore, Will H. and David A Siegel. 2013. *A Mathematics Course for Political and Social Research*. Princeton, NJ: Princeton University Press.

Moravcsik, Andrew. 1997. "Taking Preferences Seriously: A Liberal Theory of International Politics." *International Organization* 51(4): 513–553.

Morgenthau, Hans. 1948. *Politics Among Nations*. 1st edn. New York: Alfred A. Knopf.

Morrow, James D. 1989. "Capabilities, Uncertainty and Resolve: A Limited Information Model of Crisis Bargaining." *American Journal of Political Science* 33(4): 941–972.

Morrow, James D. 1994. "Modeling the Forms of International Cooperation: Distribution vs. Information." *International Organization* 48(3): 387–423.

Muthoo, Abhinay. 1999. *Bargaining Theory with Applications*. Cambridge: Cambridge University Press.

Myerson, Roger B. 1979. "Incentive Compatibility and the Bargaining Problem." *Econometrica* 47(1): 61–74.

Nasar, Sylvia. 1998. *A Beautiful Mind*. London: Simon & Schuster.

Nicolson, Harold. 1939. *Diplomacy*. New York: Harcourt Brace.

Nicolson, Harold. 1954. *The Evolution of Diplomatic Method*. London: Cassell.

Niou, Emerson M. S. and Peter C. Ordeshook. 1994. " 'Less Filling, Tastes Great': The Realist–Neo-Liberal Debate." *World Politics* 46(2): 209–235.

Niou, Emerson M.S., Peter C. Ordeshook and Gregory F. Rose. 1989. *The Balance of Power: Stability in International Systems*. Cambridge: Cambridge University Press.

Olson, Mancur. 1965. *The Logic of Collective Action*. Cambridge, MA: Harvard University Press.

Olson, Mancur and Richard Zeckhauser. 1966. "An Economic Theory of Alliances." *Journal of Conflict Resolution* 37(3): 446–483.

O'Neill, Barry. 1994. "Game Theory Models of Peace and War." In *Handbook of Game Theory with Economic Applications*, ed. Robert J. Aumann and Sergiu Hart. Vol. II. Amsterdam: Elsevier Science B.V.

O'Neill, Barry. 2001. "Risk Aversion in International Relations Theory." *International Studies Quarterly* 45(4): 617–640.

O'Neill Jr., Phillip D. 2009. *Verification in an Age of Insecurity: The Future of Arms Control Compliance*. Oxford: Oxford University Press.

Organski, A. F. K. and Jacek Kugler. 1980. *The War Ledger*. Chicago: University of Chicago Press.

Osborne, Martin J. 2004. *An Introduction to Game Theory*. Oxford: Oxford University Press.

Ostrom, Elinor. 1998. "A Behavioral Approach to the Rational Choice Theory of Collective Action." *American Political Science Review* 92(1): 1–22.

Oye, Kenneth. 1995. "Explaining the End of the Cold War: Morphological and Behavioral Adaptations to the Nuclear Peace?" In *International Relations Theory and the End of the Cold War*, ed. Richard Ned Lebow and Thomals Risse-Kappen. New York: Columbia University Press, pp. 57–83.

Oye, Kenneth A., ed. 1986. *Cooperation under Anarchy*. Princeton, NJ: Princeton University Press.

Pahre, Robert. 1994. "Multilateral Cooperation in an Iterated Prisoner's Dilemma." *Journal of Conflict Resolution* 38(2): 326–352.

Paris, Roland. 2001. "Human Security: Paradigm Shift or Hot Air?" *International Security* 26(2): 87–102.

Poundstone, William. 1992. *Prisoner's Dilemma*. New York: Anchor Books.

Powell, Robert. 1990. *Nuclear Deterrence Theory: The Problem of Credibility*. Cambridge: Cambridge University Press.

Powell, Robert. 1991. "Absolute and Relative Gains in International Relations Theory." *American Political Science Review* 85(4): 1303–1320.

Powell, Robert. 1996. "Uncertainty, Shifting Power, and Appeasement." *American Political Science Review* 90(4): 749–764.

Powell, Robert. 1999a. *In the Shadow of Power*. Princeton, NJ: Princeton University Press.

Powell, Robert. 1999b. "The Modeling Enterprise and Security Studies." *International Security* 24(2): 97–106.

Powell, Robert. 2002. "Bargaining Theory and International Conflict." *Annual Review of Political Science* 5: 1–30.

Powell, Robert. 2004. "The Inefficient Use of Power: Costly Conflict with Complete Information." *American Political Science Review* 98(2): 231–241.

Powell, Robert. 2006. "War as a Commitment Problem." *International Organization* 60(1): 169–203.

Powell, Robert. 2007a. "Allocating Defensive Resources with Private Information about Vulnerability." *American Political Science Review* 101(4): 799–809.

Powell, Robert. 2007b. "Defending against Terrorist Attacks with Limited Resources." *American Political Science Review* 101(3): 527–541.

Powell, Robert. 2009. "Sequential, Nonzero-sum 'Blotto': Allocating Defensive Resources Prior to Attack." *Games and Economic Behavior* 67(2): 611–615.

Price, Richard. 1998. "Reversing the Gun Sights: Transnational Civil Society Targets Land Mines." *International Organization* 52(3): 613–644.

Putnam, Robert D. 1988. "Diplomacy and Domestic Politics: The Logic of Two-Level Games." *International Organization* 42(3): 427–460.

Rabin, Matt and Richard H. Thaler. 2001. "Anomalies: Risk Aversion." *Journal of Economic Perspectives* 15(1): 219–232.

Rajmaira, Sheen. 1997. "Indo-Pakistani Relations: Reciprocity in Long-Term Perspective." *International Studies Quarterly* 41(3): 547–560.

Rapoport, Anatol and Albert M. Chammah. 1966. "The Game of Chicken." *American Behavioral Scientist* 10(3): 10–28.

Rapoport, Anatol and M. J. Guyer. 1966. "A Taxomony of 2 X 2 Games." *General Systems* 2: 203–214.

Reiter, Dan. 1995. "Exploding the Powder Keg Myth: Preemptive Wars Almost Never Happen." *International Security* 20(2): 5–34.

Reiter, Dan. 2003. "Exploring the Bargaining Model of War." *Perspectives on Politics* 1(1): 27–43.

Reiter, Dan and Alan C. Stam. 2002. *Democracies at War*. Princeton, NJ: Princeton University Press.

Reuss-Smit, Christian and Duncan Snidal, eds. 2008. *The Oxford Handbook of International Relations*. Oxford: Oxford University Press.

Richardson, Lewis F. 1960. *Arms and Insecurity*. Pittsburgh, PA: Boxwood Press.

Roberson, Brian. 2006. "The Colonel Blotto Game." *Economic Theory* 29(1): 1–24.

Rose, Gideon. 1998. "Neoclassical Realism and Theories of Foreign Policy." *World Politics* 51(1): 144–172.

Rosenau, James N., ed. 1967. *Domestic Sources of Foreign Policy*. The Free Press.

Rosendorff, B. Peter and Helen Milner. 2001. "The Optimal Design of International Trade Institutions: Uncertainty and Escape." *International Organization* 55(4): 829–858.

Ruggie, John Gerard, ed. 1993. *Multilateralism Matters*. New York: Columbia University Press.

Russell, Bertrand. 1959. *Common Sense and Nuclear Warfare*. London: George Allen & Unwin.

Russett, Bruce. 1993. *Grasping the Democratic Peace*. Princeton, NJ: Princeton University Press.

Rutherford, Kenneth R. 2000. "The Evolving Arms Control Agenda: Implications of the Role of NGOs in Banning Antipersonnel Landmines." *World Politics* 53(1): 74–114.

Samuelson, Paul A. 1954. "The Pure Theory of Public Expenditures." *Review of Economics and Statistics* 36: 387–389.

Sandler, Todd. 1993. "The Economic Theory of Alliances: A Survey." *Journal of Conflict Resolution* 37(3): 446–483.

Sarkees, Meredith Reid. 2000. "The Correlates of War Data on War: An Update to 1997." *Conflict Management and Peace Science* 18(1): 123–144.

Sartori, Anne E. 2002. "The Might of the Pen: A Reputational Theory of Communication in International Disputes." *International Organization* 56(1): 121–149.

Schelling, Thomas C. 1960. *The Strategy of Conflict*. Cambridge, MA: Harvard University Press.

Schelling, Thomas C. 1966. *Arms and Influence*. New Haven, CT: Yale University Press.

Schelling, Thomas C. 1978. *Micromotives and Macrobehavior*. New York: W. W. Norton.

Schelling, Thomas C. and Morton H. Halperin. 1961. *Strategy and Arms Control*. New York: The Twentieth Century Fund.

Schultz, Kenneth A. 1998. "Domestic Opposition and Signaling in International Relations." *American Political Science Review* 92(4): 829–844.

Schultz, Kenneth A. 2001a. *Democracy and Coercive Diplomacy*. Cambridge: Cambridge University Press.

Schultz, Kenneth A. 2001b. "Looking for Audience Costs." *Journal of Conflict Resolution* 45(1): 32–60.

Schultz, Kenneth A. 2005. "The Politics of Risking Peace: Do Hawks or Doves Deliver the Olive Branch?" *International Organization* 59(1): 1–38.

Schultz, Kenneth A. 2010. "The Enforcement Problem in Coercive Bargaining: Interstate Conflict over Rebel Support in Civil Wars." *International Organization* 64(2): 281–312.

Schultz, Kenneth and Henk Goemans. 2014. "Aims, Claims and the Bargaining Model." Working paper.

Schweller, Randall L. 1992. "Domestic Structure and Preventive War: Are Democracies More Pacific?" *World Politics* 44(2): 235–269.

Schweller, Randall L. 1996. "Neorealism's Status Quo Bias: What Security Dilemma?" *Security Studies* 5(3): 90–121.

Schweller, Randall L. 1998. *Deadly Imbalances: Tripolarity and Hitler's Strategy of World Conquest*. New York: Columbia University Press.

Sebenius, James K. 1984. *Negotiating the Law of the Sea: Lessons in the Art and Science of Reaching Agreement*. Cambridge, MA: Harvard University Press.

Shelef, Nadav. 2014. "Unequal Ground: Homelands and Conflict." Forthcoming, *International Organization*.

Signorino, Curtis S. 1996. "Simulating International Cooperation under Uncertainty." *Journal of Conflict Resolution* 40(1): 152–205.

Signorino, Curtis S. 1999. "Strategic Interaction and the Statistical Analysis of International Conflict." *American Political Science Review* 93(2): 279–297.

Sil, Rudra and Peter J. Katzenstein. 2010. *Beyond Paradigms: Analytic Eclecticism in the Study of World Politics*. New York: Palgrave Macmillan.

Singer, J. David. 1961. "The Level-of-Analysis Problem in International Relations." *World Politics* 14(1): 77–92.

Siverson, Randolph M. and Paul Diehl. 1989. "Arms Races, the Conflict Spiral, and the Onset of War." In *Handbook of War Studies*, ed. Manus Midlarsky. Boston, MA: Unwin Hyman.

Slantchev, Branislav L. 2005. "Military Coercion in Interstate Crises." *American Political Science Review* 99(4): 533–547.

Slantchev, Branislav. 2011. *Military Threats: The Costs of Coercion and the Price of Peace.* Cambridge: Cambridge University Press.

Slantchev, Branislav L. and Ahmer Tarar. 2011. "Mutual Optimism as a Rationalist Explanation of War." *American Journal of Political Science* 55(1): 135–148.

Smith, Alastair. 1996. "Diversionary Foreign Policy in Democratic Systems." *International Studies Quarterly* 40(1): 133–153.

Smith, Alastair. 1998. "International Crises and Domestic Politics." *American Political Science Review* 92(3): 623–639.

Snidal, Duncan. 1985a. "Coordination versus Prisoner's Dilemma: Implications for International Cooperation and Regimes." *American Political Science Review* 79(4): 923–942.

Snidal, Duncan. 1985b. "The Limits of Hegemonic Stability Theory." *International Organization* 39(4): 579–614.

Snidal, Duncan. 1991a. "International Cooperation among Relative Gains Maximizers." *International Studies Quarterly* 35(4): 387–402.

Snidal, Duncan. 1991b. "Relative Gains and the Pattern of International Cooperation." *American Political Science Review* 85(3): 701–726.

Snyder, Glenn H. 1984. "The Security Dilemma in Alliance Politics." *World Politics* 36(4): 461–495.

Snyder, Glenn H. and Paul Diesing. 1977. *Conflict among Nations: Bargaining, Decisionmaking and System Structure in International Crises.* Princeton, NJ: Princeton University Press.

Snyder, Jack. 1991. *Myths of Empire.* Ithaca, NY: Cornell University Press.

Snyder, Jack and Erica D. Borghard. 2011. "The Cost of Empty Threats: A Penny, Not a Pound." *American Political Science Review* 105(3): 437–456.

Spruyt, Hendrik. 1994. *The Sovereign State and its Competitors.* Princeton, NJ: Princeton University Press.

Stein, Arthur A. 1982a. "Coordination and Collaboration: Regimes in an Anarchic World." *International Organization* 36(2): 299–324.

Stein, Arthur A. 1982b. "When Misperception Matters." *World Politics* 34(4): 505–526.

Stone, Randall W., Branislav L. Slantchev, and Tamar R. London. 2008. "Choosing How to Cooperate: A Repeated Public Goods Model of International Relations." *International Studies Quarterly* 52(2): 335–362.

Tammen, Ronald L., Douglas Lemke, Carole Alsharabati, Brian Effird, Jacek Kugler, Allan C. Stam III, Mark Andrew Abdollahian, and A. F. K. Organski. 2000. *Power Transitions: Strategies for the 21st Century.* New York: Chatham House.

Tarar, Ahmer. 2001. "International Bargaining with Two-Sided Domestic Constraints." *Journal of Conflict Resolution* 45(3): 320–340.

Tarar, Ahmer. 2005. "Constituencies and Preferences in International Bargaining." *Journal of Conflict Resolution* 49(3): 383–407.

Tarar, Ahmer. 2006. "Diversionary Incentives and the Bargaining Approach to War." *International Studies Quarterly* 50(1): 169–188.

Tarar, Ahmer and Bahar Leventoglu. 2009. "Public Commitment in Crisis Bargaining." *International Studies Quarterly* 53(3): 817–839.

Taylor, A. J. P. 1954. *The Struggle for Mastery in Europe 1848–1918*. Oxford: Clarendon Press.

Thucydides. 1954. *History of The Peloponnesian War*. London: Penguin.

Toft, Monica. 2005. *The Geography of Ethnic Violence: Identity, Interests and the Indivisibility of Territory*. Princeton, NJ: Princeton University Press.

Tomz, Michael. 2007. "Domestic Audience Costs in International Relations." *International Organization* 61(3): 821–840.

Trachtenberg, Marc. 1988/89. "A 'Wasting Asset': American Strategy and the Shifting Nuclear Balance, 1949–1954." *International Security* 13(3): 5–49.

Trager, Robert F. 2010. "Diplomatic Calculus in Anarchy: How Communication Matters." *American Political Science Review* 104(2): 347–368.

Trager, Robert F. 2011. "Multidimensional Diplomacy." *International Organization* 65(2): 469–506.

Trager, Robert F. 2014. *Diplomacy in Anarchy: The Construction and Consequences of Perceptions of Intentions*. Cambridge: Cambridge University Press.

Trager, Robert F. and Lynn Vavreck. 2011. "The Political Costs of Crisis Bargaining: Presidential Rhetoric and the Role of Party." *American Journal of Political Science* 55(3): 526–545.

Tsebelis, George. 1991. *Nested Games: Rational Choice in Comparative Politics*. Berkeley, CA: University of California Press.

Tsebelis, George. 2002. *Veto Players: How Political Institutions Work*. Princeton, NJ: Princeton University Press.

Van Evera, Stephen. 1999. *Causes of War*. Ithaca: Cornell University Press.

von Hintze, Otto. 1975. *The Historical Essays of Otto Hintze*. Oxford: Oxford University Press.

Von Neumann, John and Oskar Morgenstern. 1944. *The Theory of Games and Economic Behavior*. Princeton, NJ: Princeton University Press.

Wagner, R. Harrison. 1983. "The Theory of Games and the Problem of International Cooperation." *American Political Science Review* 77(2): 330–346.

Wagner, R. Harrison. 1986. "The Theory of Games and the Balance of Power." *World Politics* 38(4): 546–576.

Walt, Stephen. 1996. *Revolution and War*. Ithaca: Cornell University Press.

Waltz, Kenneth. 1954. *Man, the State and War*. New York: Columbia University Press.

Waltz, Kenneth. 1979. *Theory of International Politics*. New York: Random House.

Watkins, Michael and Susan Rosegrant. 2001. *Breakthrough International Negotiation*. San Francisco, CA: Jossey-Bass.

Watson, Joel. 1999. "Starting Small and Renegotiation." *Journal of Economic Theory* 85(1): 52–90.

Weeks, Jessica. 2008. "Autocratic Audience Costs: Regime Type and Signaling Resolve." *International Organization* 62(1): 35–64.

Wendt, Alexander. 1999. *Social Theory of International Politics*. Cambridge: Cambridge University Press.

Willard-Foster, Melissa. 2011. "Costly Peace: A Rationalist Explanation for Asymmetric War." Working paper.

Wolfers, Arnold. 1962. *Discord and Collaboration: Essays on International Politics*. Baltimore, MD: Johns Hopkins University Press.

Zagare, Frank C. and D. Marc Kilgour. 2000. *Perfect Deterrence*. Cambridge: Cambridge University Press.

Zaloga, Steven. 2007. *The Atlantic Wall (1): France*. Osprey Publishing.

Index

alliances, 3, 55, 180, 184–187, 192
anarchy, 2, 8, 31, 33, 42, 107
   arms control, 55, 141, 189, 190
arms control verification, 5
   arms race, 32, 36, 39, 41, 185, 189
Assurance game, Stag Hunt game, 36–38, 44–46, 48, 155, 189
attrition, 5

bargaining, 4, 6, 18, 55–73, 75, 76, 81, 83–85, 89–90, 93, 94, 100–101, 128, 146–147, 149–151, 175, 177, 199, 201, 205, 206, 209
Bayes Rule, 151, 153, 154, 159, 171, 195–200
   perfect Bayesian equilibrium, 94–168

cheap talk, 149–151, 154, 175, 206
Chicken, Chicken game, 37, 38, 47–49, 57, 108, 150
choice under certainty, 12–14
choice under uncertainty, 12–16,
Cold War, 8, 56, 76, 81, 113, 177, 187, 195
commons goods, 180
conflict, 3, 4, 55, 63–66, 68, 69, 73, 81, 82, 94, 100, 112, 149
constraints, 3
constructivism, 8
Contrite Tit for Tat, 139–142, 144, 145
cooperation, 3, 36, 41, 43–46, 48–49, 127–147, 153, 156, 177–178, 181–192, 196, 210
   cooperation theory, 4
   cooperative behavior, 4, 39
coordination, 49
Coordination game, 37, 38, 46–48, 132
costly signal, 149–151, 153, 175
credible threat, 65, 67, 70, 71, 73, 79, 82, 83, 85, 86, 96–99, 101, 150

deterrence, 18, 112–114, 117–125,
Deterrence game, 56, 58, 59
domestic actors, 3, 4, 11, 150, 164–165, 174, 194–210

dominant strategy, 37–38, 39, 44, 183
dominated strategy, 37–38, 39, 129

Edgeworth, Edgeworth Box, 20, 31, 143
efficiency, 3–6, 16–17, 31, 48, 56, 63–64, 69, 70, 87, 105, 128, 197–199, 201–202, 205
   Nash equilibrium, 37–38, 42–59, 94, 105, 108, 129, 132–145, 181, 187, 190
expected utility theory, 11–12
Extensive Form game, 56–59

formal models, 7, 9

game tree, 58, 60, 73, 74, 82, 93, 101, 114, 202
greedy types, 25, 26, 102–103, 121–124
Grim Trigger, 135–136, 137, 145

Hobbes, Thomas, 8, 30

idealism, 8
impatience, 5
implementation and enforcement, 4
indivisible goods, 4, 17–19, 71–73, 92
international relations theory, 1, 6, 127
international security, 4, 66

Keynes, John M., 1, 2

legal system, 2, 45, 56
liberalism, 8, 10
   liberal institutionalism, 127, 128

Machiavelli, 8
Marxism, 8
Matching Pennies, 38, 49–52, 53
median voter theorem, 29
monitoring problems, 5

nationalism, 26, 27, 30
neo-liberal institutionalism, 8

INDEX

non-feasible/undervalued intermediate outcomes, 4, 70–71, 72, 73
Normal Form game, 37, 38, 53, 56, 154
nuclear weapons, 11, 18, 45, 48–49, 53, 59, 76, 80, 81, 89, 106, 127, 142, 150
    Nuclear Non-Proliferation Treaty (NPT), 178, 190

optimization, 3

paradigm wars, 7–9
Pareto (Pareto optimal, Pareto improvement, Vilfredo Pareto), 17, 19, 31, 36, 43, 44, 46, 49, 128, 144, 155, 192, 199, 201, 202, 204, 205
peacekeeping, 5, 141
political economy, 10, 33, 178, 195
power
    balance of power, 104–110, 116, 118, 122
    changing power, 4, 75–90, 125
    competition for power, 31–32, 33, 34, 40–44, 92, 112–125, 128
preferences, 3, 11–16, 28–34, 37, 59, 110, 130, 150, 164, 192, 196, 197
preferences properties/assumptions, 12–16
Prisoner's Dilemma, 5, 8, 36–41, 44–46, 48, 53, 112, 128–130, 133–136, 144, 146, 183
    repeated Prisoner's Dilemma, 127, 128, 134, 136, 141, 143, 145–147
private goods, 179, 184–185, 196
private information, 4
problem oriented research, 9
prospect theory, 24–27
public goods, 177–187, 192, 196

rational choice theory, 3, 6, 8, 11, 112
rationalist international relations theory, 2, 8–10, 63, 75, 92, 194
    assumptions rationalist international relations theory, 2–3
realism, 7, 8, 10, 33, 127–128, 195
    defensive realism, 8
    neo-classical realism, 8
    offensive realism, 8
resolve, 92, 104, 110

risk acceptant, 22–23, 24, 26, 27, 60
risk averse, 22–24, 26, 72
risk neutral, 22, 24, 26, 59–60, 72

satiated, 25, 80, 123
strategic choice, 3
strategic interaction, 6, 56
strategy, 3, 7, 36–53, 58, 69, 94–96, 102, 107, 109, 111, 117, 120, 121, 123, 127, 130, 132–139, 140, 145, 153, 158, 161–163, 166, 208
subgame perfect equilibrium, 58, 61, 96, 145, 166, 200
subgame perfection, 59, 94, 138–139

Thucydides, 8, 30, 55, 75
tipping model, 178, 187–192
Tit for Tat, 136–138, 139, 140, 146
trade, tariffs, non-tariff barriers
    free trade, 1
    international trade, 1, 36
    non-tariff barriers, 4, 129
    protectionism, 1
    tariff, 145, 181–182, 197
    Tariff Barrier game, 143–145
    tariff levels, 3, 39–40, 55
    trade agreements, 55
    trade barriers, 11, 55, 196
    trade wars, 6
    world trade, 202
treaty, 1, 3, 55, 151, 154–163, 177, 178, 187, 195
trust, and mistrust, 4, 92, 93, 101, 103

uncertainty, 4, 110, 161–164, 175, 195, 207
unitary actors, 3, 28–30, 34, 194, 198, 205–206

war, 1, 3–6, 12, 14, 18, 22, 33, 45–46, 49, 55–57, 63–73, 75–90, 110, 112–125, 127–128, 147, 149–174, 195–196, 199
    non-decisive, 5, 66
    potentially decisive, 5–6, 66
    preventive war, 4, 59, 76–90, 101, 113, 141, 147

zero sum, 17, 30–32, 41, 49, 62, 128
    positive sum, 17, 33, 41, 61

Made in the USA
Columbia, SC
24 November 2019